DEAR
LEADER

FROM TRUSTED INSIDER
TO ENEMY OF THE STATE,
MY ESCAPE FROM NORTH KOREA

JANG JIN-SUNG

RIDER
LONDON · SYDNEY · AUCKLAND · JOHANNESBURG

10 9 8

Rider, an imprint of Ebury Publishing,
20 Vauxhall Bridge Road,
London SW1V 2SA

Rider is part of the Penguin Random House group of companies whose
addresses can be found at global.penguinrandomhouse.com

Penguin
Random House
UK

Text copyright © 2014 by Jang Jin-sung
Translation copyright © 2014 by Shirley Lee

Jang Jin-sung has asserted his right to be identified as the author of this
Work in accordance with the Copyright, Designs and Patents Act 1988

This paperback edition first published by Rider in 2014

www.eburypublishing.co.uk

A CIP catalogue record for this book is
available from the British Library

ISBN 9781846044212

Penguin Random House is committed to a sustainable future for
our business, our readers and our planet. This book is made from
Forest Stewardship Council® certified paper.

MIX
Paper from
responsible sources
FSC® C018179

Printed and bound in Great Britain by Clays Ltd, St Ives plc

CONTENTS

PART THREE: FREEDOM

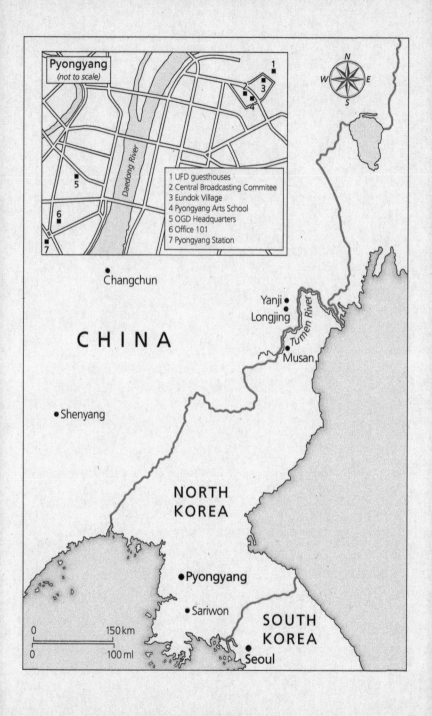

Pyongyang
(not to scale)

Daedong River

1 UFD guesthouses
2 Central Broadcasting Commitee
3 Eundok Village
4 Pyongyang Arts School
5 OGD Headquarters
6 Office 101
7 Pyongyang Station

N
W E
S

• Changchun

Yanji •
Longjing •

Tumen River

• Musan

CHINA

• Shenyang

**NORTH
KOREA**

• Pyongyang

• Sariwon

**SOUTH
KOREA**

• Seoul

0   150 km
0   100 ml

TRANSLATOR'S PREFACE

I FIRST met Mr Jang in June 2012. He had come to London to take part in Poetry Parnassus, hosted by the Southbank Centre as part of the summer Olympic Games. A Korean studying in England, I had been asked to interpret for both North and South Korean representatives. As I waited for him to come through at the arrivals hall at Heathrow Airport, I looked at my phone to check the photograph of him I had found on the Internet: in it, he was dressed in a dark suit, smiling a little and looking up at the camera under the curls of his black hair.

When he walked into the arrivals hall pushing a luggage trolley, his hair was dishevelled and he looked half-submerged in his navy blue suit. His white cuffs poked unevenly from his jacket sleeves and his light pink tie did not sit quite straight. We exchanged greetings in Korean, bowed and shook hands. As we walked to the car I pushed the trolley. He opened the door of the black van for me and held out his hand to steady me as I climbed the steps.

When we set off for the Southbank Centre, he hung a camera around his neck, while I prepared myself to make conversation. I pointed out London's sights for him as he snapped shots and admired the landmarks. Among those buildings I pointed out was the MI6 headquarters at Vauxhall Cross, and I took my chance to break the ice between us: 'Apparently, this is where women who want to snag a James Bond type hang out.' Suddenly, the rather formal atmosphere between us evaporated and he burst into laughter. He said that if those women ever found out that real spies were just people like him, they might stop waiting and go find themselves a proper man.

By the end of his stay, we had become friends, talking easily instead of in the formal manner of those from neighbouring nations who had become distant strangers after half a century without contact. Even today, North Koreans are not permitted to communicate freely with anyone from the outside world – not by email, not by phone, not in person.

It doesn't help that media portrayals of North Korea, based on an outsider's perspective, focus on the inscrutability of its system: the strange dynasty of Kims, the endless heavy boots marching in line or the uneasy prospect of its nuclear arsenal. There is far more to its people than the public shows of mass obedience and hysterical tears – the North Korean experience is a complex and dysfunctional relationship between a system and the people ensnared by it, of which Mr Jang is a unique witness. Not only did he live at its heart, but he escaped from it.

In this book, he ends his account in 2004, and some things have changed in North Korea since then. Informal and illegal marketisation from below, rising from the ashes of North Korea's economic collapse in the mid 1990s, has continued to impact significantly on the nature of social transactions conducted between individual and state. The purge and execution in December 2013 of Jang Song-thaek, uncle to the current ruler Kim Jong-un, made headlines across the world. The graphic accusations against him were published in a very public manner by being broadcast on state television and released quickly to a foreign audience; and the incident was noted for breaking from the past in many ways.

But these events did not occur in a historical vacuum and, in order to make sense of North Korea's present, you have to know its past. Particularly, you have to recognise its persistent dualities – between words and deeds, propaganda and reality, and the manner in which these dualities work for the outsider versus the insider. Without an appreciation of this, North Korea will remain inscrutable and our exchanges cyclical.

Mr Jang was not a politician but a poet, and this is precisely why he is intimately familiar with the regime's myth-making, and why his memoir is about the dismantling of façades. The outside world's approach to North Korea is based on many deceptions, for which all sides are responsible, and on which the status quo depends; Mr Jang's escape from North Korea really began when he realised: 'I was restless with yearning to write realist poetry based on what I saw, and not loyalist poetry based on what we were all told to see.'

It remains impossible for an outsider to gain access to the state's internal workings by doing business with or making trips to North Korea. Not only are there strict layers of control and hidden power structures in place, but proxies and agents are deliberately disguised as prominent insiders whenever North Korea deals with foreigners and presents itself to the world. It has also long been thought that no defector can speak with authority on the workings of the system, due to its highly compartmentalised nature. In this respect, Mr Jang is a clear exception.

At first, I was suspicious rather than sceptical. I asked how it was that the outside world still did not know the things he knew, and he replied that it was in order to address this that he had decided to leave the sphere of intelligence just over a year before our meeting. We both recognised the need for his knowledge to reach a wider audience. As he says: 'If North Korea has lies and nukes, I have the truth and the written word.'

Mr Jang has never overplayed his knowledge or experiences. If anything, he has been too modest, and it was only through writing this book that he realised how many essential insights he had to share. I admit to feeling frustrated by how often he underplayed or was required to underplay his knowledge. I respect his decisions and understand the circumstances, but that did not stop me from wishing he could reveal more of the truth.

There is much that is not and cannot be said in this book. The passage of time will allow for more light to be thrown; in the meantime, I hope this account can serve as a basis on which to reassess our understanding of North Korea.

The North Korean regime's doublespeak and opacity are two of its crucial pillars of power. Regardless of whether the world could not see through those façades, or was reluctant to do so, Mr Jang's memoir reveals that understanding North Korea's past and its persistent dualities is the key both to clarifying its present and to unlocking changes to come.

SHIRLEY LEE

PROLOGUE

May 1999

A LITTLE after midnight, just as I'm settling into bed, the phone begins to ring. I decide not to answer before the fifth ring, and hope it will stop before then. When it rings a sixth time, I imagine my parents waking up, annoyed, and I pick up. I am ready to give whoever is on the other end a good telling-off.

'Hello?' In the silent house my voice sounds more intrusive than the ringing phone.

'This is the First Party Secretary.'

At these words, I involuntarily jerk upright and jar my skull against the headboard.

'I am issuing an Extraordinary Summons. Report to work by 1 a.m. Wear a suit. You are not to notify anyone else.'

Although in this country we are accustomed to obeying even the strangest command as a matter of course, it's disconcerting that the First Party Secretary himself has just given me an order. He is the Central Party liaison for our department. Under normal circumstances, I would expect to receive orders from the Party Secretary of Division 19 or Section 5, in keeping with my position in the Party's organisational hierarchy. On top of that, he has used the term 'Extraordinary Summons'.

This usually refers to the mobilisation of troops. When the United States and South Korea perform joint military exercises on the Korean peninsula, our nation responds by conducting nationwide mobilisation drills. The call to take part in these is referred to as an 'Extraordinary Summons'. But we are usually notified through deliberate leaks in advance of such a call. Individual Workers' Party units and sections, under fierce pressure to outperform their rivals, are always seeking to gain an edge: employees of those well connected enough to be in the know remain at work on the specified day, reporting for duty ahead of those who have unwittingly gone home for the evening.

However, if this were a standard military mobilisation summons, I would not have been asked to wear a suit. We cadres who belong to the Central Party, unlike ordinary North Koreans attached to regional or departmental Party branches, know that an 'Extraordinary Summons' can also lead to an encounter with Kim Jong-il, our Dear Leader.

When someone is summoned to meet him, there is no advance notification. Not even the highest-ranking generals are made aware of the operational details of these meetings. An invitation to meet Kim is relayed through a First Party Secretary, who is summoned to a Party Committee room that has been placed under lockdown by Dear Leader's personal bodyguards. Under their close surveillance, the First Party Secretary receives a list of names and issues the individual summons for each cadre, with the logistics of the encounter carried out in strict secrecy. In this situation, the term 'Extraordinary Summons' is the code phrase that sets this clandestine process in motion.

But the same phrase can have a third, more perturbing meaning. The Ministry of State Security uses it when carrying out secret purges of high-ranking officials. On receiving an Extraordinary Summons at night, a cadre might leave his house alone, taking care not to wake his family, before disappearing into a prison camp or being executed.

Thankfully, I am confident that the third scenario will not apply to me. In fact, I can't wait to leave the house. Only a few days ago, the First Party Secretary had dropped a subtle hint of glory to come.

As instructed, I put on my best suit and tie. In Pyongyang, there are no taxis available after midnight, and motor vehicles must have a special night licence to travel after this time. So although it is pitch dark outside, I hop on my bicycle and pedal to work. Bicycles are one of the main forms of transport, but unlike most bikes, mine is brand new and has been specially shipped to me by a relative stationed overseas.

Outside, there are no streetlights lit. The silence of the capital city is so absolute that I can only sense the presence of passers-by before their dark shapes loom into my vision. The electricity supply is in a perpetual state of emergency, even though there are two power stations serving the city. The ageing Pyongyang Thermoelectric Plant was built with Soviet support in 1961, and the East Pyongyang Thermoelectric Plant was built in 1989, but neither produces enough power to supply more than one district of the city at a time. So, like a roaming ghost, power settles in rotation on sections of Pyongyang for about four hours a day.

One area of the city is always bright, though: the Joong-gu Area, which lies at the heart of Pyongyang. This is where Central Party offices, senior cadres' residential areas and buildings for foreigners, such as the Koryo Hotel, are located. My workplace, Office 101 of the United Front Department (UFD), lies at the heart of this bright central district. Nearing the compound, I notice that it is more brightly lit than usual, with the grounds as well as the usual guard posts lit up. As I enter the gates, I exclaim to myself, 'Yes! I am going to meet the General!'

In the courtyard stand thirty or more soldiers dressed in the dark mustard-coloured uniform of Dear Leader's personal guards. They wear the characteristic X-shaped leather harness that supports a pistol on each side. Three beige Nissan vans with curtained windows are parked one behind the other, each big enough for a dozen passengers. The Party Secretary for South Korean Affairs greets me in person, beside whom the prestige of the First Party Secretary, who phoned me earlier, pales in comparison. He leads me towards a two-star general with a clipboard, who seems to be supervising the operation. The other soldiers refer to the man as Comrade Deputy Director.

After briefly looking me up and down, the general barks, 'Stand him over there!' I look over to where he is pointing and see the nation's most senior cadres in the sphere of inter-Korean relations standing in line: the Party Secretary for South Korean Affairs Kim Yong-sun, UFD First Deputy Director Im Tong-ok, UFD Policy Director Chae Chang-guk, UFD Policy Deputy Director Park Young-su, and two other cadres from the Department for the Peaceful Unification of the Homeland. The atmosphere is tense, and with six powerful men standing in line like schoolchildren, I feel uncomfortable about greeting them. I go to stand at the end of the line.

'Are we meeting the General?' As I whisper to the man in front of me, a voice yells, 'Don't talk! Understand?'

I look indignantly at the soldier, about to demand that he speak to me in a more respectful way, but the vicious light in his eyes quickly puts me in my place.

One by one, Comrade Deputy Director checks our identification documents against his list. We climb in silence into the middle vehicle according to our position on the list. We take our assigned seats. The soldier who yelled at me for whispering is the last to step into the van. I'd thought he had treated me condescendingly because I am only in my twenties, but now I hear him speaking in a rude, officious manner even to Central Party cadres who are twice his age.

'Don't open the curtains! Don't get out of your seat! Don't talk!' he barks. Even more alarming than his insolence is the fact that my comrades meekly reply, 'Yes, sir.' Even Kim Yong-sun and Im Tong-ok, two of the most senior cadres in the country, are lowly men in the presence of Dear Leader's personal guards.

Through the open door of the van, I watch the remaining soldiers scramble into the other two vehicles. Soon, the door is pulled shut and the engine starts. As the van begins its journey, my stomach churns with anxiety, but I know that an encounter with Dear Leader is a wondrously momentous event.

Thick brown curtains seal off the windows and separate us from the driver. Unable to see out of the van, I begin to feel a little car-sick. After a two-hour journey in silence, and much to my relief, we finally arrive at a railway station. It is around 4 a.m. We climb out of the van and as I regain my bearings I realise we have come to Yongsung, a First Class Station. In a population of over 20 million, there have only been two First Class Citizens: Kim Il-sung and Kim Jong-il. First Class Stations are reserved exclusively for their use, and there are dozens of these stations scattered across the country. The station roofs are camouflaged in green to make them difficult to spot through satellite imagery. At ground level, the buildings are unmarked, but heavily armed guards patrol them and they are enclosed by high walls.

Yongsung Station is in the northern outskirts of Pyongyang, usually less than half an hour away from where we began our journey. I recognise my surroundings because I have passed by the place on several occasions. At first, I'm puzzled that it has taken so long to get here, but I can't suppress a grin when I realise that the vans have tried to confuse us by taking a deliberately circuitous route. As we move from the van to a train, we go through another series of identity checks.

The special train reserved for this occasion is different from ordinary trains. The sides of the carriage are painted grass-green and the roof is white. From the outside, the markings suggest that it was made in China: above the door handles the word 'Beijing' is painted in bright red Chinese characters. But when I step into the carriage, I spot prominent Mitsubishi logos that betray its true origin in Japan. The seats in the carriage have been replaced by single beds and everything is arranged open-plan, presumably so that the guards can keep watch over us.

As at the start of the journey, the rules are barked out: 'Don't touch the curtains. There are blankets under the beds. Remain in your bed throughout the journey. Sleep until the train comes to a stop. Notify us if you wish to use the toilet. Break any of these rules and you'll be removed from the train – immediately.'

The guard takes care to put added emphasis on that final word. I feel that if I make one wrong move, I might be thrown off this train and out of my privileged existence altogether. During the long night ride no one speaks a word, not even to ask to use the toilet. There is only the sound of the train rattling along the tracks. I close my eyes and count the rhythmic beats, trying hard to fall asleep.

The special train dispatched for just seven civilians comes to a halt at around six in the morning. We have stopped at Galma, a First Class Station in Gangwon Province. When I step down from the carriage, the cool dawn air on my face is refreshing. I realise how tense I've been in the presence of the soldiers. Policy Director Chae Chang-guk elbows me as he overtakes me and flashes a grin. He's like a child, unable to contain his excitement.

We are transferred once again, to another waiting van. After an hour's drive, again in silence, we climb out at a small pier surrounded on all sides by cement barriers, where we board a waiting launch. The waves lap gently, but the brackish smell of seawater is overwhelming.

The boat starts with a lurch and a deafening roar as the engine sparks into life. A moment later, I absorb the fact that I am on a boat for the first time in my life. It accelerates recklessly, seemingly intent on tossing me into the waves. I lean forward to hold on to the railing, but a soldier suddenly puts his arms around me from behind and pins down my hands. A shiver runs down my spine. I tell myself that the closer we get to Dear Leader, the stronger must be our show of faith in him. I glance around and see that each of the six other passengers is similarly held in place by a soldier acting as a human safety belt. Staring back into the distance, where the two strands of white foam in our wake merge into one continuous stream, I shout at the top of my voice over the engine's roar, 'Is this a Navy boat?'

My guard smirks, even as his forehead wrinkles with the effort of understanding what I am trying to say above the racket of the engine. 'The Navy? Hah! The Navy doesn't have a boat as speedy as this. This one's ours. It belongs to the Guards Command. It's pretty fast, isn't it?' The Guards Command is responsible for the protection of Kim's household. It is composed of 100,000 infantry, seamen and pilots.

Although he has to shout, I notice how my guard has abandoned his officiousness and talks conversationally, perhaps because we are speaking without an audience. This makes me feel a little better. As he says, the boat is very fast: a cap blows off the head of one of the guards and flies off into the sea, where it lands on the water. I watch it grow smaller among the waves and then disappear.

After about twenty minutes, we slow down near a tree-covered island. I wonder if we have been going round in circles within a small area, just as we had done on the journey to Yongsung Station. The bow of the boat drops and the island comes into clear view. From the pristine wharf to the manicured woods on either side of the pavement, everything is spotless. It looks as though the place was completed yesterday. I realise I had been expecting to find our Dear Leader waiting for us on the pier with wide-open arms, just as he does in the revolutionary movies. It is a bit startling to see that no one is here to greet us.

The guards lead us to a large hut, where we take our seats in a room that is about a thousand square metres. We are told to remain silent. Everything is white: the chairs, the floor, the walls. There are no windows. Instead, there are squares of green-tinged light shining from built-in wall panels.

At half past noon, more than four hours after we arrived on the island, there is a sudden burst of activity around us. Guards wearing white gloves spray something onto the chair where Dear Leader will sit.

Comrade Deputy Director makes us stand in line again. We are ordered to take off our watches and hand them in, as part of the security procedure. Each of us is then handed a small envelope. The outer packaging has Japanese characters printed on it. Inside, there is a small cotton wipe that smells of alcohol. Comrade Deputy Director instructs us: 'You must clean your hands before shaking hands with the General.' He then comes forward, singling me out for a stern instruction: 'You must *not* look into the General's eyes.' He gestures to the second button of his uniform jacket and says, 'You must look here. Understand?'

I wonder whether this is intended to impress on me my inferiority to Dear Leader, but the thought quickly passes. We continue to wait as Comrade Deputy Director finalises seating arrangements. Again, I'm at the back of the line. There are seven civilians in the room, and more than twenty guards around us. We stand rigidly, staring in silence at a pair of closed gates for perhaps ten more minutes. They are large and white, and decorated with gilded flowers.

When the gates finally open, a guard with the rank of colonel marches through and stands to attention. 'The General will now enter the room,' he announces.

Everyone and everything turns to stone. Keeping my head still, I focus my gaze on a point halfway up the arch where Kim Jong-il's face will soon appear.

Another minute seems to pass. Unexpectedly, a small white puppy tumbles into the room. It is a Maltese with a curly coat. An old man follows, chasing after the puppy that belongs to him. We raise our voices in unison to salute Dear Leader.

'Long live the General! Long live the General!'

Our combined cheer hurts my eardrums, but the puppy is

unperturbed by the noise, probably used to such fanfare. However, Dear Leader must be pleased that his puppy has shown such courage, because he bends down to stroke it. He then mutters something into its ear.

I feel let down when I see Dear Leader up close, because I am confronted by an old man who looks nothing like the familiar image of the People's Leader. Even though we are clapping fervently and cheering for him, he doesn't respond or even seem to notice. He continues to play with his puppy, as if resentful of being surrounded by men who are younger than him. Seeming to read my mind, he looks up and my heart skips a beat. As if we had all been waiting for this moment, we cheer even more loudly.

'Long live the General! Long live the General!'

He glances round the room, then strides in my direction.

I prepare myself for the glorious encounter, but he walks straight past me, halting before a slogan displayed on the wall behind us. In yellow letters on a red background, it reads: *Let's serve Great Leader Comrade Kim Jong-il by offering up our lives!*

He calls out, 'Kim Yong-sun!' Party Secretary Kim Yong-sun hurries to his side. Kim Jong-il asks him, 'Is this hand-painted? Or is it printed?' In this close proximity, his voice indeed belongs to a great leader. Every syllable resonates with absolute authority.

Seeing Kim Yong-sun falter, the Comrade Deputy Director answers in his place: 'Sir, it's hand-painted.'

Kim Jong-il says, 'This looks good. When I went somewhere last week, I saw slogans printed on enamel. But this hand-painted one looks much better, don't you think?'

This time, Kim Yong-sun is ready with his answer. 'Yes, sir, I agree. In fact, I already made enquiries about this. But I was informed that we will continue to produce enamelled slogans, as hand-painted slogans require the use of costly imports.'

Kim Jong-il ignores him. He steps back a few paces, inspects the slogan for a few more seconds, and gives an order with a quick wave of his hand: 'Replace existing versions of this slogan throughout the country with hand-painted ones.'

I attempt some mental arithmetic. How much would this project cost? At that very moment, the General wheels round, catching me off guard, and thunders, 'You, boy! Are you the one who wrote that poem about the gun barrel?'

I bark my carefully worded response: 'Yes, General! I am honoured to be in your presence!'

He smirks as he approaches me. 'Someone wrote it for you, isn't that right? Don't even think about lying to me. I'll have you killed.'

As I begin to panic, Dear Leader bursts into hearty laughter and punches me on the shoulder. 'It's a compliment, you silly bugger. You've set the standard for the whole *Songun* era.'

I find myself unable to respond, and it doesn't help that Kim Yong-sun is glaring at me. Before the General takes his seat, Kim Yong-sun finds an opportunity to scold me. 'You stupid bastard. You should have thanked him. You should have responded by offering to write poems of loyalty even from your grave,' he hisses into my ear.

When he is done with me, he puts his joyous face back on and rushes to attend to Kim Jong-il. Returning to his own seat, he gently smoothes his hands over his buttocks before they touch the chair, just as a woman does with her dress as she sits down. The other cadres are no less formal. Instead of real people sitting on chairs, it is as if sculptures are set around the room, incapable of movement. Dear Leader's Maltese puppy is the most active being in the room, whimpering excitedly and pacing around its owner's feet.

Kim Jong-il seems not to be interested in small talk and the white Maltese puppy holds his attention. The General remains focused on what the dog is doing, what it might be thinking. But every now and then he shouts, 'Hey, Im Tong-ok!' or 'Hey, Chae Chang-guk!' and the chosen man rushes towards him to be consulted. It makes for a strange scene, in which he holds the puppy in higher esteem than any of his most loyal men.

Ten or fifteen minutes later, a pair of double doors opens. Men in white dinner jackets and red bow ties appear with salvers held high. At the other end of the room technicians are bent double, humbly moving to and fro on the stage, adjusting the microphone and lighting. The band are seated and strike up; the feast is about to begin. I can't help but feel it's all a bit of an anti-climax, having expected to hear a sublime new saying or pearl of wisdom from Dear Leader. But as the food and music get under way, I lose myself in the occasion. I become mesmerised.

Every time a new course is brought into the room, the lights in the wall panels change to an eerie new colour. When the vegetable dish comes out, the lights go from a vivid grass-green to light purple; with the meat dish, the lights go from pink to a deep red. It is astonishing to discover that lighting can be part of a meal's presentation. As for the fish course, the platter it is presented on glitters so spectacularly that I can't taste the food. Tiny spotlights are set around the big grey serving platter, making the fish scales shimmer.

The wine is slightly tangy. My steward, who like all Kim Jong-il's staff belongs to the Guards Command and has a military rank, points to a label on the bottle that reads *Baedansul*. He describes its contents as an 80 per cent proof liquor developed by the Foundational Sciences Institute. This is the academic body devoted to the study of Dear Leader's health, and as such also falls under the Guards Command. Three thousand researchers work there, planning and preparing medicines and dishes specifically designed to extend Kim Jong-il's longevity. In order to test the effects of different medicines and foods, they operate a testing unit made up of men selected from a nationwide pool that shares his illnesses and physique. I am proud to understand more than most about this important work, as a friend's older brother works at the Institute.

The climax of our banquet is dessert. I am presented with a glass containing a large scoop of ice cream, over which the steward pours clear liquor. He lights the spirit and the flames dance blue and wild.

As I scoop some of it up with a small spoon, flames rise with it. Kim Yong-sun taps me on the shoulder and advises me, 'Blow it out first, *then* eat it. Don't have too much, though. It's very strong stuff.' He shares the information boastfully.

I lose myself momentarily in the contradictory sensations of heat and cold in my mouth. Then Kim Jong-il waves me over.

When you visit the house or workplace of a cadre who has had the privilege of attending a banquet hosted by Dear Leader, the wine glass that clinked against his in a toast is always kept in pride of place in a display cabinet. I realise that Dear Leader wants to provide me with such a treasure. The steward, who has been lingering close by for this moment, quickly hands me a large wine glass. Unprepared, I hastily take it over to Kim Jong-il, who fills it with dark red wine, saying, 'Keep up the good work.'

As I stand bent double at the waist in a deep bow, my eyes cast down, I can see his feet under the tablecloth. He has taken off his shoes. Even the General suffers the curse of sore feet! I had always thought him divine, not even needing to use the toilet. That's what we were taught at school and that's what the Party says: our General's life is a continuous series of blessed miracles, incapable of being matched even by all our mortal lifetimes put together. With this glorious invitation into his circle, I had thought I would enter and partake of a divine dimension in time.

But here I am, looking into his shoes, which have high heels and an inner platform at least six or seven centimetres high. Those shoes have deceived his people. Although his thin, permed hair adds to the illusion of height, Dear Leader can't be more than one metre sixty without those shoes.

After his earlier majestic commands, the way the General speaks at the table confounds me too. He uses coarse slang. In all the books and lectures quoting his words that I've read and heard since my childhood, his words serve not only as examples of perfect usage, but also reveal the truth of our homeland. Dear Leader's speech is always elegant, beautiful and, above all, courteous to his people. Yet tonight he muddles subject and predicate. He doesn't even call anyone Comrade, but addresses cadres as 'You!' or 'Boy!' It doesn't make sense.

Towards the end of dessert, the coloured lights dim. A woman appears on stage wearing a Western-style white dress that reveals her shoulders. The band starts to play an instrumental prelude, and she begins to sing a Russian folk song.

As she sings, Kim Jong-il starts to twitch. Although the spotlight is on the woman, the protocol of the occasion dictates that we should focus our attention on him alone. We watch as he draws out a gleaming white handkerchief. I blink, and the cadre sitting next to me reaches for his own handkerchief. Oddly, others also begin to withdraw their handkerchiefs. Then the General bows his head a little and starts dabbing at the corners of his eyes. I cannot believe what I am seeing. Here am I, beholding his tears! What will become of me after witnessing such an intimate thing?

My eyes shut tight in awe and terror.

When I open them, I see the most extraordinary thing I have ever seen in my life. My comrades, who have been beaming with the joy of feasting with Dear Leader, have begun to weep. How did this happen? Can I escape this banquet with my life intact? But before I can think any further, my own eyes feel hot and tears begin to flow down my cheeks. Yes, I must cry. I live my life in loyalty to the General. Loyalty not merely in thought and deed, but loyal obedience from my soul. I must cry, like my comrades. As I repeat these words in my heart, *I must cry, I must cry*, my tears grow hotter, and anguished shouts burst from somewhere deep within me.

Amid my uncontrollable shaking, the song comes to an end. There is no applause, but the room has filled with the sound of wailing. As the lights are slowly turned up, our crying quickly diminishes to whimpers, as if we had practised together in advance.

Wiping my eyes, I glance round, to look at the faces of the cadres around me. They were crying only moments ago, but they are now watching Dear Leader intently, awaiting instructions for the next act of synchronicity. For the first time in my life, loyal obedience makes me cringe.

On my journey back home, I find myself haunted by a disturbing question. Why did Dear Leader cry? I am aware that North Korea's Propaganda and Agitation Department chose to portray him as full of tears after his father Kim Il-sung's death in 1994, when the state distribution system fell apart all over the country. By early 1995, the rumours that people were starving to death in the provinces were made plausible by what was happening in Pyongyang itself.

When food distribution centres started shutting their doors and the numbers of people absconding from work to find food increased like a virus, the Party slogan 'If you survive a thousand miles of suffering, there will be ten thousand miles of happiness' was introduced. The state of food emergency was officially referred to as the 'Arduous March' and the population was urged to follow the example set by our General, at the forefront of the struggle.

As evidence, the song 'The Rice-balls of the General' was played over and over again on television. The song's lyrics claimed that Dear Leader was travelling hundreds of miles around the country each day to offer support to his people, all while sustained by just one rice-ball. Before the Arduous March, television broadcasts had only ever shown the smile of our Leader, as he led us towards a Socialist victory. People began to cry spontaneously, uncontrollably and en masse when they saw the tears of our divine Dear Leader for the first time on television.

As I continue on my way homewards, I am profoundly unsettled by my reaction to seeing Kim Jong-il's tears in the flesh. A distressing thought grips me, and it is hard to shake off: those were not the tears of a compassionate divinity but, rather, of a desperate man.

PART ONE

DICTATOR

PSYCHOLOGICAL WARFARE | 1

I was loyal and fearless. I didn't have to live in terror of the consequences of being late for work. Nor did I need to keep my head down like other cadres in an attempt to be invisible at Party meetings, for fear of becoming the next target of criticism. I had immunity, thanks to Dear Leader, who had sanctified me after being moved by a poem I wrote in his honour.

The world might damn North Korea as a ruthless regime that kills its own people, claiming that the system is oppressive and run by physical force. But this is only a partial view of how the country is governed. Throughout his life, Kim Jong-il stressed, 'I rule through music and literature.' Despite being the Commander-in-Chief of the Democratic People's Republic of Korea (DPRK) and Chair of the National Defence Commission, he had no military experience. In fact, he began his career as a creative professional, and his preparation for his succession to power began with his work for the Party's Propaganda and Agitation Department (PAD).

To express this in the language of 'dictatorship' understood by the outside world, Kim Jong-il wielded a double-edged sword: yes, he was a dictator by means of physical control, but he was also a dictator in a more subtle and pervasive sense: through his absolute power over the cultural identity of his people. In a mode characteristic of Socialism, where ideology is more important than material goods, he monopolised the media and the arts as a crucial part of his ambit of absolute power. This is why every single writer in North Korea produces works according to a chain of command that begins with the Writers' Union Central Committee of the Party's Propaganda and Agitation Department.

Anyone who composes a work that has not been assigned to the writer through this chain of command is by definition guilty of treason. All written works in North Korea must be initiated in response to a specific request from the Workers' Party. Once the writer has handed in his piece, it must then be legally approved before being accepted as a new work. Those writers who produce distinguished works under these standards are of course rewarded. The role of a North Korean writer, in each set task, is to create the best articulation of the assigned idea according to a combination of aesthetic requirements determined in advance and in consultation with the Workers' Party. It is not the job of a writer to articulate new ideas or to experiment with aesthetics on his or her own whim.

Literature thus plays a central role not only in North Korean arts but also in the social structure of the country. Before 1994, when Supreme Leader Kim Il-sung was alive, the art of the novel was pre-eminently in vogue. Nearly all the top state honours, such as the Kim Il-sung Medal, the Order of Heroic Effort and the title of Kim Il-sung Associate, were swept up by the state's novelists. The novel provided a perfect narrative format through which writers might expound upon the great deeds of the Supreme Leader.

It also helped that in his last years, Kim Il-sung lived immersed in the world of novels. He took a special interest in works written by novelists belonging to the April 15 Literary Group, a First Class literary institution whose remit is the revolutionary history of Kim Il-sung and Kim Jong-il. As is the case with First Class train stations, the term 'First Class' is incorporated into the job title of the nation's professionals who work only on matters directly related to the Kim family. In fact, Kim Il-sung's own memoir, *With the Century*, was compiled by a group of First Class novelists from the April 15

Literary Group. In elite circles, the memoir was known as one of Kim Il-sung's favourite books. Once, at a gathering of North Korean cadres who had family connections in Japan, Kim Il-sung described, to the amusement of his guests, how much he enjoyed reading *With the Century*. After his death, and as his son Kim Jong-il's rule became established in the institutions of the state, the status of novelists changed. Poetry became the literary vogue. This was not due solely to Kim Jong-il's preference for the form. The phenomenon was reinforced, if not triggered, by a shortage of paper when the North Korean economy collapsed and people scrabbled just to survive. When there wasn't even enough paper in the country to print school textbooks, not many people could afford to own a hefty revolutionary novel. With poetry, however, the necessary tenets of loyalty to the Kim dynasty could be distilled potently into a single newspaper page. This is why poetry emerged as the dominant literary vehicle through which Kim Jong-il exercised his cultural dictatorship.

With the decrease in the number of novelists, and an increase in demand for poetry and poets, a more stringent professional hierarchy was needed. Epic poets write long poems, lyric poets write shorter ones; and this generic distinction came to determine a poet's rank, although the Workers' Party alone could decree which genre a poet might adopt and which poets might be permitted the honour of praising Kim Jong-il through poetry. The epic genre of Kim Jong-il poetry in particular was restricted to just six poets, who were also the poets laureate of North Korea. At the age of twenty-eight, in 1999, I became the youngest of this tiny elite of court poets. Based on age and experience alone, I had accomplished the impossible. Unlike my fellow poets, however, I was also an employee of the United Front Department – a job that allowed me entry into a world completely unknown to most ordinary North Koreans, where I was given access not only to state secrets, but to a world that lay far beyond the remit of the Workers' Party.

The United Front Department (UFD) is a key section in the Workers' Party, responsible for inter-Korean espionage, policy-making and diplomacy. Since 1953, Korea has been divided by an armistice line known as the Korean Demilitarised Zone (DMZ), held in place by military force on each side. The division of the Korean peninsula is not based on a difference in language, religion or ethnicity, but on a difference in political ideology. The North Korean version of Socialism, founded as it is on the maintenance of absolute institutional unity, regards pluralism and individual determination as its greatest enemy. The Workers' Party has therefore been active and diligent in psychological warfare operations aimed at Koreans in both the North and the South for over half a century.

Entrusted to this most sanctified mission, I worked in Section 5 (Literature), Division 19 (Poetry) of Office 101. In spite of the uncanny and unintended echo of Orwell's Room 101, this office was, ironically, so named precisely in order to avoid any hint of the nature of our work. The institution had been established in 1970, and the ratification from Kim Il-sung had been issued on 10 October, hence Office '101'.

When it was first set up, my department specialised in conducting psychological warfare operations against and in relation to the South through cultural media such as the press, literary arts, music and film. After the 1970s, it strove particularly to amplify anti-American sentiment and foster pro-North tendencies among the South Korean population, exploiting the democratic resistance movements that had risen against the then military dictatorship.

Work produced here was circulated under the names of South Korean publishers, and even took on their distinctive literary style, preferred fonts, and quality and weight of paper. In music, too, the styles of instrumental and vocal arrangements were copied from South Korean recordings. Books and cassettes produced in this way were systematically distributed by our department through pro-North organisations in Japan or through other South-East Asian nations, and passed on to democratic resistance movements in South Korea. My department in this way sowed the seeds of what might at first appear to be a political paradox: even today, sympathy towards the DPRK among South Koreans is almost entirely concentrated within the democratic, progressive and anti-authoritarian camp of the nation's political divide.

Just as on a beach, wearing a swimsuit is more appropriate than a business suit, in the spirit of being faithful to the South Korean context, the institutional slogan of the UFD was 'Localisation', whereby we were required to absorb the character and identity of South Koreans. My first day at work in Office 101, and therefore my entry into its South Korean bubble, was 12 August 1998. I was twenty-seven. I was never more proud of myself than that day, as I stepped into the secret world of the UFD.

My office was in the built-up neighbourhood of Ryunghwa District in Pyongyang's Central Area. The strikingly different world of Office 101 was evident as soon as I crossed the threshold of the compound. There was a large steel gate with high walls all around, representing the exclusivity of a world that ordinary people could not peer into. Employees used a small entrance that was part of the gate, and which allowed only one man at a time to squeeze through. A single soldier stood guard.

The presence of the soldier was also a mark that distinguished this institution from the rest of North Korean society, where employees usually took turns to serve as guard and surveillance for and against fellow employees. As if to confirm that guard duty was a separate duty from UFD duties in this institution, a male cadre of our department's Party Committee had to be fetched to explain my presence to the guard, and to have my identification double-checked, before I was allowed to set foot in the compound for the first time.

Once I entered, in contrast to the small and unassuming entrance, the yard was very large. Everything was paved with cement, without a trace of visible bare earth. The cadre who came to fetch me explained that the four-storey building opposite us was the headquarters of Office 101. The main building was flanked to the left by a library of South Korean literature and an assembly hall. Communications Office 813, to the right, was where counterfeit books were printed under the imprints of South Korean publishers. Pointing to the library, the cadre told me that the library building had been the only school for courtesans in Pyongyang at the time of the Japanese occupation. Adding that Wolhyang-dong in Moranbong Area, not far from here, was a famous courtesan area in the past, he smiled knowingly at me.

My office in Division 19 (Poetry) was on the second floor of the main building and in my time there were eight of us in the team: seven men and one woman. Opening the office door, I immediately saw long wooden desks on two sides of the room. Each desk sat four, and we would face the wall as we worked. As I set foot on the marble floor of the office, I almost turned back to leave: it was as if I had just blundered onto the scene of North Korea's most terrifying crime – treason – the extent of which no one else in the country could begin to imagine or exaggerate. The forbidden materials so casually littering every surface in the room would have brought a death sentence in any other room in all of North Korea and, anywhere else in the country, the shocking slogan framed in pride of place on the wall would have been far beyond the pale in its daring contradiction of half a century's demonising of the South. The enemy newspapers and books strewn carelessly about the office were only slightly less astonishing to my eyes than the mandate for Office 101 from Kim Jong-il, respectfully framed and displayed prominently on the otherwise bare white wall: 'Inhabit Seoul, although you are in Pyongyang.' An act of abominable treason outside these walls was not only permitted within them, but actively encouraged by Kim Jong-il himself! The leader required us to inhabit South Korea's collective psyche so as to undermine and triumph over it. Every day I worked in the UFD I never lost my sense of wonder at our world's stark and secret contrast with the closed society outside our compound.

With our Workers' Party passes in our shirt pockets, we arrived at Office 101 every day at 8 a.m. and began our working day by reading the South Korean newspapers. Although North Korea's official name is the Democratic People's Republic of Chosun, it refers to itself as Chosun and South Korea as southern Chosun, and defines the borders of Korea from the DPRK point of view. However, in the course of our work in Office 101, we saw the term 'South Korea' everywhere in the papers and it became second nature to us. In North Korea, the southern administration was portrayed as a treasonous regime led by a sycophantic leader, who continued to betray the Korean people and their land in order to make them puppets of the United States; but through the media that filled the room, we came to know their leader as the South Korean President.

As no one within our office was allowed to talk about their job, or to know anything about a colleague's, there were no items on anyone's desk that were not strictly necessary to the task at hand – apart from a calendar. The only item that stood out in the room was a small mirror on the table of our female colleague, fiercely marking her territory as a woman. If it weren't for the different locks on each of our desk drawers, the rest of us might forget which desk was our own.

Just as our drawers were always locked, members of my team rarely talked about their personal lives, although there were only the eight of us. Once, I cautiously asked the reason for this on my way home with a senior acquaintance at the UFD. His answer was unexpected. He said the reason why everyone kept to themselves inside the office compound was not so much because of security constraints, but because of the nature of our work. Outside, we were Pyongyang residents and North Koreans. Inside, however, we were South Korean citizens, each one of us. As there was not much to talk about while in these foreign shoes, the lack of conversation on personal topics had become an institutional habit. After this explanation, I understood better how the essence of 'Localisation' was our chameleon-like duality.

Nevertheless, this privileged 'Localisation' was strictly controlled. South Korean newspapers were only loaned out for a day at a time, and we had to return them to the library before leaving work. In the case of South Korean novels or poems, we could borrow them for several days, but we had to keep them in our locked drawers when leaving the UFD premises. Taking any South Korean materials out of this area was forbidden, and the librarian sometimes visited the office unannounced to check that our reading materials were kept securely.

Our main task, from the moment we arrived at work to the moment we left, was to transform ourselves into South Korean poets and write South Korean poetry. To be more precise, we were to be South Korean poets who were supporters of Kim Jong-il. My South Korean pseudonym was Kim Kyong-min. Our names and surnames had to be different from our real names, and when asked to choose a pseudonym I had used the name of the first relative who came to mind. Supervisor Park Chul deliberated for over three hours on whether the name sounded plausible as that of a South Korean poet before he granted permission for me to assume it.

In return for our specialist work, and on top of our standard rations, we received additional rations of imported food every Saturday. Because of our identity as inhabitants of the outside world, the resources we received – different each time – came from the outside world. They were taken from humanitarian materials donated by the United Nations and the rest of the international community, as well as from South Korean NGOs and religious organisations. In the five-kilo packages that we received, there would be rice from the US, cheese, butter, olive oil, mayonnaise and even underwear and socks.

Sometimes, there were cookies and sweets, or milk powder intended for babies. Because we were given so much, it was a chore to collect our regular rations from the public distribution system, on which the rest of North Korea depended on for survival.

The foreign packages always came to us with their labels intact. The existence of such international aid was viewed as a shameful secret that the regime could not afford to reveal to its ordinary citizens at a time of widespread famine, as it would undermine the state's ideology of 'self-reliance'. But as our department's role was to live and work as outsiders, it seemed logical that we should receive outside goods. We had been handpicked for this work and were trusted not to be tarnished by association with these outside voices and supplies. It felt like a blessing to be allowed to inhabit such a privileged world.

Consuming outside products was easy, but thinking like an outsider was not. One day, feeling it was too difficult to write successfully like a South Korean, I consulted Supervisor Park Chul. He was a man who struck me as imposing, despite his balding head. He had double eyelids and thick eyebrows that bristled with charisma.

'I don't really know much about southern Chosun,' I said. 'And I just don't have the knowledge or experience to make literature out of southern Chosun life. So exactly what kind of writing should I do here?'

Supervisor Park Chul laughed so hard that his comb-over flopped down over his eyebrows. He patted it back into place. 'Neither you nor I have been to Seoul!' he said. 'Although we're all countrymen, Northerners and Southerners, our cultures are different now. But it doesn't make much difference, because we're actually working with the Northern audience in mind, not the people of southern Chosun.'

He paused to crumble some cooked egg yolk into a fish tank containing three bright red fish. After tipping the rest of the egg yolk into his mouth, he wiped his hands and continued, 'To succeed here, you have to give up on anything like your own name or renown as a writer. You know, when I used to work for the Writers' Union, I was a star on the rise. You've probably read my poems. Take, for example, "Longing for my Townsfolk".'

'Yes,' I replied, though the title didn't ring any bells.

He continued, 'If I'd stuck to being a poet, I'd probably be a household name by now. But since I've spent my life as a UFD operative, no Koreans here or in the South will ever recognise my work. Still, at least we have an easy life, working here.'

Hearing him sigh, I thought of him as a lonely, ageing man who had to keep his secret life to himself and his colleagues. Just as he'd said, working at the UFD meant not only hiding our work from our countrymen in the South, but also from those in the North. With the increasing economic discrepancy between the North and South, the ideological warfare against the South was perceived as futile by the 1990s, and the propaganda campaigns against the South had run out of steam.

By my time, the UFD was using the experience and techniques previously employed against South Korea's citizens to conduct psychological offensives against our own people. The experience and techniques that had been learned were replicated in psychological operations aimed at North Koreans though, in other ways, we were still fighting a cultural war on two fronts.

The work of Office 101 was never confined to a single genre or medium. It employed speeches, video, music and other forms of cultural expression – all under the names of South Korean or foreign authors – that could be used to infiltrate and influence the values of Koreans.

In April 1998, for example, four months before the start of my work at UFD, Office 101, Section 1 (Newspapers) produced an article that received praise from Kim Jong-il. The piece was written under an assumed outsider's name and declared our Great Leader Kim Il-sung to be the Sun of the World. The evidence in question was the sinking of the *Titanic*. The date on which the RMS *Titanic* sank, 15 April 1912, also happens to be the date of Kim Il-sung's birth. Using this coincidence as a form of historical proof, Section 1 explained that 'As the Sun set in the West, it rose in the East'. Such creations of the United Front Department were then published in the Party newspaper, the *Rodong Sinmun*, or broadcast on television – which only shows state-run channels – as the works of foreign authors, journalists and intellectuals. The North Korean people could never have imagined that all these apparently foreign works were produced by Office 101 in the very heart of their capital, Pyongyang. Isolated from the outside world, it's not surprising that they believed that the people of the world, including South Koreans, admired our country's strong leadership and many achievements.

After Kim Il-sung's death in 1994, epic poetry became the chief vehicle of political propaganda with the publication of a poem by Kim Man-young of the Writers' Union Central Committee. The work took the form of a prayer for the eternal life of Kim Il-sung. Kim Jong-il published that lengthy poem in the *Rodong Sinmun* and proclaimed Kim Man-young the most loyal worker in North Korea. Soon afterwards, the poetry of Shin Byung-gang was promoted by the military's Propaganda Department in order to demonstrate their loyalty to Dear Leader. Kim Jong-il declared Shin's works, along with those of Kim Man-young, to be 'People's Literature'; and the two poets were presented with imported cars and household appliances, as well as extravagantly decorated luxury apartments whose furnishings included sets of gold-plated cutlery.

Within my department, a panic ensued. Although the UFD also employed poets, it had not been able to satisfy Kim Jong-il with a single epic poem – a serious omission that could potentially lead to an accusation of insufficient loyalty on the part of the United Front

Department as a whole. It had become an increasingly worrying concern to my colleagues by the time I joined the Department.

The problem had been exacerbated by the type of personnel they employed. Due to the constraints of psychological warfare under which the UFD operated, operatives were highly trained in ideological persuasion but had not invested much thought in the literary qualities of the work they produced. It was perhaps the tragic and inevitable consequence of making art anonymously, as Supervisor Park Chul had suggested when he described not being able to publish his works in his own name. Moreover, UFD writers had to accommodate two lies unique to them in the writing process: they had to pretend to be South Koreans in their feelings of adoration for Kim Jong-il, and this had to be expressed in a fabricated South Korean way of writing.

Although I was the youngest writer on board, at twenty-seven, the onus of rectifying this situation fell on me. When I was summoned to UFD headquarters to receive orders from First Deputy Director Im Tong-ok, I could hardly believe my own ears. Im Tong-ok was the highest authority in the UFD, and even the head of Office 101 could not meet him without being explicitly summoned. The UFD has several sections, and more offices under each section. Office 101, to which I belonged, was part of the policy-making section of the UFD. Between me and Im Tong-ok was the head of Division 19, then that of Section 5, as well as the other various heads of Office 101. To be summoned outside of this chain of command was a striking anomaly.

The headquarters of the UFD lies in Jeonseung-dong of Moranbong District in Pyongyang. The long, three-storey building, privy to the secrets of the history of the Workers' Party and our nation's history of espionage, looked even more imposing than Office 101. As if to hide its secrets from the world, the building faced north, away from the sunlight, and was covered in ivy.

The Deputy Policy Director of Office 101 led me to the door of Director Im Tong-ok's office, on the first floor of the building. The wooden floorboards creaked beneath our feet with every step. The majestic old building seemed to be in built in an old Russian style, with its high ceilings and large windows, and the imposing double doors to Director Im's office added to the sense of grandeur.

My guide knocked and entered, revealing another open door. He mumbled something into the room, and a loud voice answered from within.

'Ask him to come in. Come in!' said First Deputy Director Im Tong-ok.

His title of First Deputy Director meant that he acted with the absolute authority of Kim Jong-il in one of the nation's key ministries. There were only six institutions considered important enough to be headed by a First Deputy Director: the Organisation and Guidance Department (Kim Jong-il's executive chain of command, which sits above the constitution and has unrestricted jurisdiction to intervene in any sphere), the Propaganda and Agitation Department (whose First Deputy Directorship was left vacant until 1998, after which Jung Ha-chul was appointed to the post by Kim Jong-il), the United Front Department, Office 38 (in charge of Kim Jong-il's personal wealth), Office 35 (conducts intelligence activities overseas) and the Ministry of State Security (the secret police).

Director Im came to meet me at the door. His piercing gaze and countenance suggested that he indeed had authority over all matters related to South Korea and to the external presentation of North Korea, as the representative of Kim Jong-il. However, perhaps he was dumbfounded by the situation he found himself in, assigning such a critical task to an inexperienced young man, or perhaps he was just at a loss for words. He wiped his wide forehead, mustered all the concern he could gather into his deep wrinkles, and made it clear, in his long-winded way, that this task was not one he was assigning lightly. Then he suddenly stood to attention, saying with utmost conviction: 'Now the General's order will be communicated.'

Whenever Kim's words are disseminated in an order, letter or certificate of appreciation, the speaker must stand to attention and make sure his appearance is properly respectful, that his uniform is impeccable and that all his shirt buttons are done up properly. Loyalty to Kim Jong-il had to be demonstrated even in the smallest action as well as through one's overall attitude. As Director Im stood to attention, I instinctively did the same, waiting for his next words.

'The General has issued an order for an epic poem to be used in the conducting of psychological warfare,' he continued. 'This work must promote the notion that our *Songun* policy has been formulated to protect South Korea. The United Front Department assigns this operation to Comrade Kim Kyong-min,' he said, using my assumed South Korean name.

Director Im looked as if he were about to continue speaking, but paused when he noticed that I was biting my lip in consternation. The *Songun* or 'Military-First' policy was supposed to unify the entire Korean peninsula under Kim Jong-il through the superior might of our military force, and to defend our Socialism. I now had to write a poem based on the premise that such a policy *protected* the South. Without realising it, I had grimaced at the evident impossibility of such a task. Director Im assumed a severe expression, but seemed to be at a loss for further words. 'You have two months,' he said, and the meeting was over.

It was mid-December 1998. From that day on, I worked round the clock on the task that had been assigned to me. The basic argument was straightforward: it was my job to praise Kim Jong-il as the master of the gun, the bringer of justice and the People's Lord who knew only victory. But the essence of the task was to find evidence for these truths and shape them into a literary form. To help me accomplish this, I spent an entire month reading South Korean literature, identifying themes that supported the argument I was to expound.

I decided on a comparison of South Korea's *Mangwoldong Memorial for the Martyrs of Democracy* with North Korea's *Sinmiri Memorial for Revolutionary Martyrs*, with a pun linking *Gukgun* (the name of South Korea's National Army) and *Songun* (the Military-First policy of North Korea). This allowed me to compare South and North as two sides of the same coin: while the democratic martyrs of South Korea had been killed by the bullets of their *Gukgun*, the revolutionary martyrs of North Korea would be looked after even in their afterlife by our policy of *Songun*. My poem portrayed South Korea's military as aggressive, and that of North Korea as concerned solely with defending the Korean people. When I submitted my proposal, Director Im and the other UFD officials heaped praise on the approach I had chosen.

On 16 May 1961, a military coup ended civilian rule in South Korea and ushered in the military dictatorship of Park Chung-hee. His long rule of eighteen years was ended by his assassination by an associate, but in the instability that followed, Cheon Doo-hwan positioned himself as the new military dictator. In this way, the divided peninsula was ruled by a military dictator not only in North Korea, but also in the South.

On 18 May 1980, however, South Korean democratic activists rose up in protest in the provincial city of Gwangju in South Korea. They were violently suppressed in the streets by South Korean soldiers, whose authoritarian leader claimed that the protesters, who were armed and were damaging government property and the police station, were North Korean agents who had infiltrated the country. Taking my inspirational starting point from the fact that the South Korean military had once massacred its own citizens, I wrote in the passionate voice of a South Korean poet visiting Pyongyang in May.

To the poet, a Korean spring could not come about through

Nature's will alone. It could only be brought about and sustained by the committed protest of the people rising for their rights. The South Korean poet, knowing only a blood-soaked spring, recognises in Pyongyang a true Korean spring: here, both Koreas are protected by Kim Jong-il's policy of *Songun*, as he wields the very gun handed to him by his father, Kim Il-sung, who once used the weapon to free the Korean people from Japanese rule. This is how the poet concludes his praise of that gun:

> So this is the Gun
> that in the hands of an inferior man
> can only commit murder,
> but, when wielded by a great man,
> can overcome anything.
> As history has shown,
> war and carnage belong
> to the weak.
> General Kim Jong-il,
> the General alone,
> is Lord of the Gun,
> Lord of Justice,
> Lord of Peace,
> Lord of Unification.
> Ah, the true Leader of the Korean people!

The poem was presented to Kim Jong-il in time for the anniversary of the Gwangju Uprising on 18 May 1999.

After publication, I received the moving news that Kim Jong-il had read my poem many times, underlining key phrases as he went. He even wrote next to the title of the poem in his own hand, 'This is the artistic standard of the *Songun* Era.' It was a historic moment of triumph for the UFD in establishing itself above the military and the Party's propaganda departments in the sphere of literary arts.

Most importantly for me, I gained the personal approval of the single most powerful man in our country. The personal endorsement from Kim Jong-il was followed by an order for nationwide publication. Four days after my submission of the poem, on 22 May 1999, 'Spring Rests on the Gun Barrel of the Lord' was distributed throughout the nation in the *Rodong Sinmun* newspaper. This led to my invitation to become one of the 'Admitted' of Kim Jong-il.

My entry into this circle changed the course of my life in the way that winning the lottery might do in a capitalist nation. My career ahead was full of opportunities from which I could cherry-pick as I chose. But most importantly, my new status guaranteed a privilege of immunity that was powerful beyond imagination: not even the highest authorities of the DPRK could investigate, prosecute or harm one of the Admitted. The only way prosecution could possibly occur was for the crime to be treason and for the Organisation and Guidance Department to receive explicit permission from Kim Jong-il himself. Nobody wanted to push too far and risk the ill will of the General himself, so such a process was rarely pursued.

The Party's Organisation and Guidance Department, responsible for the protection of Kim Jong-il, operated a special section dedicated to serve those who were Admitted. The criteria were strict and the circle small. As was the case with me, Kim Jong-il had personally to request your presence and spend time with you behind closed doors for more than twenty minutes. Bursting with pride at my admission to this tiny and exclusive elite, I felt like a new man each day. My first year of work at the UFD passed by very quickly.

In North Korea, the anniversary on 8 July of Kim Il-sung's death – referred to as the Celebration of Kim Il-sung's Eternal Life – is a field of battle among cadres desperate to demonstrate their loyalty to the cult of Kim. Director Im Tong-ok announced during the UFD's agenda meeting for the year 2000 that we would be the ones to offer the best epic poem to Kim Jong-il, outshining the military and Party's propaganda departments once again. As I was now one of the Admitted, there was no question of the glorious task falling to anyone other than me, and my primary task for the year was the completion of this assignment.

Director Im took the reins with great gusto from the start of the first thematic planning meeting.

'Quiet, please. We will now begin our meeting to discuss the literary work of the United Front Department that will be published to commemorate the Supreme Leader's immortal life on 8 July. I have already asked Comrade Kim Kyong-min to call his poem "An Ode to the Smiling Sun". In any event, we must stick to the "Smiling Sun" motif.'

As Director Im said, the only way to eulogise the Supreme Leader's immortal life was through the motif of the 'Smiling Sun'. The Workers' Party had conducted propaganda activities focused on Kim Il-sung and his successor, Kim Jong-il, for over half a century. In the context of this tradition, 'Smiling Sun' was a relatively new motif. It had first been seen at the funeral of Kim Il-sung in 1994.

Usually, funeral portraits showed the deceased wearing a sombre expression. However, declaring that 'The Supreme Leader is alive and with us forever', Kim Jong-il ordered that the standard funeral portrait of his father be exchanged for one of him smiling. From then on, the Supreme Leader was referred to as a 'Sun' whose immortal life was a 'smile'.

On 8 July 1997, exactly three years after Kim Il-sung's death, the Central Party Committee, Central Military Committee, National Defence Commission, Central People's Committee and Parliamentary Committee issued a joint declaration that Kim Il-sung's birthday was to be inaugurated as the 'Sun Festival'. At the same time, it was declared that our calendar was to be changed. Kim Il-sung's birthday,

15 April 1912, was set as the first year of the new *Juche* calendar, *Juche* being the state-ratified philosophy of North Korea based on the principle of self-reliance. The year AD 2000 became *Juche* 89.

'Now, Comrade Kim Kyong-min will expound on this theme.'

Only after someone tapped me on the arm did I realise that everyone was waiting for me to rise and speak. I leapt to my feet. 'Although the title of this work refers to the "Smiling Sun", I would like the poem to make a literary allusion to tears.'

I could hear murmuring around me.

'If you examine the "Smiling Sun" works produced until now by the Party or military, they refer to the Supreme Leader's smile predominantly in the context of our achievements,' I explained. 'For example, the Supreme Leader smiles from the height of his immortality because he is satisfied with the great virtue and legacy politics of our General's rule, or as he peers down with pleasure at our unique kind of Socialism, which remains steadfast despite threats and pressure from imperialistic forces. In my view, it is time for the United Front Department to steer towards satisfying our audience's literary sensibilities, and to move beyond agitating their political fervour.'

'That's all very well, but how will you satisfy their literary sensibilities?' Director Im asked curtly.

'This is what I propose to say: when I traced the history of the "Smiling Sun", I discovered that our Supreme Leader was surrounded by tears from early childhood. Embarking on his life in this manner, the Supreme Leader triumphed over individual suffering and anguish and dedicated his entire life to his people and homeland by smiling. In other words, our Supreme Leader lived for his people and not for himself. This progression will lead to the following conclusion: "All the tears that were to have been shed by his people, our Supreme Leader took on himself alone to shed. What smiles he had, he gave them all so that his people might smile." By juxtaposing his tears and his smiling, the "Smiling Sun" will appear to shine more brightly. This also allows for the Smiling Sun to be ascribed with the following poetic qualities: "When the Supreme Leader gave the people his gift of smiling, it manifested as his Love; when he sowed his gift on our lands, it manifested as rays of the Sun; and as he left his gift for history, it manifested as Immortal Life."'

As soon as I finished speaking, Director Im leapt out of his chair. His excitement could not be contained and he smacked the desk several times. He exclaimed, 'That's it! If this goes according to plan, the General will no doubt be moved to tears, as will the rest of the nation. The Propaganda and Agitation Department and the General Political Bureau are no match for us. Let me assure you, the United Front Department will come out ahead if we go through with this. This is real poetry! Comrades, what are your thoughts?'

With the powerful head of the United Front Department showing such enthusiasm for my proposal, it was no wonder that praise and wonder erupted from the rest of the room too. One man confessed how difficult it had been for him to hold back tears as he listened to me speak, and began to clap his hands.

Suddenly, Supervisor Park Chul stood up, wearing a severe expression in stark contrast to the others in the room. He was my immediate superior, as the head of Office 101, Section 5. 'Comrade Director Im,' he said, 'although the proposal is laudable in its literary potential, I believe that a reference to our Supreme Leader shedding tears is highly problematic.'

The room was silent.

Supervisor Park Chul continued, 'Kim Chul, one of our nation's three canonical poets, employed the word "dew" to refer euphemistically to the Leader's tears. For this mistake, he was banished to the countryside for ten years.'

'What do you mean? Of course we can make a reference to tears. Don't you remember how our General shed tears at our Supreme

Leader's funeral ceremony? And it was even broadcast all over the world! On top of that, I'm sure I've seen references to our Supreme Leader's tears when he was moved by the novels he read.' As Director Im retorted with annoyance, other cadres nodded enthusiastically.

Park Chul spoke again. 'The novel is a descriptive genre, but poetry is a lyric genre. Poetry is to do with human emotions, not with human psychology. To refer so explicitly to tears in a poem would promote "pessimism on the part of the individual". Besides, in verse, you can only have tears of loyalty. Yet Comrade Kyong-min proposes not only to refer to the tears of an individual, but of our Supreme Leader himself. Heaven forbid! If we are accused of promoting "pessimism on the part of our Supreme Leader", each one of us will have to face the consequences.'

No one said a word, perhaps at the terrifying mention of 'consequences'. One man shut his notepad, as if to acknowledge that the meeting was over.

I rose again to speak. 'Of course you are right to say that tears of loyalty, which must be shed by an individual, are the only tears permitted in poetry. But the poetic work in discussion here is to be composed in the genre of epic. Epic poetry is a narrative genre, just like the novel. Moreover, the focus of the work is not on our Supreme Leader shedding tears, but on how he has continuously exercised restraint and held them back. It is due to this forbearance that his tears were made manifest as Love, Sunshine and Immortal Life. Therefore, I do not see a problem.'

Supervisor Park, visibly annoyed that an employee of his should speak out in defiance, refused to change his stance. 'Referring to our Supreme Leader's tears once or twice? There's nothing wrong with that. But you're talking about an epic poem, whose length will require repeated references to our Supreme Leader's tears. Have you ever seen such a thing in any of our nation's poems? Right now, as our nation pulls through this time of famine and bad harvests, the Party slogan is "The journey is hard but let us go forth in laughter". And you propose to write a poem about our Supreme Leader shedding tears?'

At these words, even the cadre who had earlier been close to tears upon hearing my proposal nodded in agreement. Everyone now looked to Director Im. Pushing at the table with both hands, he stood up and spoke gravely. 'This is the plan. Starting from today, Comrade Kyong-min will put all other duties aside for six months and compose an epic poem according to his proposal. But he will make sure to avoid excessive references to our Supreme Leader's tears. At the United Front Department, you have assumed a South Korean identity and this allows you some leeway. We're not restricted by Writers' Union rules and don't have to go through their censorship or approval process. We just have to judge among ourselves at the UFD as best we can. The current proposal is excellent in terms of its literary merit. Let's make this work.'

Director Im dismissed everyone from the meeting but asked me to stay behind. The two of us were alone in the room.

'Don't pay any attention to what Supervisor Park says,' he told me. 'I'm sure he's jealous. What achievements can he boast of? You have six months of hard work ahead of you. You should take a week off. Go and recharge yourself. Where would you like to go?'

I told him I wanted to visit my hometown. After meeting the General, I had been thinking a lot about my friends back home. It was glorious enough to have been admitted to the UFD, but I had even become one of the Admitted. How much everyone would admire me! I said that revisiting my place of birth would help me equip myself emotionally for the task ahead. Im Tong-ok granted my request without hesitation.

GOING HOME | 2

I PHONED my childhood friend Young-nam from Pyongyang Station. We had been best friends in nursery school, where we were in the same class, and we had remained inseparable all the way to the end of primary school.

'You're meeting me at the station, right?'

'In your wildest dreams!' His response was as predictable as ever, and I burst into laughter.

Young-nam's nickname was 'Jappo' – short for Japanese expatriate. Like me, he had been born in Sariwon in North Korea, but all the kids called him Jappo because his parents were immigrants from Osaka in Japan. They had arrived in Sariwon in the 1960s, as part of the repatriation of Koreans from Japan referred to as the 'Great Movement of the Korean People'. At the time, in a bid to promote the North over the South as the homeland of a unified Korea, Kim Il-sung welcomed into North Korea around 100,000 ethnic Koreans who had been living in Japan.

After the Korean War, the circumstances of the Cold War made North Korea a more attractive choice in terms of its economic superiority, and this enabled Kim Il-sung to pursue a policy of embracing expatriates. Using these immigrants as evidence of people choosing Socialism over Capitalism, the North Korean state fervidly referred to them in propaganda campaigns. On the surface, it looked as if Kim Il-sung was gaining significantly from a propaganda policy based on an embracing celebration of Korean ethnicity. In reality, however, the arrival of the immigrants caused unexpected ripples in North Korean society. Actually, it was what they brought with them that had the greatest impact. The Japanese products that the immigrants brought with them were regarded as wondrous goods from the outside world, never before seen by ordinary North Koreans. Until then, they had believed that any product of Kim Il-sung's Socialism must be the best in the world, but now they were exposed to the state of progress in Japan. The immigrants settled all over North Korea, according to their wishes or ancestral connections, and an unofficial new slogan was seized on nationwide: 'Capitalism may be rotten to the core, but they do make good products!' Almost instantaneously, North Korea became caught up in a fever of all things 'made in Japan'.

It became a fad for North Koreans to pick up labels or packaging thrown out by the 'Jappos' and display them in their homes like treasure. The immigrants naturally came to be regarded as a privileged class through their enjoyment of Japanese products, and they were soon firmly entrenched in the comfortable middle class of North Korean society.

They were admired not only because of the products they possessed, but also because of their Japanese cultural traits. Whether it was their characteristic forms of greeting, language, manners or even their eating habits, their way of life was considered sophisticated and prosperous. In contrast, the official reward of higher status in return for loyal service seemed not as exciting. Increasingly, those who did not have family outside the country to send in Japanese products tried to emulate the Jappos at least in cultural terms.

Children were all too sensitive to this trend, complaining to their parents that none of their older relatives had had the foresight to run away and settle in Japan. The North Korean state had built the legitimacy of Kim Il-sung on the basis of his credentials as an anti-Japanese resistance fighter, and so it was a great irony that his immigration movement caused ordinary North Koreans to admire

Japan. Korea had been freed from the ignominy of colonial servitude under the Japanese, but now it had been 'colonised' again by the Japanese or, more specifically, the Jochongryon, the organisation run by the UFD that represents people of Korean origin in Japan. In effect, the Japan taboo reinforced by means of institutional communalism had begun to fade away from the public consciousness.

To North Koreans, for whom even ordinary clothes were a uniform dictated by the state, the notion of a private car for individual use was inconceivable. Nevertheless, this very privilege was freely given to the Jappos, whose private cars, speeding along empty roads in Pyongyang, were more than just a mode of transport in the eyes of North Koreans. They introduced the dangerous suggestion that one might control the speed of one's journey, instead of goose-stepping in line to the whistle of the state. In this way, the presence of these immigrants offered a daring invitation to flout the traditional framework of loyalty.

The North Korean state's jealousy eventually led to oppression of the Jappos. The immigrants, who had experience and memories of living in a Capitalist society, were assigned to the 'wavering' class, reserved for those whose ideas were perceived to be a risk to the state. Their career prospects were severely restricted. Kim Jong-il even legally prohibited Jappos from driving white cars. The reason for this seemed petty: it was because white cars were the same colour as the background of Japan's national flag. In Party lectures, cadres alleged that Japan only exported white cars to the world, yet within their own nation they were fixated on red cars; and the reason for this was that they wanted to paint their national flag on the world map as a symbol of their central position in the world. It was clearly a warning from above that a Jappo could not be trusted in the same way as a Korean.

Despite these efforts, the preference of many North Koreans for the 'Mount Fuji people', as opposed to the 'Mount Paektu people' and the anti-Japanese feats of Kim Il-sung, did not disappear. My friend

Young-nam was therefore a member of a group of people who were generally admired, in contradiction to the official stance. Moreover, his family was once the wealthiest in Sariwon.

Nevertheless, life became very difficult for his family after the death of his grandparents in Japan, when their supply of Japanese money and goods came to an end. As they were immigrants from Japan, Young-nam and his parents had no prospect of entering respectable careers, because the assignment of jobs was controlled by the Workers' Party. They had to start selling off their possessions one by one and, eventually, they became impoverished and lived in a much worse state than the local North Koreans.

The one thing I remember clearly from my childhood is that we had a Yamaha piano at home, given to our family by Young-nam's father when he was still a wealthy man. I remember my mother telling me that when Young-nam's family first settled in Sariwon, my father helped them secure a new apartment through the allocations made by the Workers' Party. As the piano had arrived in the house before I was born, I grew up assuming that everyone had Japanese pianos, just as everyone had a portrait of Kim Il-sung on their wall at home.

One day, however, when I went to a friend's house to play, I realised that they did not have a piano. I was astonished. When I came home, I ran into the house and shouted at my mother, as if I had just witnessed something incredible: 'Mum, did you know? They don't have a piano at home!'

She replied coolly, 'They probably didn't want a piano in the house. They prefer reading books.'

It was only when I began my first year at Dongri People's Primary School that I came to understand that the possession of a Japanese Yamaha piano was a very big deal indeed. The kids – and the grown-ups too – referred to me as 'the boy with the Japanese piano' or 'the doctor's boy'. Most kids at school lived in 'harmonica apartments' built in the 1950s, so-called because each floor had flats that were packed closely together like the square holes in a harmonica. We lived in a large flat on the third floor of an apartment block set aside for officials. My mother, who was the head doctor at a medical centre for the exclusive use of Party cadres, hoped that my two older sisters would become teachers and that I would one day become a famous pianist. She finally cajoled my father into finding me a famous piano tutor.

One day, my father brought a tutor home with him. The man had a long face and spoke with the heavy accent characteristic of Hamgyong Province in the north. But what amazed me more than his accent was that he was an ethnic Korean from China. And he stank of cigarette smoke, which I didn't like. Worse, he was a chain-smoker, and my sisters didn't like him much at first, either. But he didn't seem to care. Bending down, he pulled my ear to his mouth and said emphatically in his phlegmatic voice, 'My name is Choi Liang. Did you hear that? Two syllables. Choi Liang!'

His loud voice frightened me as much as the stench of smoke did. When my father announced that the man and his family were going to move in with us, I was devastated. I pretended to need the toilet, ran outside, and sobbed.

Choi Liang became my first proper mentor. He had been a violinist in China's Shanghai Symphony Orchestra. During the Cultural Revolution, he'd fled the Red Guards' assaults on the educated by coming to North Korea, along with many other ethnic Koreans. His first job in North Korea was as a violin tutor at Pyongyang Arts School. At the time, he and Paek Go-san were considered to be among North Korea's leading violinists. Paek Go-san had taken both the top prize for his category and the honorary prize in the Tchaikovsky International Music Competition of 1982. In 1978, he had also been the first Asian to be appointed a lifetime member of the panel of judges for the violin section of the competition.

Paek Go-san had a younger brother called Paek Do-san, who had insulted Choi Liang by referring to him as a 'dirty bastard', a common derogatory term used by Koreans to refer to the Chinese.

Choi Liang, infamous for his short temper, punched him in the face. For this Choi Liang was banished to the countryside until my father rescued him from rustic exile by hiring him to teach me music. Choi Liang's wife, son and daughter moved into our house with him and our quiet home burst into unaccustomed life as it became home to our two families.

In my early years, teacher Choi Liang seemed to me the cruellest of men. He started me off with ear training and he went about this task without mercy. Several hundred times a day, I would have to strain to discern the note or interval he sounded on the piano. Gradually, I learned to pick out the notes and intervals without hesitation. Eventually, he moved on to chords and by the end he had taught me how to arrange music for a string quartet.

My father tried very hard to get Choi Liang hired as a professor at Sariwon Arts School. However, his foreign birth proved too great an obstacle for the post and he was taken on as a lecturer instead. Even so, because he was one of North Korea's leading violinists, students flocked from all over the country to study with him. Choi Liang frequently invited them to our house and even showed them my string quartet arrangements.

I still remember very clearly what Choi Liang had to say about string quartet arrangements, as he often repeated this piece of wisdom: 'Above all, the score should be covered with black notes everywhere. Semitone intervals should be used with care, but as frequently as needed. Understood?'

More than just an education in music, Choi Liang instilled in me great artistic ambition. Every day I listened to his anecdotes about Beethoven, Mozart and the fame that surrounded them even after their deaths. While other children aspired to become Party cadres or to drive cars for Party cadres, I dreamed of becoming Dvořák, and of achieving world renown for the composition of my own *New World* Symphony. I once mentioned this dream to my mother and she gave me a fierce telling-off, saying that if I shared these thoughts with anyone else, our entire family would be accused of Revisionism or Moral Corruption. She made sure to give me a terrific fright by saying that if I didn't keep these thoughts to myself, I might be arrested.

My mother was troubled by the realisation that her thirteen-year-old son had grown enamoured of the music of Dvořák. I had come to love his works because of the tape recordings that Choi Liang had smuggled in with him from China, and because the only other kind of music I had access to was the stuff I heard at school. It wasn't just that the music was limited to revolutionary anthems. Rather, after having been exposed to the thrilling world of harmonic possibility, I found it frustrating to listen to North Korean songs of perfect victory that did not allow for any suggestion of imperfection through musical dissonance or tension.

Once, in singing class at school, I couldn't contain my thoughts any longer. I volunteered to do the accompaniment for the session, and played as I wished instead of following the prescribed pattern. My pedalling on the organ (there was no piano at school) wasn't perfect but I knew that I had played well and without mistakes. In spite of this, our music teacher punished me for my deviation by humiliating me in front of the class, making an example of me as someone who knew nothing whatsoever about music. In my heart, though, I believed it was the school – not me – that lacked an understanding of music. As a result, I could not stop myself from beginning to doubt everything else the school taught us to regard as the most accurate and objective form of knowledge, whether this took the form of the revolutionary history of Kim Il-sung, linguistics or any other subject.

As time went on, I was confirmed in my conviction that Western music was artistically superior to the North Korean music I was being taught. It wasn't that I preferred one set of stylistic rules to the other. Western music had its rules too; but what it had that North Korean music didn't was the infinite possibilities of breaking an established rule, to make a new one of your own. With Choi Liang by my side to explain the intricacies of musical rule-breaking, I grew more confident that the transgression of expectation and rules was not unmusical, but, rather, that this was part of the essence of musicality.

From dawn to dusk, I listened to Dvořák. My father worried about my hearing and took my headphones away from me several times; but I was so desperate that I once took a stethoscope from my mother's bag and held it against the speaker of the tape player so that I could listen under the blankets at night. My father was proudly supportive of my ambitions and was convinced that I was destined for great things, but Choi Liang was stubborn in his honesty.

'This boy will never become a good pianist,' he said. 'His fingers are too short. He does have creative talent, though, and I recommend that he should train to be a composer.'

I entered Pyongyang Arts School at fifteen. I was determined to become a world-famous composer, fulfilling the dream that Choi Liang had sown in me. But my sudden encounter with a book from the '100-Copy Collection' resulted in my musical ambitions being replaced overnight by literary ones.

The book was the *Collected Works of Lord Byron*. As part of North Korea's 'Hundred-Copy Collection', the print run of this book was restricted to one hundred copies. In North Korea, the circulation of foreign books is restricted in this way so that only the ruling Kim and his family, his closest associates and select members of North Korea's elite have access to them. Each of the books in a hundred-copy set has a stamped number on the first page to show which of the hundred copies it is. Books bearing the 'No. 1' stamp are, of course, offered only to the ruling Kim. It is thus considered a mark of high status among cadres and other members of the elite to possess a book stamped with a single-digit numeral, or the closest number they can get to it.

The secret translation and printing of these limited editions of foreign works continues to be done by a team of translators working under the auspices of the Propaganda and Agitation Department and the Chosun Social Sciences Institute, in the Joong-gu Area of Pyongyang. It is the responsibility of cultural or science attachés stationed in DPRK embassies abroad to acquire foreign books for limited distribution through this system.

I don't know how our copy of the *Collected Works of Lord Byron* had ended up in my father's personal bookcase. One day, I picked it up from the shelf out of mere curiosity, noticing that the spine of the book was different from the others stacked there. North Korean books usually reflect North Korean state aesthetics in their bright and gaudy designs. This book, however, was subdued in colour. The dark and faded cover was suggestive of an ancient foreign culture. The pattern of a frame, similar in design to that of an oil painting, surrounded the printed title. Ordinary books were mass-produced, but this book seemed to be handmade, as its thick and bulky cover housed pages that were held together by delicate threadwork.

I opened the book with vague curiosity, but I was pulled in from the first page and the poetry seized me at once. The vocabulary was bold and the words pushed their definitions and associations to the limits, unlike anything I had ever read. In North Korea, the institutional control of thought begins with the consolidation of language, a policy designed to unify the private and public spheres of thought. In order for the realms of individual expression to adhere to a shared ideology, the Party's Propaganda and Agitation Department sets strict boundaries for the written and spoken word. No North Korean literary work may deviate from the legal framework of Kim Jong-il's *Juche* Art Theory, printed in several volumes, which sets the conditions under which Socialist art can exist. The authority of thought which monitors and enforces this theory, through the penalty of prison camp for all those who are responsible for letting a deviant work slip through the net, is the National Literary Deliberation Committee. As one who had been brought up in such a fixed framework of linguistic expression, Byron's poetry was like a dictionary of New Korean to me. As I worked out the meanings and inferences in words I had never seen before, I experienced the strange sensation of learning how to speak Korean from a foreign-language speaker.

What really intrigued me too was the politeness of the language. In the North Korean language, there are two distinct registers of speech: one relating to the Leader, and one to everyone else. Before encountering Byron's poetry, I had thought that adjectives such as 'Dear' and 'Respected' were a special form of pronoun in the Korean language reserved for Kim Il-sung and Kim Jong-il. Along with 'Great', which is always seen in one of the terms referring to Kim Il-sung as 'Great Leader', I had assumed that these adjectives were names just like Kim and therefore etymologically and purely Korean. But I learned, through Byron's poetry, that these words were terms of respect that were part of a universal language and not uniquely Korean. I felt strangely elated by the discovery that these terms might be applied to an individual.

Most of all, the patterns of words and poetic devices – all balanced against the underlying rhythm of the poem – awakened in me a sense of literary sublimity that surpassed what music alone could convey. Just as I had done with Dvořák's *New World* Symphony, I read Byron's epic poems *Childe Harold's Pilgrimage* and *The Corsair* over and over again in their North Korean translations. *The Corsair*'s ending – the protagonist, a vagabond pirate, disappearing from the island upon learning of his beloved's death – left me restless, and this agitation lingered with me long after each reading. I had known only loyalty to the Supreme Leader, believing that this was the most sublime emotion a human being could feel. But these poems were proof that emotions could be experienced in a personal sphere that did not include the Leader. This understanding may be taken for granted in the rest of the world, but it was an astounding epiphany for me, and after this realisation, I wanted suddenly to confess my love to a woman. I wanted to fall in love, and I wanted to be weak for love. Out of this longing, I began to write poetry of my own.

I even considered dropping out of Pyongyang Arts School, but I did not dare let my parents down after the faith they had placed in me. The least I could do, though, was to attempt to find a literary mentor.

There are three poems that all North Koreans must learn by heart. These are 'For my One and Only Homeland' by Ri Su-bok, 'Mother' by Kim Chul and 'My Homeland' by Kim Sang-o. In 'For my One and Only Homeland', the poet states that although he has only one lifetime to live, he will sacrifice it to his homeland, of which there is also only one. In this poem, the self is sublimated to the country. 'Mother' describes how the motherly love of the Workers' Party is deeper than that of any human mother, who cannot rear her child as an individual separate from the state. Here, motherly love is inadequate on its own, and profoundly inferior to the love provided by the Party. 'My Homeland' describes the Great Leader as the poet's true homeland, and the country is subsumed into the identity of its leader.

If I were to have a teacher at all, I wanted it to be one of North Korea's foremost poets. Fortunately, as wide as my world seemed, it was also small. Ri Su-ryon, the granddaughter of Kim Sang-o, happened to be my classmate. When she told me that her grandfather had agreed to meet me, and she asked me to go home with her after lectures, I was so overjoyed that I took her hand and shook it wildly. It was the winter of 1990, when I should have been wholly devoted to my musical studies at Pyongyang Arts School.

Kim Sang-o's apartment was in Otan-dong, in the Joong-gu Area, with unobstructed views over the Daedong River. After Korea's liberation from Japanese occupation in 1948, Kim Sang-o had returned from Japan and served as the deputy editor of a newspaper in Hwanghae Province. When Kim Il-sung came to Hwanghae Province, Kim Sang-o was assigned to be his speechwriter. This collaboration eventually led to his promotion to the post of Vice President of the Central Committee of the Korean Writers' Union.

However, the influence of China's Cultural Revolution, which began in 1966, led to many intellectuals being purged in North Korea too. The North Korean state had designated Khrushchev as a 'revisionist', following his criticism of Stalin's cultification, and at the time the DPRK preferred the Chinese style of Communism to that of the Soviet Union. The record of Kim Sang-o's years in Japan as a student let him down as it associated him with pro-Japanese collaborators, and was seen as undermining Kim Il-sung's authority as an anti-Japanese resistance fighter. After losing his licence as a writer, Kim Sang-o was banished to the countryside, where for fifteen years he worked as a farm labourer.

Kim Il-sung, however, had a good memory. When he conducted an on-site guidance session in South Hwanghae Province, he asked for the young speechwriter who had composed Kim's first speech in Hwanghae Province, shortly after the liberation of Korea. Kim Sang-o was subsequently recalled to Pyongyang and he composed the lyric poem 'My Homeland' at this emotional time, praising the person of Kim Il-sung (instead of the state or territory) as his true homeland. My classmate Ri Su-ryon was born in Seoheung-gun in Hwanghae Province where Kim Sang-o had been in exile, but following his rehabilitation she had moved with him to the capital city of Pyongyang.

Kim Il-sung appointed his former speechwriter as the head of UFD Office 101, Section 5. From then on, he had to channel his literary talents to serve the goals of the Workers' Party, working under a pseudonym and deprived of an identity or history of his own. By the time of my visit to his home, he had retired from the UFD, though he was still an honorary director of Office 101 due to his official status as a Kim Il-sung Associate. As his UFD title came with no actual responsibility, he was living as quiet and ordinary a life as possible for someone with such a background. More importantly from my perspective, he also had the time to meet me.

When Kim Sang-o himself opened the door, I was startled and bowed deeply from the waist. His tall stature and imposing countenance made a strong first impression on me, suggesting that men of Kim Il-sung's inner circle were, even in appearance, extraordinary beings. Yet it was his humility that made him a truly great man in my eyes.

In spite of his status, Kim Sang-o's house was cold because of the erratic heating system in Pyongyang. As I entered, his wife offered me one of his coats to keep me warm, and I was surprised to notice three cigarette burns on the fabric.

Until fairly recently, the electricity supply had not been too bad. But as it was a centrally organised system, even a minor disruption in one area would affect the hot water heating supply for the rest of Pyongyang. The age of the pipes and their tendency to burst frequently was a problem, and many households resorted to siphoning hot water from the traditional Korean under-floor heating system to use for washing. So there was always a lack of heat, and with the inefficiency of the infrastructure, even in the harsh middle of winter, the best heat to be had was a lukewarm floor.

This was the case even though Kim Sang-o lived in a senior Party cadres' retirement flat, built in the 1980s in a residential area set apart from those of ordinary Pyongyang residents. Although this was the first time we had met, he lamented that what he found more unbearable than the cold was the fact that he could not set foot properly on the bare earth. He had been assigned a twelfth-floor apartment and, as the lift was always out of order, he was stuck between the earth and the sky.

When he started to talk about his home province, I could see that the burn marks on his coat were nothing compared to the scars in his heart. In the early 1980s, the North Korean state had decided that the presence of disabled citizens in Pyongyang was an affront to the beauty of the city, and banished them en masse to the countryside. Kim Sang-o's only daughter, who had a physical disability, was left behind in Hwanghae Province when the rest of the family was instructed to relocate to Pyongyang. That woman was my friend Su-ryon's mother.

On the day of my first visit, Kim Sang-o took great pains to read every line of the poems I'd taken from my jacket pocket. When he had finished reading my attempt at an epic poem, he laughed heartily, saying that he knew I had written in imitation of Byron. To my astonishment, he did not scold me, but was accepting of it: 'If you had come to me with something like "Oh, my homeland! Oh, my Party!" I would have refused to talk to you. I enjoyed your personal narrative of love. I can see that you're faithful to your own voice.'

Kim Sang-o's words of moral encouragement became the cornerstone of my life as a writer. He taught me that 'A piece of writing will stubbornly pursue its author and hold him accountable to the end. Look to your conscience; speak your own truth. That is the only way that you can go beyond what you have been taught and accomplish a literature that truly belongs to you.'

In Kim Sang-o's last years, the UFD pleaded with him continually in the hope that he would produce more state literature for them, but he refused to the end, saying that his health didn't allow it. I wonder, though, if his choice to keep silence was the decisive act of Kim Sang-o's conscience and his truth, after a life spent in loyal obedience to the Workers' Party.

With Kim Sang-o's recommendation, I was able to submit my own poems to the selection process for literary works organised by the Party's Propaganda and Agitation Department. The best would be offered for the judgement of Kim Jong-il himself, and my compositions made the selection.

On 19 February 1992, the state newspaper *Rodong Sinmun* published an announcement to the effect that a collection of fifty poems entitled *The Songs of a Blessed Generation* had been presented to General Kim Jong-il on his fiftieth birthday. He had read the book and written the two poets a letter of commendation.

Even today, I remember with vivid clarity the look on the face of the Party Secretary for Pyongyang Arts School as he presented Kim Jong-il's letter of appreciation to me, a student of music who had wronged the school by straying from his assigned course of study. He had to do this in front of all the staff and students, and while he had no alternative but to say, 'I am so delighted that we had such a jewel in our school,' he twisted my ear with such force that I almost cried out loud on stage.

It didn't end there. In his letter, Kim Jong-il said that anything I asked of him would be granted, and I took him at his word. The Party required a graduate of music to serve the state in a musical capacity for the remainder of his or her working life. But the Party made an exception for me and granted me my first choice of career: I was assigned to be the Arts Writer of the Chosun Central Broadcasting Committee in the Propaganda and Agitation Department.

In North Korea, there is only one television channel. Central TV is broadcast from 5 p.m. to 11 p.m. on weekdays and from 10 a.m. on Sundays. In my new role as Arts Writer, I was responsible for curating North Korean poetry, and I helped with presenting poetry in a format suitable for television. My parents and teachers were shocked at Kim Jong-il's granting of my wish, as was, of course, the Party Secretary for Pyongyang Arts School.

It was 1994 when I began my working life. Before my first day at work, I went to see Kim Sang-o's widow, and in the traditional Korean show of reverence, I offered her a deep bow.

Kim Sang-o had died in 1992 of tuberculosis in a special ward on the eleventh floor of Kim Man Yu Hospital, a state-of-the-art facility. Even his final breath, he gave to me. All cadres had to sign an oath of loyalty to Kim Jong-il when they were close to death, swearing that their single-hearted devotion would continue after they died. Poet Kim Sang-o had added the following words to his handwritten will: 'I leave behind unfinished works, to be completed by my children and my student.' His funeral was handled by the United Front Department, as befitted a dignitary of the state. Kim Il-sung also decided that the Homeland Unification Medal – one of North Korea's highest state honours – was to be awarded to Kim Sang-o on the day of his funeral. The *Rodong Sinmun* duly announced this as an ordinance of the state.

It was Kim Sang-o's will that prompted the UFD to recruit me into its ranks, although I had originally applied to be an Arts Writer. Following a stern complaint from Kim Jong-il that the UFD had ceased to produce works of Kim Sang-o's quality, UFD First Deputy Director Im Tong-ok had personally sought me out for recruitment. The vetting process for a Central Party cadre required at least six months of rigorous background checks, but the process was rushed through on orders from above and my transfer to the UFD happened quickly.

There was another problem, though: the Party required UFD staff to be graduates of literature or the social sciences, and music just didn't cut it. So I was admitted to the graduate faculty of literature and languages at the University of Kim Il-sung in September 1996, under the pretext of doing my trial period at the UFD. But this wasn't about due process; it was only a means of achieving an end. The one-year UFD trial period was also replaced by my graduate degree, and I was admitted to the UFD upon graduation.

Because of this history, my request to return to my place of birth was about much more than merely revisiting friends and seeing my hometown again. It was really to make a pilgrimage to the place that had brought me to Choi Liang and Kim Sang-o, who had taken my hand in theirs to guide me towards my calling.

PYONGYANG STATION was so crowded that it was difficult to see along the platform. There seemed to be more passengers who had spent days waiting for a delayed train than people who were there to buy tickets or embark on their journey; and it wasn't just because this was the central railway terminus in the capital city of North Korea.

In North Korea, apart from sections of track linking newly constructed stations or in the development zones, the rest of the country relied on a single-track railway laid during the Japanese occupation of the Korean peninsula during the first half of the twentieth century. North Koreans were used to the fact that trains never operated according to a regular timetable. Both Kim Il-sung and Kim Jong-il stressed that the railway was the nervous system of the nation. But in reality, North Korea was like a person with nerve damage paralysing one half of the body. Natural disasters were not even a major problem, given the constant physical breakdowns, problems with the engine or tracks and frequent blackouts. Even when the electricity was actually working, the power was low, and passengers bounced up and down as the carriage hiccupped its way along the track. Sometimes villagers along the line would race the train on their ox carts, laughing as they overtook the passengers in their carriages.

Besides, there were higher priorities, as passenger trains must always give way to the ruling Kim's special train, for which myriad routes were kept clear for security reasons, only for them to be changed at the last minute. Many freight trains operated several months behind schedule, and the Party and military used all kinds of justifications to get Kim Jong-il's ratification to be granted priority track use. While trains that operated under Kim Jong-il's orders, often carrying military goods, travelled across the country's tracks on maximum priority, passenger trains were at the very bottom of the pecking order.

Luckily, my hometown was south of Pyongyang, where there was less rail traffic compared to other regions. This was thanks to the nature of Japanese colonial planning, which focused its infrastructure in the northern parts of the country, to aid in its mission of using Korea as a foothold for controlling Manchuria to the north. North Korean trade networks were concentrated on these connections, and the southern regions had been left relatively undeveloped.

The distance from Pyongyang to my hometown of Sariwon is sixty-three kilometres, which would take less than an hour by car. But when I arrived at the station, I was told that the start of the journey would be delayed by three hours. I didn't mind the wait. I hadn't been back for ten years and was determined to make the journey by train, so I was full of excited anticipation. To be honest, I was returning home in clouds of glory as one of the Admitted. I had even planned to take with me my special wine glass into which the General himself had poured wine, and use it to toast friends back home. But my mother sternly refused me permission, saying that such an heirloom should not be removed from the house. So instead, I had filled my rucksack with alcohol and tinned meats. Carrying this bag and waiting in line for my ticket, I stood tall and proud.

Queues are the same everywhere in North Korea. There are three signs showing the way to lines for Cadres, Military Personnel and Ordinary Residents; and at the head of each line, armed soldiers stand guard. Although only in my twenties, I confidently approached the Cadres' line with my Central Party identification documents enclosed in a tan leather wallet and embossed with the gold Party emblem. People in this queue were also offered a separate waiting room, so there was no tedious standing in line for several hours like the other passengers.

On any train, the carriage at the front of the train is reserved exclusively for the use of Party cadres. Whereas the platform had been teeming with people, because this was a restricted area, the carriage was empty save for a few people. Near the door, there were four people with dark faces who seemed nervous and kept looking round. It appeared that they had boarded the train illegally by bribing an officer. As if their goal was not Sariwon but the safe start of the journey, they were so relieved when the train began to move that they bent over and giggled among themselves.

In North Korea, there is no freedom of movement. You can only buy a train ticket by showing an official travel pass the size of an identity card, stating your reasons for travel. If you travel without such a pass and are discovered, the sentence is three months of hard labour. A security agent soon appeared in the carriage. He must have been offered a bribe too, because he did not ask to see the travel passes of the four joyriders. As if in gratitude to me for pretending not to have noticed this, once he had checked my travel pass, he stood to attention and saluted me very formally.

For a long time I couldn't take my eyes off the constantly changing scenery outside the window. We had to wait for over two hours at Hwangju Station on the way, but even this did not bother me. I was in enough of a trance to be going back to my hometown, like a pilgrim returning to a pure and holy spring.

When the train finally arrived at Sariwon Station, after travelling for over half a day, I leapt excitedly from my seat but was surprised to see the crowded platform. Having travelled in leisure in an almost empty carriage, I was puzzled to see so many passengers disembarking onto the same platform as me. I even saw dozens of people jumping down from the roof of my carriage. At first, I shook my head at the way they had put themselves at such risk just to get a free ride. But when I approached the commotion further ahead on the platform, I saw that money had not been the problem. Security agents were beating up several passengers and yelling questions: 'Answer me! Do you bastards have a travel pass? Fucking answer the question!'

There are also security checkpoints on all roads that cross the borders of counties and provinces, even in the hills. Those people who were risking the law anyway by travelling without authorisation were forced to travel on the roof of carriages for convenience and ease of escape. This was probably why the people picked on by the security agents betrayed no sign of the strength it must have required to risk their lives by travelling on the roof of a carriage, and instead were pleading with tears and every kind of piteous explanation they could think of.

The atmosphere of my hometown was so different from that of Pyongyang. This unfamiliarity destroyed all the calm excitement of my pilgrimage. The yelling, screaming and coarse swearing all around me made the place feel dark and terrifying. For a while, I stood there feeling lost. I looked around at the screeching mob of people who had come to the station to meet the train. They were not here merely to greet family and friends, but to collect their cargo. Most of the passengers had been ferrying large sacks of corn or rice.

Until 1994, and the start of the Arduous March, all North Koreans relied for sustenance on the socialist Public Distribution System (PDS), which determined the allocation of every basic necessity of life. This included household items and items of food, whether rice or eggs. The ration size was determined by the state, and it also served as a marker of class in North Korea. The highest ration that was granted, the Daily Ration, conferred a generous amount of supplies for a household. The Central Party's Finance and Administration Department made sure that every morning, a refrigerated Nissan truck delivered fresh supplies to the honoured few. The Daily Ration was granted only to the households of Central Party Secretaries, Directors and Corps Commanders in the military.

Further down the hierarchy came Three-day Rations, Weekly Rations and Monthly Rations. Three-day Rations applied to the households of those who held a rank equivalent to Ministers, Party Secretaries at the city level, and Central Party cadres ranked Deputy Director. Departmental directors in the Central Party institutions and section chiefs received Weekly Rations. Those who were Admitted to Dear Leader's circle, such as myself, received individual rations on a weekly basis, instead of household rations. This included 5 kilos of seafood and meat, 21 kilos of rice, thirty eggs, two bottles of cooking oil and fresh produce.

Monthly Rations, once allocated to the vast majority of ordinary North Koreans, disappeared with the collapse of the state's PDS in 1994. Weekly Rations and the grades above still remain in force – enjoyed only by the loyal and fortunate. But the ration classes that applied to cadres were kept as a secret from the ordinary populace, because they had relied solely on rations and suddenly had to fend for themselves – while cadres were still supplied. At the time, a nationwide campaign of 'self-sufficiency' was promoted in order to urge people to make do on their own, following the example of the General. This meant that the suppression of information about the rations enjoyed by the higher classes was all the more strictly enforced.

During the Arduous March and these times of economic hardship, the trains diligently transported not only people but the cargo of self-sufficiency. Observing the weight of their cargo, everything else I saw at the station made me grimace. As I stood there, surprised and somewhat appalled at the chaotic sight before me, someone tapped me on my shoulder. It was my friend Young-nam, who had promised to meet me at the station. His face was clearly marked by the effects of hunger, but his youthful smile was the same as ever. Seeing him was like a fog lifting from my eyes. 'You've grown up!' I said.

Just as I'd done when we were children, I pinched his earlobe instead of shaking hands. His chubby earlobe was larger than anyone else's and had always reminded me of a mother's swollen nipple. When we were very small, I even pinched it till it bled on a few occasions.

'Let's go,' he said.

The strength he displayed when relieving me of my rucksack reminded me of our childhood playfulness. After leaving the ticket barrier, I looked round near the station entrance. The first thing I noticed was the Sariwon Post Office opposite, which was unchanged as if time had stood still since I had left. At the same time, although I had remembered it as a large building, it seemed to have grown smaller and tarnished with age. The concurrence of things being exactly as they had been but at the same time smaller and more shabby was the same with the grocery store and food store next to the Post Office. But the cement of the large station square, which in my memory was smooth, was now full of cracks and wounds.

A fresh breeze blew in my face, and I noticed the big elm tree still leaning to one side, as if about to collapse sidelong. Its continued survival cheered me a little. When I was of primary school age, my mother and I had often waited under that tree for my father on his return from a business trip. Vivid memories came rushing back. In one scene, I picked up a broken piece of blue glass from a bottle and used it to reflect the sunlight, which glittered through the branches and leaves in different directions.

When we set off to the right of the station square, I wondered if we had taken a wrong turn. This was not the park I remembered, covered with vibrant foliage; there was no sign of the deer or pheasants that used to roam here. Instead of a single pavement running straight through the park, there were many dirt tracks leading in confusing directions. On either side of this tangled road, long lines of squatting hawkers in shabby worn clothes, old and young, male and female, tempted travellers with their trinkets.

Young-nam urged me on, but I did not want to miss anything. I deliberately paced myself in order to browse the hawkers' wares spread out on either side of me. I grimaced as I took in every sort of poverty known to North Korea's provinces gathered together and put on display here in this miserable plot. The stench of unwashed bodies in the air was rank. The wares optimistically placed on display by grimy hands were not the kind one would expect to pay for. I asked one woman why she was selling an empty insulated flask for 20 won. She replied by saying that if I filled it with hot water, I could hug it during the night to keep warm.

It also bewildered me to see tap water on sale. It cost 10 won to wash your face with soap and water and five to wash with water alone. Young-nam told me, as if it was an everyday occurrence, that face-washing was a service that had been introduced the previous year. Not only had there been famine here, but the water supply had also dried up. Although the women were shouting 'Water for your face!', their own faces were greasy and dirt-flecked. It was disheartening to see the state of these women reduced to selling tap water and women with no water of their own forced to sell off their most precious possessions.

When I discovered that the cotton comforters on sale had been stuffed with filters collected from old cigarette butts, I could not suppress a snort of disgust. A woman sat by her wares, concentrating on the task. How many old cigarette butts did it take to fill a comforter? Was this the best they could do? People should not have to live like this: they weren't living a life, but living in order to stay alive, themselves discarded like used cigarette butts. But, as if anticipating my condescension, the old woman swore at me, shouting that those who did not collect old cigarette butts deserved to die.

'Don't you think of looking down on me,' she added, with a strange air of dignity.

Turning towards the far corners of the park, I could see a swarm of homeless people who looked to be either dead or dying. There was nothing between these men and women and a cold grave but their own shadows, and even those who were still alive were clearly waiting for death. There were also men hovering over the bodies like flies, at times poking at the inert figures with a stick. I asked Young-nam what they were doing. My Jappo friend explained, scratching too audibly at his skin through his clothes.

'They're from the Corpse Division,' he said. 'Dispatched by the city's Party Committee.'

'Corpse Division? What do you mean?'

'Why, they get rid of the corpses! Maybe you don't have this in Pyongyang, but the committees in all the other provinces dispatch them to their main park near the station. All sorts of people move through the station, so they come here to beg, until they die.'

Young-nam's expression, so unmoved even in the face of death, was distant and unfamiliar. A Corpse Division? Such a thing could never exist in Pyongyang, which was a holy centre of revolution and the capital of Chosun. Although North Korea's official name is the Democratic People's Republic of Chosun, in reality, it was and remains a Republic of Pyongyang Residents. When there was famine all over the country and rations stopped, supplies were rerouted to Pyongyang residents as the first priority. The issuing of travel passes was severely restricted, and security at the Pyongyang border controls was heightened, so that supplies routed to the capital could not seep into other provinces. From 1996, when even Pyongyang rations broke down, the Party finally resorted to an opening of trade with the Chinese so that flour and corn could be brought in. Even when Pyongyang residents did starve or freeze to death, they couldn't be left on the streets as in the provinces: Pyongyang was the showcase of Kim Il-sung and Kim Jong-il's North Korea for foreign visitors, and its appearance had to be kept up at all costs.

Young-nam continued, 'Apparently, the Party Secretary for Hamheung thought of the idea, and received a state medal for it. Good for him! The dead are beyond gratitude, but the living are appreciative. How else would we get rid of all the corpses? You get a full day's ration if you sign up for the work; that's quite generous, you know.'

As my friend chattered on, he seemed to be speaking in a different language from the one used in Pyongyang. Nothing here seemed familiar to me any longer. I stood watching the Corpse Division at work, ignoring Young-nam's wave of the hand urging me to move on. The Corpse Division had a loaded rickshaw, on top of which some empty sacks were laid. Six bare and skeletal feet poked out from beneath these in oddly assorted directions. For the first split second, I did not understand what I was seeing, but as soon as I realised these empty sacks were human bodies, I grew nauseous and retched. I trembled with angry regret for having looked too closely. I had heard rumours that when the Public Distribution System collapsed, corpses could be seen on the streets in some provinces. But I had never thought to see it happen in my own hometown. The place I'd cherished in my memory had been like a beautiful landscape painting; now that was sullied forever, and torn into shreds. At this betrayal of my memories, I felt rage tempered by confusion rising up from deep within me.

As I met the townspeople and my old neighbours, I became ever more despondent. After I'd finished unpacking at Young-nam's house and had changed my clothes, neighbours swarmed into the house. Young-nam's mother had knocked on everyone's door to say that the Doctor's son had come back to visit. They put everything on hold to come and marvel at me – one of the Admitted. Without exception, everyone I saw looked old and exhausted.

'We heard you had dinner with the General! What kind of porridge does he like to eat?' It was Mr 'Tall-Man' Park, who used to live down the street from us. He had eaten nothing but porridge since the last state holiday. His face was jaundiced.

'The General? Oh, you know the song, "The Rice-balls of the General"? Just like in that song, he shared a rice-ball with us,' I mumbled in response.

Even though these were simple country folk who believed whatever the Workers' Party told them, I could not have imagined that I would be asked this question so soon. I rubbed my hands, sticky with sweat. But the townspeople seemed relieved to hear that the General dined on solid rice-balls instead of porridge; some tutted, while others stood in mute wonder. I heard a voice saying that it was just as the Party cadres had told them, so we had to do more for the Patriotic Rice movement, even if it meant forking out money for the rice. The Patriotic Rice movement was a campaign whereby ordinary North Koreans offered their rice to the state as an act of patriotism.

The townspeople continued to quiz me endlessly about the General, asking anxiously after his health. I was appalled by the fact that they were concerned more for their leader's well-being than for their own, although they were in a wretched state. I did my best to answer their questions with lies, but found myself disgusted by the man I had become.

The life had been drained out of my townsfolk and there was no comfort from seeing any of their faces again. When I met Soon-yong from next door – I used to have a crush on her and she was always my play-wife in our childhood games of marriage – she had become a disfigured old woman. As soon as our eyes met, she withdrew her gaze and hung her head, revealing her thin, bare neck; another sign of her impoverished state. Myung-chul, once famous for his strength and envied by all the other boys in town, had turned into nothing but skin and bones. Their prematurely darkened, cadaverous skin and the deep zigzagging wrinkles on their faces were a silent testament to the years of starvation they had endured.

When I asked after some neighbours I could not see in the crowd, the matter-of-fact reply was that each one of them had starved to death. The shock of it felt like a blow to the head. In my memories, these names belonged to those who were alive and well, but they didn't exist on this planet any more. I mourned the hollowness inside me.

Suddenly, I heard someone yelling outside. Mr Tall-Man Park told me that it was Grandfather Apple-Tree Cottage. He had gone mad. Everyone in our town knew about Apple-Tree Cottage. The house was so called because the grandfather planted an apple tree in their yard when his granddaughter was born, so that they could grow up together. Every autumn, the town's children would come round and ask, 'When can we pick the apples?' Grandfather Apple-Tree Cottage would answer, 'Come along this Sunday with your mum and dad. Don't forget, Sunday is apple-picking day!' Apple-Tree Cottage had always been welcoming to us. I asked why Grandfather Apple-Tree Cottage had become deranged.

Myung-chul answered with a deep sigh, 'There's no more apple tree. Grandfather chopped it down after his granddaughter hanged herself from it. Her mother left home to be with some son of a bitch, and her father died a few years ago. The mother never kept in touch, so there was only her grandfather left. He looked after her – how could an adolescent girl fend for herself? But one night, a thief came and picked all their apples. The next morning, the grandfather found that his granddaughter had hanged herself from the apple tree. He went raving mad after that. Says he will eat the thief when he is found.'

The story was already wretched beyond belief, but when Myung-chul finished by saying that everyone still called the old man

Grandfather Apple-Tree Cottage, although there was no more apple tree, I could no longer keep my composure and tears welled from my eyes. I pretended to wipe some dirt off with the back of my hand. I felt deeply sorry that I was hiding my own tears from them, but I was too ashamed of myself to show them my tears. How could I, with my privileged existence, express my misery in front of those who had nothing left, who had been deprived even of the means to express their misery?

With these thoughts, I was overcome by an impulse to hide my hands and sat down. The lives of my townsfolk were threatened by their not having enough to eat, and it was mortifying that my hands had been employed for literature when the nation was in such a state. Or rather, I needed desperately to hide my hands from my old neighbours. My very hands seemed to me to embody my arrogance and selfishness, and their soft skin to expose how I had used them to secure my own existence at the expense of countless other lives.

That night, at the dinner prepared by Young-nam's mother, I had to choke back my tears again. She proudly explained how she was able to offer me, her guest, a half-full bowl of rice – she had stashed away ten grains of rice at every meal. In addition to the rice, there was a small dish of salted cabbage and pickled anchovies, which were presented to me as if they were an expensive delicacy. When I asked how long it had taken to save up the rice, she replied, 'Three months.' I could not believe that they were eating rice by the grain, instead of in servings. I muttered an excuse, saying that I had indigestion after eating lunch on the train.

Almost as soon as I left the table, Young-nam's father scolded his wife severely, saying that she had put me off my food. He brought me my spoon, forcing me to grip it and pleading with me to join them at the table again. From my rucksack, I took out my imported liquor and tinned meats, the ones I had brought with me from Pyongyang as parting gifts.

'Look, don't worry about me. I'm not refusing because there's not enough food,' I blurted.

Although I had brought these food items as gifts, I was at my wits' end when it came to explaining my possession of such extravagant luxuries to a family who ate rice by the grain. When Young-nam's father lifted the bottle of cognac and marvelled in wonder, I felt even more overwhelmed by a sense of foreboding.

'Ah, I haven't seen Western liquor for years,' he sighed. 'You know, when we first arrived in North Korea from Japan, I had so many of the bottles that I gave them out as gifts whenever I could.'

The mother, suddenly embarrassed by her own meagre offering in comparison to the gifts I had brought with me, sheepishly nudged the bowl of rice towards her husband. 'You have the rice,' she said. 'Perhaps I should have saved it for another time.'

The bowl of rice was passed to the son by the father, then by the son back to the mother. Young-nam's mother eventually took it back into the kitchen to keep it for her daughter, who had gone out to work a nightshift at the fabric factory. My chest felt tight, but I was also moved by the love that led this family with so little rice of their own to offer the last of it to an outsider.

Young-nam's father continued to gaze in wonder at the bottle of imported liquor I had brought. When I told him that it was given to me by Dear Leader, his mouth dropped. Kim Jong-il gave special gifts to his senior cadres three times a year: on New Year's Day, Kim Il-sung's birthday, and his own birthday. These might include suit fabric from Italy, rare medicinal herbs or shoes, all especially imported. But while other items might change, the liquor was always a key feature.

The custom of imported liquor gifts was instituted because many cadres, previously unfamiliar with these drinks, had been mesmerised by them, drinking excessively at state banquets or during foreign postings, and committing social gaffes. Generally speaking, the alcoholic gift pack consisted of two bottles each of three types of cognac – six bottles in all. For a North Korean cadre, the gift of imported liquor was effectively the gift of foreign currency, as each bottle sold easily for around US$100 on the black market. But anything sold on to traders on the black market eventually wound its way back into cadres' hands as bribes, so the gift of cognac was worth much more than its face value. This was also the reason why prices of imported liquor in North Korea plummet around the time of the three state holidays mentioned.

Young-nam's father seemed interested in more than merely drinking the contents of the bottle; he was transfixed by the foreign label, and perhaps wanted the bottle as a keepsake. He asked outright if I would give it to him as a present. When I said yes, he rushed to find himself an empty glass and filled it with the cognac, as if to get rid of the drink as quickly as he could. Young-nam's Osakan father savoured his cognac, explaining that it reminded him of his past. But after draining two glasses, he lost control.

'You know that Yamaha piano you had at home? I gave that to your family. You know that? Right? And our house, you know your father gave me this. You know that too, right?'

'Yes. Yes.' I could do nothing but respond monosyllabically, and I could feel the blood surging to my head.

'I'm forever designated a Jappo, so I've never been allowed to have a real job. You know, around this time last year, your father came to sleep over at our place. We hadn't eaten for days. I was hungry. I was so hungry that I contacted your father. You know, I realised that a friend is better than the homeland. It's thanks to your father's support that we were able to survive for one more year. I made him promise not to tell you.'

Young-nam's mother tried to calm him down. 'You're drunk. Stop talking about the homeland in that way in front of the kids. Besides, we decided to move to North Korea at your bidding. What good is it to regret the decision now?'

Behind her words, there lay many other words that could not be said.

'Yes, I'm sorry,' her husband replied. 'I'm sorry for bringing us to this country. But tonight, I'm a happy man. With you here, it feels like we've had ourselves a proper meal. Do you have any idea what we've been doing for food? You know, this wife of mine, she puts rice water on the table and calls it rice. She boils wild shoots and serves the liquid broth as if it's a proper stew. There's never any real food on the table, but she still demands we sit at the table for our meal. And why not? We can pretend we've eaten proper food and feel better about our lives.'

Young-nam sat with his head in his hands, glaring at his father from between his fingers, as if thinking that his father was ruining the last remaining shreds of dignity in their lives. When I noticed the signs of starvation on the crown of his head, it rent my heart. *Young-nam, I didn't know. Forgive me for my ignorance.*

The next morning I packed my bags to leave. I had planned to stay for two more days but made up an excuse, saying I was needed urgently at work. When I saw the tattered shoes that Young-nam put on as he hurriedly followed me out of the house, I was glad I had made the decision to leave. Wanting to buy him a new pair of shoes before I went back to Pyongyang, I said we should go by the market. As we walked, I stole a glance at his dangling earlobe. It had dry white patches of flaky skin, which spread down to his neck. I felt bitterly sorry for all the times I had pinched him as a child.

'So, how does it feel to be back home? Is it much different from Pyongyang?' His voice was feeble and sounded as if it was coming from afar.

'People live the same anywhere you go. I even get told off at work all the time.'

'I want to move to Pyongyang. At least you can get a job there. Even meet the General like you did.'

I faltered, searching for words that might comfort him. Just walking alongside him was mortifying, and I felt guilty that my visit had thrown his life into disarray. But he started to pour his heart out. 'You don't get it, do you? There's no future for me. At least you're in Pyongyang, where you can get on in life by working hard. You even got to choose your own career. Here, scrambling for the next meal is the best I can do. Even if I make it today, there's the next meal to worry about. And the next. All my waking hours are spent fearing whether I will be able to eat again. We live no better than animals. You saw with your own eyes at the station. You know how the standard greeting used to be, "Have you eaten?" But now, you can't say that, because what can you say in response? "No, I haven't and what the fuck can you do about it?" Can't you see? It's different outside Pyongyang. And you don't have those in the capital city either, do you?'

I looked to where he was pointing. The walls on either side of the marketplace entrance were plastered with black-lettered slogans instead of the usual prices of goods. 'Death by firing squad to those who disobey traffic rules!', 'Death by firing squad to those who hoard food!', 'Death by firing squad to those who waste electricity!', 'Death by firing squad to those who cut military communications lines!', 'Death by firing squad to those who hoard state resources!', 'Death by firing squad to those who spread foreign culture!', 'Death by firing squad to those who gossip!' I hadn't realised that there had been so many new regulations introduced in our nation. The slogans implied that any and every mistake would lead to death by firing squad.

In Pyongyang, to avoid the eyes and ears of foreigners and tourists, new regulations were announced internally, through workplace and residential unit meetings that all North Koreans are required to attend. I realised I had never before seen a regulation posted in a publicly visible place. It took me a while to remember why we had come to the market in the first place. Once I'd regained my composure, I wanted to buy the shoes as quickly as possible and get out of this place; and so I took the lead, holding Young-nam by the hand.

There were more people hanging around than were actually buying or selling. As we made our way through the crowds, the stench was suffocating. 'Take care with your wallet!' Young-nam warned me. I walked even faster, and finally found a shoe stall. I asked Young-nam to pick a pair of shoes he liked. He resisted, saying he was sorry enough not to be able to treat me well as a guest and he couldn't possibly receive a gift on top of that. As he reluctantly picked out a cheap pair, I asked the vendor for the most expensive pair he had. Even that turned out to be of mediocre quality, a pair made in China.

Young-nam recalled a Korean saying: 'They say that if you buy shoes as a parting gift, you'll never see each other again.'

'You think I'm your lover or something? What do you mean, "never see each other again?"' I said.

Seeing the grin spread ear to ear on Young-nam's face, I felt a little better. After the purchase was made, I forced the change and the rest of the money in my wallet into Young-nam's pocket. But before we were able to leave, a siren started somewhere.

'What's that?' I asked.

The reaction of the people around us was even stranger than the sound of the siren. Everyone looked annoyed and some swore loudly.

Young-nam's eyes were closed. He too looked exasperated. Then he hissed, 'Fucking hell.'

When I asked again what was happening, he said it was an execution.

'What?' I asked.

The shoe vendor looked up from polishing a shoe with a tattered rag, and replied in Young-nam's place, 'You're not from here, are you? Bad timing, that's all. There's going to be a People's Trial. No one can leave the market till it's over.'

In North Korea, a public execution is not regarded as a punishment. It is categorised as a method of moral education, and also as a tool of public propaganda used in power struggles. But an execution in the market? As I looked confusedly at Young-nam, he reassured me that these executions took place almost on a weekly basis. They always happened in the market square so that a large audience could watch the proceedings.

Sure enough, soldiers rushed in from all directions to surround the square, herding us into the centre with the butts of their rifles. There was chaos everywhere. It made me flinch that the prisoner, led in by two soldiers, was dressed not in prison uniform but in everyday clothes. It felt like a deliberate message to the townsfolk that any of them could be in his position; that it didn't take a special criminal mind to suffer this fate. The man's eyes were full of terror as he scanned the scene around him from beneath his sagging eyelids and bony sockets. There was blood around his lips. For him, this truly was hell on earth, and his fellow men must have seemed as frightening as demons.

The People's Trial was over in less than five minutes. It was not really a trial. A military officer merely read out his judgement. The prisoner's crime was declared to be the theft of one sack of rice. As the country was ruled according to the *Songun* policy of Military-First politics, all the rice in the nation belonged to the military, and even petty crimes were dealt with according to martial law.

'Death by firing squad!'

As soon as the judge pronounced his sentence, one of the two soldiers who was restraining the prisoner shoved something into his mouth in a swift, practised motion. It was a V-shaped spring that expanded once it was put inside the mouth, preventing the prisoner from speaking intelligibly. The prisoner made sounds but there was no human noise, only whimpering. This device had been officially sanctioned for use at public executions so that a prisoner could not utter rebellious sentiments in the final moments of his life before it was taken from him.

Bang! Bang! Bang!

I had never been so close to a gun being fired. The blood froze in my veins. Not daring to look at the prisoner at the moment of his death, I flicked my gaze upward. There was not a cloud in the sky, which was exceedingly clear and bright blue. But the faces of the townsfolk made to witness the execution were grave.

When the soldiers blew their whistles and yelled for the crowd to disperse, the people didn't react, and began murmuring among themselves. As the whispers spread, I could catch what was being said. The prisoner's identity had been established by those who knew him, and the shock I felt after learning the story is hard to describe. My hair stood on end, and a tingling chill reached from there to the ends of my toes.

THE PRISONER

Wherever people are gathered
there are gunshots to follow.

Today, as the crowd looks on
another man is condemned.

'We must not feel any sympathy!
Even when he's dead, we must kill him again!'

The slogan is interrupted: *Bang! Bang!*
as the rest of the message is delivered.

Why is it that today
the crowd is silent?

The prisoner's crime: theft of one sack of rice.
His sentence: ninety bullets to the heart.

His occupation:
Farmer.

The man riddled with bullets for stealing rice had been a starving farmer. Even someone who worked the land could not find enough to eat.

4 | THE CRIME OF PEERING OVER THE BORDER

As soon as I returned home to Pyongyang, far away from the People's Trial in Sariwon, I got into the shower. It felt like bits of the prisoner's skin and blood had been sprayed onto my skin, and I scrubbed myself again and again. For over a week, whenever I sat at the table to eat, I was overcome with nausea and could not bear the thought of food. On any other Sunday, I would have slept in, but that day, I left when it was still dark, before dawn, to get some fresh air.

There was no one about except for a few old men sitting on the bank of the Daedong River with their fishing rods. I found an empty bench facing the water and sat down. An early summer breeze flowed with the river. I inhaled it deeply then blew out forcefully, expelling the ill feeling from my lungs. After I had done this a few times, I felt I could breathe more easily.

A stagnant stench rippled over the river's surface, and a crumpled frying pan floated past. I wouldn't have taken much notice of such small ugly things before. Instead, I would have let my thoughts drift with the water out towards the deep blue sea, whose depths would inspire me with poetry glittering like the sun rays on the waves. But that Sunday was different. As I watched the frying pan being carried away by the river's current before me, its fate seemed to represent that of my friends and townsfolk. The water itself was like the passing of time, a passage no less pointless than the river water that flowed towards me only to flow onwards and away. On the other side of the riverbank, a slogan hanging from the rooftop of a building read:

'After your thousand miles of suffering, there are ten thousand miles of joy!' The words seemed strange and vacuous.

The Party referred to this era as the Arduous March, but wasn't the reality much worse than merely 'arduous'? Moreover, this wasn't a march that all of us participated in. While ordinary North Koreans had to march in suffering for a thousand miles, cadres were strolling along the journey in privileged comfort. My townsfolk were concerned about their Leader's eating and health, yet Kim Jong-il had the luxury of eating cold ice cream adorned with flames. I was filled with grave doubts, but I knew they were dangerous and would achieve nothing. I lived in Pyongyang. I was one of the Admitted, and I had come such a long way while only in my twenties. For my parents' sake, I must not harbour any such deviant thoughts. If I continued on this path a little longer, I would end up in the most enviable of positions as the paragon of loyalty to Dear Leader. I had to carry on.

I resolved to work hard on the task set for me, the epic poem for which I had the full support of the United Front Department behind me. On my first day back at work, I arrived in the office earlier than others, at six-thirty in the morning. In my quiet corner, I wrote the title of my poem in big letters on a sheet of lined paper with my fountain pen: 'An Ode to the Smiling Sun'. But I had produced nothing by the end of the day. My task was to describe how our Supreme Leader smiled, yet all I could think of was the misery of my townsfolk.

Why were we a poor nation? If our Supreme Leader was great, why were his people starving to death? Reforms had led the Chinese to prosperity, so why was our Party not considering any change in policies? I hated the way that these questions kept bubbling up in my mind like water from a mountain spring. When I thought I had dismissed one, another question arose in its place. Never before in my life had I so many questions to ask of myself, the Party and Dear Leader.

Every week, Director Im asked after my progress on 'An Ode to the Smiling Sun'. I eventually grew sick of my excuses, and waited desperately for the end of each working day. When I took up my pen to write, it was the tears of the people – and not of our Supreme Leader – that filled my mind. I was restless with yearning to write realist poetry based on what I saw, and not loyalist poetry based on what we were all told to see.

Because I couldn't let anyone find out about such writing, I spent my nights at home writing poetry in secret. In this way, every day, I wrote songs about rice rather than about our Dear Leader, my mind filled with the scenes I had witnessed in my hometown.

> This boy was brought up on watery rice broth.
> I give him a bowl of real rice on his birthday,
> But he stamps his feet and refuses it.
> 'This isn't rice!' he protests, holding his ground.

The night I wrote this poem, I cried until daybreak. It was based on a story that a work colleague had shared with me about his nephew, in a rare moment of disclosure, which I had written down.

I began to open my eyes to the poverty in Pyongyang itself, and I wanted to find out all that I could. After obtaining permission from the UFD to travel and conduct interviews freely in Pyongyang, I visited its markets and went out of my way to talk to those who had nothing. In contrast to my hometown, Sariwon, where deaths from starvation and even public executions were a common occurrence, Pyongyang's residents would gossip guardedly about a neighbour's death, as if it were a dangerous state secret, saying they knew it had been starvation. They lived in rigid fear, in the knowledge that there was much to lose as the result of a loose tongue: removal of the privilege of living in Pyongyang and being banished to the provinces.

But in the conversations of those living in the poorest areas of Pyongyang, in Dongdaewon and Sungyo, the truth of their situation was clearly evident. A woman described how she cried when she heard her young son boasting to friends that he had eaten three meals that day, while she herself had eaten nothing for a week. There was a beggar whose final wish was to be able to give someone something, because all he had been able to do in life was to receive from others. As these records of truth became condensed into my secret book of poetry, I felt myself mature into a fellow human being.

But I also lived in fear. I knew about a writer who had secretly written in a realist style, and when his crime was discovered, he was sent to a gulag. I took care to keep my poems to myself, and it was all I could do to register the truth of how I felt, and confirm to myself that I was still human. The only defence I had against the paralysing terror was my faith that truth mattered. But I also began to study seriously the non-North Korean books that I had until then read as a duty and out of professional curiosity.

Until the day I was admitted to the United Front Department, I did not know what country was really meant by the name 'Daehanminguk' (which is how South Korea refers to itself, literally 'Great Nation of the Han People'). I had thought it was the name of some country in South-East Asia, registering only how it had a similar name to Taiwan (*Daeman* in Korean). We had only been taught about the existence of South Korea in terms of its being 'southern Chosun', the lower half of the Democratic People's Republic of Chosun, and even a passing curiosity about South Korea was treated as an act of subversion against the state. I only discovered this after my entry to the UFD, but in the summer of 1998, when the South Korean government offered to send rice to North Korea, North Korea had refused on the basis that the sacks had 'Daehanminguk' written on them.

As far as it was in the remit of 'Localisation' for South Korea, I read every outside text with gusto, and watched South Korean television obsessively. To do so was a special privilege granted to me and my colleagues, but strictly prohibited for ordinary North Koreans, being, at the time, deemed an act that was inconceivably beyond the pale. It struck me that while North Korean television never mentioned criticism of their own system, South Korean television never praised their own administration. The lack of uniformity in their press was publicly displayed, and they would even criticise government policies and disagree with their politicians. By the time I progressed from South Korean newspapers to the more detailed analyses provided in periodicals concerned with politics, the economy, society and culture in general, my desire to seek other versions of the truth was even greater.

One of the periodicals I read regularly was the *Monthly Chosun*. Every time I opened its pages, shocking facts confronted me. I had believed that South Korea, a US colony, was being ruined by its Capitalist system. So it surprised me to discover that the South Korean economy was actually highly developed. I was also intrigued that our much-vaunted pride in the admiration of the international community rested on no more than the achievements of our Supreme Leader, while South Korea had given rise to many small and medium-sized companies of international repute. South Korea was derided as an economic slave to the US, yet the figures showed that South Korea's trade volume competed alongside that of the Americans in world rankings. What struck me harder than anything, and was more powerfully moving than ideological fervour or propaganda, was the existence of the gap between North and South: we were one people, all of us Koreans, but why were our lives so different?

As I learned more about South Korea and the outside world, my focus turned inwards again, towards the North Korean political system. Although the slogan of the United Front Department is 'Localisation', outside texts that dealt with Kim Il-sung or Kim Jong-il on a human level had the sacrilegious sections blacked out by censors. It was this that provoked my curiosity more than anything

– if you casually wave someone away from a secret, they might just walk away, but if you struggle with all your might to hide it, their curiosity will only increase.

The happiest time of my working day was in the break after lunch, when many of my colleagues would leave the office for a little fresh air. One day, when I was sure no one was around, I held the blacked-out section of a page I was reading against the windowpane. As the black strips turned pale in the sunlight, the letters underneath became legible. What I saw on that page were the most terrible blasphemies that could not be seen or heard anywhere else in our nation. Even the smallest facts – precisely because they had been so carefully sealed away – eroded my unquestioning faith in our system. I had believed that the civil war that split our homeland was triggered by an invasion from the South on 25 June 1950. Through the revealing light of that windowpane, I read that not only in South Korea, but in the rest of the world too, historians routinely attributed responsibility for the invasion to us, and not to the South.

The Workers' Party's rewriting of our history looked shabby in comparison. Even the greatness of our Supreme Leader was not the greatness of morality and righteousness. He had acquired his autocratic powers not through his benevolence but by selfish means, such as purging and executing his comrades. When I discovered this history, I knew I could no longer write in loyal obedience to a regime built on lies. I tried to convince Director Im that, just as Supervisor Park had said, referring to the Supreme Leader's tears in a poem might go against the principles of *Juche* Art Theory. Perhaps fearing the responsibility, he eventually acquiesced.

It happened that in 2001, under the orders of Supreme Commander Kim Jong-il, the North Korean people were mobilised. In order to establish the *Songun* way of thinking in society, all civilians under forty, including high-school students, had to enter into a compulsory three-year period of military service. Kim Jong-il stressed that Central Party cadres must set an example of the Military-First mindset, and that they too must leave their current posts and serve in the military. This led to the astonishing sight of Party Secretaries and Directors parading in the streets in uniforms too small to hide their flabby bodies.

In North Korea, a university degree is equivalent to the rank of lieutenant. Director Im made sure that I could do my 'military service' as a lieutenant in a unit based in Pyongyang, faking it like many other enlisted soldiers who did their 'military service' at home. Even while I was technically a soldier, I continued my literary work with extended periods of stay at UFD guesthouses. At the time, Office 101 was preparing for literary exchanges with South Korean writers, with the objective of arousing sympathy for our positions and views in the South Korean populace. Part of the mission included compiling a literary anthology of 'Unified Korean Literature'.

By the second year of Kim Jong-il's nationwide mobilisation order, its enforcement was no longer taken seriously by anybody of note. When I returned to Office 101 in the summer of 2002, I eagerly caught up with the South Korean literature and media that I had missed out on; and troubling thoughts, rising from the apparent contradiction of facts, returned to haunt me. The longer I bore these truths alone, the heavier my heart became, and the deeper my loneliness. I needed a trusted friend with whom to share my discoveries.

'This is a southern Chosun periodical. Don't lose it.'

Although I knew that removing a volume from the United Front Department was an act of treason, I passed a book from there on to my friend, Hwang Young-min. He had been a classmate of mine at Pyongyang Arts School. But my decision to trust him was based on more than just our friendship. He had, on several occasions, very cautiously tried to share the notion that the infallibility of our system might be questioned.

Young-min's father, Hwang Jin-thaek, had been a two-star general and chief of staff at the Ministry of Social Security (today, the Ministry of People's Security). Paek Hak-rim, the nominal director of the Ministry, was an honorary appointee in his eighties, and Hwang Jin-thaek was the de facto head of this powerful state surveillance organ. In North Korea, however, no one could wield more power than was to Kim Jong-il's liking. One day, after Young-min's father spoke out a little too boldly on a Party issue, he was accused of being an anti-revolutionary. If the prosecution had reached its natural conclusion, Young-min would have been sent with his family to a gulag for his father's crimes. The North Korean system of guilt-by-association made this a common feature of sentencing practice. Although Hwang Jin-thaek was able to clear his name before the investigation could finish, he died of the injuries he'd suffered under interrogation. Fortunately for Young-min, he was able to retain Pyongyang residency and was reinstated as composer for the Wangjaesan Orchestra.

The Wangjaesan Orchestra, kept separate from other North Korean cultural institutions, was operated directly by the Party's Organisation and Guidance Department as Kim Jong-il's court musicians. There was one other such group, the Bocheonbo Band, which worked in modern genres and with electric instruments, while members of the Wangjaesan Orchestra used classical Western instrumentation and also worked in the medium of dance. As the group of performers who played for Kim Jong-il consisted of young and beautiful women, people referred to them unofficially as the 'Joy Division'.

Young-min knew things about Kim Jong-il's personal life that no outsider knew, and it had taken a visible toll on him. He never talked much about himself, and I might have thought he had been like that all his life if not for our friendship at school, before his appointment. He was taller than me and had curly hair. People always assumed that he was the older of the two of us, although we were the same age. His serious eyebrows, as black as soot, reflected his unwavering faithfulness. Sometimes, when he smiled, his cheeks blushed a slight red, revealing the innocence of a passion that he kept hidden from the world. Even after the death of his father, and in spite of his introverted personality, he could nonetheless manifest instances of fearless defiance, and the Party's OGD took notice. Although Young-min was formally reinstated, he found himself excluded from Kim Jong-il's presence on more than one occasion, based on some feeble pretext.

When the two of us got drunk together, and his cover slipped, he would even say dangerous things: 'Indeed, our General is the Sun! If you get too close to him, you burn to death, but if you go too far from him, you freeze to death. And that's not my line. I hear it directly from the most powerful cadres. You think you know Kim Jong-il? It's not the North Korean people our Leader loves, it's the North Korean girls. I've seen it with my own eyes, and too much of it.'

In North Korea, it is forbidden to mention any information about the ruling Kim that isn't included in the body of official propaganda released by the Workers' Party. Dear Leader was the Father of the People; and as soon as you knew him as a man called Kim Jong-il, unless you were authorised to have this knowledge, your life would come to an end as the system of guilt-by-association was put into action. Many cadres ended up in prison camps because to remain close to the centre of power was a dangerous game of balance, requiring a constant and attentive awareness.

When I shared my reading materials from the outside world with Young-min, and when Young-min told me about Kim Jong-il's secret personal life, we were able to share our burdens. Our friendship provided me with the strength to carry on. The truth is more powerful the less it is tampered with; and as we learned about our place in the world together – a world very different from that portrayed by Dear Leader – our friendship deepened.

On 10 January 2004, I heard loud and insistent knocking at the front door. When I opened it, Young-min was standing there, deathly pale and out of breath. He was wearing a dark jacket with fake fur around the neck for warmth. As he stood there and stared at me, unable to speak, I knew that something awful had happened.

'That book you lent me, that southern Chosun book – I lost it.'

I gripped the doorknob to keep myself from sinking to the floor. He had fallen asleep in the underground, he told me, and left his bag on the train. He'd rushed back to retrieve it straight away, but as he reached the platform the door had slid shut. His words were barely audible to my ringing ears. Without thinking, I went to pick up my pen from the table, but put it back down. I could derive no comfort even from holding my most cherished possession.

'Were your identification papers in the bag?' I asked.

'No, just the book,' he replied.

'Was there anything in the bag that could be traced to you?' I asked again.

'No, it was a new bag. Actually, there was my notebook too. But I'm fine, at least until they check for fingerprints,' he said.

It looked as if it was I who was in the greater danger. Books belonging to the UFD were marked 'Top Secret: Restricted to Internal Agents' with a bright red stamp, as well as a bright blue one that read 'Chosun Workers' Party Central Committee, United Front Department'. Whenever a book was loaned to an agent, we had to show our official identification and sign for it. In my contract of admission, there was a clause that made the danger very clear: 'If you expose southern Chosun literature outside the Department, you will be executed for treason.'

The contents of this particular book could only make the situation worse. It included a biography of Kim Il-sung and Kim Jong-il written by a South Korean academic who had pieced together their family history, although we were only allowed to know their revolutionary history. It even made mention of the fact that Kim Jong-il had mistresses. The Party requires its people to live by a code of honour derived from Confucian tradition, which emphasises conservative family values such as obedience to one's parents, marital fidelity and hereditary rights of the eldest son, in order to reinforce the legitimacy of a dynastic succession. But the personal history of the Kim family, in which those values were flagrantly ignored and bloody purges and violent politics formed the basis of their power, was in stark and contradictory contrast to the official version of events.

Whether or not these things were true, and regardless of whether we believed that an unauthorised version of North Korean history could exist, it was considered treason of the most serious degree to have shared this information. Although the sacrilegious sections were censored with black marker pen, the Ministry of State Security was not going to believe we could not read the writing behind it.

I felt sure that the secret police would appear at any moment. The closer a cadre is to the top, the more violent his end when it comes. Young-min too, as one of Kim Jong-il's personal composers, was a senior cadre of the Central Party. The affair could not end with our deaths alone, because in the following weeks, after we had confessed to our treason and accepted the penalty, our families would have their lives summarily destroyed.

Looming always in the back of all North Korean minds is the principle of guilt-by-association, by which the family and associates of the traitor are destroyed along with the criminal, so that his or her corruption might be rooted out for good. I knew that the principle wasn't just an empty threat, as the state made sure to display to its people whenever the opportunity arose for its enforcement. Yet this tragic possibility had felt unrelated to me until now, when I found myself in the position of potentially experiencing its devastating effects. Young-min and I communicated through our eyes, not saying much. We were not so much concerned with concocting an alibi for the crime, as with survival itself. With the coming of daylight, our lives would turn dark, and I was too afraid even to look at the time ticking by on the clock.

I suddenly needed a drink. Seeing me reach for a bottle, Young-min took the two biggest glasses out of the cabinet. We downed our first shots together. We had put our families at terrible risk, and knowing this, we could not waste a single moment. We needed a plan, and then to carry it out.

As we downed a second desperate shot together, we made our decision. No words passed between us, but we both knew it well. The drink didn't blur our senses – it gave us strength.

Young-min spoke first: 'You know that saying: "When a small man drinks he vomits, but when a great man drinks he designs a revolution"? Well, what I'm saying is, that southern Chosun book ... it made me feel ...'

I interrupted him. 'Let's go to South Korea.'

Young-min's fingers froze on the rim of his glass.

I continued, 'There's no other way. For the sake of those we love, we can't risk confession. You know what this country is like. You more than anyone else know what this country is like.'

He didn't need any persuasion. He seized my hand and, as if that were not enough of a gesture, pulled me close in a tight embrace. 'You're right, we're leaving,' he said. 'We'll die either way, so it doesn't matter for us. I can't even breathe any longer here, knowing what I know. Be killed at home or on the road, what's the difference?'

There was no point in wasting time once we had confirmed our decision, and we began to plan our next steps. We agreed to turn up for work as usual in the morning. Luckily, as we had established, the bag that Young-min had mislaid contained no direct personal identification linking it to him, so as long as I kept my wits about me, I could buy some time. When the Ministry of State Security tracked me down from the book, I would argue that I had simply misplaced my bag. In any case, it would take a day for them to put a surveillance team in place, and my status as one of the Admitted would prevent them from acting too hastily. We would make our way north during this time. The only way out of the country was to cross the border into China, as it was impossible to cross the DMZ into South Korea. A travel pass could be obtained from a former classmate at Kim Il-sung University, who worked in Pyongyang at a cross-border trading company. He was always in need of money, and a decent bribe would sort him out. By a stroke of good fortune, we found that there was a 9 p.m. train scheduled to leave Pyongyang the next day towards the border region. If we were to get on this train, we must pretend everything was normal until the time came for us to leave.

After planning these things, I hurried to pack my bag. As I would have to go to the train station straight from work, we decided that Young-min would take my rucksack. He could leave work in the afternoon. I stuffed into my rucksack everything I could think of. I did not forget my secret manuscript of poetry. It was my voice, and I would take it out of the country with me.

'See you at 7.30 p.m. at Pyongyang Station,' I said.

Young-min nodded, turned to go, but then swung back and seized my arm. He dropped his gaze as if he were lost for words, but then spoke in a low but firm voice.

'If we get caught, we will commit suicide.' The word 'suicide' felt like a tangible object being passed from his tender heart to mine. I felt strangely thrilled by the thought that death could be a conscious choice: I had the means to decide my own fate.

A FAREWELL SIN |

ONCE I'd seen Young-min off into the night, I went to my room and lay awake in bed. I was not especially dreading exile, which would begin in less than twenty-four hours. What I feared the most was the scale of what I had to leave behind. I felt sick that my mother and father must live out their remaining days in a world from which their only son had suddenly disappeared. Yet I could not say goodbye to them.

They would not let me go if they learned of my plan. They would kill themselves first. Once I left the country and officially became a missing person, I knew how the Ministry of State Security would interrogate them. If they so much as suspected that my parents had been aware of my intention to escape, they would be convicted of assisting a traitor. It was better by far for them to remain ignorant, so that they could face the authorities in complete innocence. I tried to take a little comfort from the knowledge that they'd live one day longer in the belief that everything was all right.

Filled with such excuses, I buried my face in the pillow in order to muffle my crying. I hugged it tight, to restrain myself from lashing out at the walls. As I cried and silently begged my parents for forgiveness, dawn broke. It was my last morning at home.

I heard my mother call me from the dining room, saying that I'd be late for work if I didn't hurry. I was suddenly terrified of coming face to face with my parents. This might be the last time I ever saw them. What would I say? How could I say it? My father shouted through to me that breakfast was going cold. I looked in the mirror and hastily rubbed my eyes. Seeing my own reflection, I wondered if I had ever before been so self-conscious in front of my parents, and fresh tears blurred my vision. If I emerged like this, with bloodshot eyes, they would ask questions. In my panic, I took a pair of dark sunglasses out of the drawer. As I walked into the dining room, they both questioned me at once.

'What are the sunglasses for?'

'My eyes are a bit sore.' I managed to make up an excuse, but my voice carried the hint of a tremor.

My mother jumped from her chair and approached me. 'Let me see.'

I instinctively turned my face away from her. 'It's all right, no big deal. I just wanted to dress up a bit.'

'Are you sure you haven't hurt them? Let me see.'

I held her hands in mine and pleaded, 'Yes, I'm sure. I need to impress someone today.'

My father responded brusquely, 'But what's the point of wearing those things at the breakfast table? Are you going to keep them on?'

I flinched. He'd caught me out, and I couldn't sit here eating breakfast wearing shades without a better excuse. *I want to sit here with you. This is our last meal together.* I could not utter the words. As I imagined my distraught parents later regretting how they saw me off into the unknown without eating, the tears welled once again.

'It's all right, my eyes really are fine. Don't worry.' I smiled as I spoke, though my eyes were wet. I quickly hugged my mother, wiping the tears away behind her back. She seemed much smaller than I had thought her to be. She was unfamiliar, although it was she who had raised me. My arms felt unusually long and heavy and I wanted to step away from her, but could not bring myself to.

'What's up with you today? You're acting oddly,' she chided me.

A mother can see into her child's heart merely by looking at his shadow. Stepping back from me, she tried again to look into my eyes.

My father intervened. 'Let him alone, he'll be late for work.' If he hadn't spoken at that moment, I would not have been able to stop her from finding me out.

I quickly crossed the living room and made my way towards the front door. Only when I had reached the threshold did I steal a look behind me. I longed to see my parents one more time. But the living room was empty and I could hear them talking together in the kitchen. My father was complaining about my older sisters, saying they were useless at keeping in touch, and that he wanted to see the grandchildren more often. How could he have known that I was a much worse child to him than my sisters had ever been?

Once I left the house, I might never be able to return. I saw my parents' shoes by the front door. My chest felt tight, as though I was suffocating. The farewell bow I could not offer them I offered to their shoes instead.

As soon as I left the house, my tears erupted in bitter sobs. I knew that the Workers' Party could take away my right to life, but it had also taken away my right to say goodbye to my family, and I had to deceive them to the end. I wept as I remembered my mother's last words: 'Let me see your eyes.' Why had I stopped her from looking into her son's eyes? My body trembled with angry regret.

When I arrived at work, my colleagues came up to me. 'What's wrong with your eyes?' they asked. I lied that I had an eye infection, and this led to a stroke of luck. After our morning meeting, Supervisor Park Chul urged me to go to a doctor, saying that he had suffered from something similar in the past. On the pretext of getting my eye infection seen to, I was able to leave work at eleven that morning.

I made my way to the trading company where my classmate from Kim Il-sung University worked as the head of surveillance. In North Korea, all workplaces have someone in charge of surveillance. In the case of companies that deal with foreigners or employ North Koreans who travel overseas on business, there are many surveillance officers. I knew I could go to this friend of mine for a special travel pass.

In North Korea, there is an ordinary travel pass and a special travel pass. They are differentiated by a red line drawn across the special travel pass. Provinces such as Hwanghae or South Hamgyong are generally classified as ordinary regions, because they lie inland. The capital city of Pyongyang and regions that lie near the borders with South Korea or China are considered special areas. Only local residents or those with a special travel pass may legally set foot in these regions.

The special travel pass for Pyongyang has a single red line drawn across it; a pass to enter the border regions displays two red lines. In this regard, a travel pass is not like a passport, which allows an individual to leave the country. Instead, it is a method of control over domestic travel. According to standard procedure, a special travel pass can only be issued after the approval of the Ministry of State Security has been obtained.

Fortunately, by this time, the forces of marketisation set in motion by the mushrooming black markets in North Korea had reached officialdom. Anything could be bought if you had enough foreign currency. North Korean trading companies, whose raison d'être was to conduct business with companies based in China in order to earn foreign exchange for the Workers' Party, were assigned a larger quota of special passes than any other official institution. And in North Korea, whether you were the state or an individual, you had to sell whatever you had in order to survive. My old classmate had constantly been prodding me to send people with foreign currency his way, to buy his allocation of blank special passes.

I went to his office and told him what I wanted. He said that although he generally sold them for US$200, he would sell me mine for only US$100 because we were old mates. Although my monthly salary of 2500 won (around US$2) was higher than most North Korean salaries, this was still not enough to sustain anyone's livelihood. Ordinary North Koreans made their living in the black markets, and cadres lived through special rations and bribery. A UFD cadre could make around US$100 each month by selling off the special rations from abroad issued through the Department.

But I was also privileged by family connections. Officially, North Korea operates two separately compartmentalised economies, referred to as the People's Economy and the Second Economy, the latter encompassing the military sphere. My relative headed the Middle East office of Bureau 99 in the Second Economy, overseeing North Korea's arms deals in the region. He was one of the wealthiest men in North Korea, and was able to offer a minimum of 10 million American dollars in 'loyalty remittances' to Kim Jong-il every year.

There was no way that he could have made his money – enough to give regular gifts to his relatives and pass round Mercedes Benz cars – by actually selling North Korean weapons. I learned from him that North Korean rockets sold fairly well in the Middle East until the end of the 1980s because they were cheap, but various factors led to deals becoming harder to secure after that time. In the early 1990s, as the Soviet bloc collapsed, he had seized an opportunity to move between Ukraine and the Middle East, setting up arms deals. Out of these successes, he built himself a reputation as a highly sought-after weapons negotiator. Kim Jong-il recognised his work and bestowed on him the highest medal in North Korea, the Award for Heroic Effort, not just once but twice. My prized new Shimano bicycle made in Japan had been one of many gifts from him too. As one of Kim Jong-il's Admitted and known among my friends as 'the man who always carried at least US$1000 in his wallet', I was able to buy a blank special pass without arousing undue suspicion. The only thing my classmate asked when I handed him a US$100 note was for me to give him the amount in two US$50 notes instead, because counterfeit US$100 bills had flooded the domestic economy when a Party directive to use them in trade with China had backfired. Now, even individuals avoided them as much as they could in their private transactions.

As I hurriedly rose to leave after we had concluded our business, he called out to me, 'Hey, where are you going? You have to put the traveller's name on the pass.'

'Oh, I'll just write it in later.'

'Are you crazy? Just because it's blank doesn't mean you can fill it in any old how. You need a cipher for it to work.'

I had no choice but to give him Young-min's name and identity as well. As my old classmate wrote our names, occupations and dates of birth in the special pass, he explained to me how my birthdate should be combined with this week's cipher for travel in the border regions. I hadn't known that such a cipher even existed, and I feared that my ignorance would sooner or later present an insurmountable and unforeseen obstacle to my escape. I stuffed the pass deep into my pocket and turned to leave. 'Take care not to defect across the border!' I heard him shout after me, and I glanced back over my shoulder to see him grinning. I gestured light-heartedly as if I were dismissing his joke, but inside I was stung.

With the special travel pass in hand, every step I took from here on would be in execution of that very plan – to defect. My legs trembled as I returned to Office 101. When I entered through the small gate and passed the guard, I walked more quickly. On my return to the office, Supervisor Park Chul looked up from his desk. 'The First Party Secretary wants to see you. Be quick about it.'

A sense of dread washed over me. Before making my way to the First Party Secretary's office, I went to the bathroom and hid the special travel pass between my foot and the sole of my shoe. It was all I could do by way of preparation. As I climbed the stairs, my head was filled with macabre thoughts.

I took a deep breath and knocked on the door of the Party Committee room. The sound echoed to the end of the corridor. The door opened and the secretary flinched when she saw me. She picked up the phone and spoke into it: 'Comrade First Party Secretary, Comrade Kyong-min is here to see you.' After putting the receiver down, she suddenly became courteous and even held the door open for me to enter the room.

From the doorway, I glimpsed the Workers' Party flag arranged under the portraits of Kim Il-sung and Kim Jong-il. The red Party colours seemed a sterner shade of red than usual. When I stepped inside, before I noticed the First Party Secretary, I saw three unfamiliar men waiting for me. There was a man who looked to be in his early fifties wearing a dark green coat, and two others, wearing black coats and in their early or mid-forties. As their eyes fell upon me, I imagined that each man had been trained to perceive my real thoughts. I already felt like a condemned criminal.

Lying on the long table that divided the room was the southern Chosun book that I had lent to Young-min, along with his notebook. My heart sank to my stomach.

The oldest of the three men spoke first. He did not get out of his chair, but his swagger was noticeable. 'We've come from the Ministry of State Security.'

It was all the more terrifying to hear that name – the merest hint of which is enough to silence a crying North Korean child – from the mouth of one of its agents. Not only that, these men would be from the infamous Section 10 of the Ministry, who specialised in interrogating North Korea's most senior men. No one else had the clearance to set foot inside UFD premises.

'Why was this book found outside the premises without authorisation?' the man asked.

To that point-blank question, I answered that I must have slipped it into my briefcase while in the office, and taken it home without realising. I'd then misplaced the briefcase.

Another man cut me short. 'Choose your words carefully, comrade. We have checked with your colleagues and none of them has ever seen you with that briefcase. We checked for fingerprints, and the bag isn't yours. We will discover the identity of its owner in a few days. Are you going to wait till then, or confess now?'

I spoke more forcefully. 'I will repeat what I said before. The briefcase belongs to me. The prints you found must belong to the thief who took it.'

The three men took turns to question me in rapid succession. Where had I bought the briefcase? What time had I left work on the day it was mislaid? Was there a witness? When had I noticed that I had mislaid the briefcase? Where might I have mislaid it? Who was at home when I returned from work? If I had misplaced my briefcase, why had I not alerted the authorities earlier? Had I been trying to read sections of the book that had been blacked out? What other items had I put in the briefcase?

I responded feebly that it was just the book. Seeing me stumble, one of the men asked what I had scribbled inside the notebook. I caught myself just before falling into the trap.

'You want to know what I scribbled in the notebook?'

When his colleague responded, I noticed how he put a slight emphasis on the fact that he was referring to *my* notebook, and I realised what was happening. Young-min's notebook contained Young-min's handwriting, not mine. If I claimed the notebook was mine in order to reinforce that the briefcase was mine, they would have the contradiction they needed because of the contrast between my handwriting and Young-min's, and the case would be sealed.

I made as if to recollect my thoughts, and the men scrutinised my face for involuntary blinks or muscle movement. But I answered confidently.

'I don't remember what's written in it,' I said. 'The notebook isn't mine. I picked it up on the street and put it in my briefcase, because I didn't want the paper to go to waste.'

Tapping the table with his pen, the older man said sarcastically, 'So the briefcase belongs to you, but the notebook in the briefcase does not belong to you. Well, we seem to have a problem here. But the fingerprints on the briefcase will reveal all. I shall give you one last chance to come clean, before the results are confirmed tomorrow. The fact that you took a restricted publication outside these premises is a treacherous crime in itself. But if you tell us who you lent the book to and who else might have had access to it, you may be let off lightly. Confess before tomorrow morning to Comrade First Party Secretary. Understood?'

After the men left the room, the First Party Secretary pleaded with me as if his own life were at stake. 'Those men can't arrest you, comrade, although they'd like to. Why? Because you're one of the Admitted. So you have to be *more* honest . . . more so than anyone else . . . with the Ministry. If you remember anything, anything at all, call me tonight. Or see me first thing when you come to work tomorrow. Okay?'

Three men with the licence to order an execution on the spot had left without taking further action, because I was one of Kim Jong-il's Admitted. If it hadn't been for that, I would have been arrested and dragged into the Ministry's premises, if only to terrify me into a confession. My status had given me immunity, however temporary. Even the infamous Section 10 of the Ministry needed to put a formal request through to the Party's OGD, which then had to be passed on to Kim Jong-il for his personal approval, before they could arrest one who was Admitted. To do so, they required conclusive evidence, because anything less would lead to their being charged with treason themselves for attempting to attack Kim Jong-il by harming his associates. While I acknowledged that I owed my current safety to Dear Leader, I knew I couldn't afford to stay in Pyongyang another day.

When I returned to my office, I began to count the seconds to the end of the longest day of my life. Whenever I heard the sound of a car outside, my blood turned cold in anticipation of the Ministry's men returning with a warrant to arrest me.

At seven in the evening, it was time to go. I normally said goodbye to the guard at the main entrance as I left for home, but that day, the words didn't come. The guard shouted and raised his gun as he stood to attention for me. The noise of the cocked rifle scraped at the marrow of my bones, and instinctively I glared at him. At that moment, I noticed two men outside the premises turn quickly towards me.

As I walked along the pavement beside the high wall of the UFD compound, I was very aware of the combined stares of the two men pinned on my back. When I crossed the road, I pretended to look both ways and glanced over my shoulder. They fell back a little, and I was now certain that they were following me.

I saw a foreigners' taxi up ahead. They were supposed to be off-limits to North Koreans, but anyone who had foreign currency could use them. I checked that there was not another taxi nearby. There wasn't – and I got in.

'The Pyongyang Hotel. Quickly, please, I'm late,' I said as I slammed the door.

As the taxi took a right turn at a crossroads, I turned to see the two men standing helplessly on the pavement. I felt very relieved. It took no more than five minutes to arrive at the Pyongyang Hotel, by the Daedong River. I paid the driver and entered the hotel. In the hotel, there was a restaurant named Pyongyang Bulgogi, through which you could enter and leave the premises. I knew the area well, and left the hotel through the restaurant. Across the road stood a building in the traditional Korean style, with a terracotta roof built to resemble the shape of a crane's wings, the Pyongyang Great Theatre. At its rear alleyway, I flagged another taxi, and finally headed towards Pyongyang Station.

I arrived at the station ten minutes later than the agreed time – as I could see from the overhead clock. Under a lamppost on the edge of the station park, yet barely visible in the dim glow of the city's weak electricity supply, Young-min stood waiting. He was carrying my backpack, which I had entrusted to him the night before. I was so glad to see him again. Each of us knew how the other was struggling to conceal the desperation he felt, and we embraced tightly.

I whispered first in his ear, 'Let's go.'

Young-min raised a clenched fist and replied, 'Let's go.'

These were our final words as we prepared to leave our homes, lives and families. In the necessity of departure, our two lives became one.

6 | IN THE RIFLE SIGHT

YOUNG-MIN and I arrived at the border town of Musan on 15 January 2004. We had travelled a distance of 465 kilometres. The journey by express train, which should have taken just one day according to the timetable, lasted four extra days. But despite this delay, every single person on board praised the marvel that was the arrival of any long-distance train at its destination. Someone yelled in a characteristically northern accent how, last month, the same trip had been delayed by more than ten days. Young-min and I glanced at each other and smirked.

They say that in January, up north in Hamgyong Province, icicles fall to the ground when you pee. When we city boys from Pyongyang stepped off the train, the sudden exposure to the brutal northern cold came as a shock. Young-min's ears turned bright red with cold. Unlike the large covered station in Pyongyang, Musan Station was a small building about thirty metres from the tracks. The fencing around us, there to prevent those without travel passes from leaving the station premises, made more of an impression than the station building. The guards blew on their whistles and herded the passengers towards a booth where we were to show our train tickets and travel passes. Young-min and I remained silent, trying to appear inconspicuous, as we felt our true motives for travel would be obvious to anyone who looked closely at us. We communicated only with our eyes as we walked and, as we drew closer to the guards, we stopped even that.

With the authority granted to us by our Central Party identification papers, we stood at the back of the shortest queue, for Cadres, where only three people waited ahead of us. The other queues, for Military Personnel and Ordinary Residents, stretched far behind. However, the guards seemed to be taking more care over scrutinising the cadres' passes, perhaps because they had more time to spare on a short queue. In the time the guards conducted one drawn-out interview with a cadre, four people in the line for Ordinary Residents had their documents confiscated without even being given a chance to explain. One of them, even as he was taken away by security agents, struggled to return for his luggage. A guard shouted and cursed at him and, when the man still did not stop struggling, began to kick him with his military boots. If my pass were declared invalid, my fate would be no better.

Finally, it was our turn. I took my identification papers out of my leather briefcase, making sure that the crest of the Workers' Party emblazoned on it in gold was visible. On seeing this, the guard, who had greying hair, tensed and saluted me. I was barely thirty.

'Please show me your travel pass,' he said meekly.

The special travel pass had already got us through several checkpoints. In North Korea, two types of guards check passengers' travel passes and identification documents every time the train crosses provincial boundaries or city limits; and this applies to both civilian and military passengers. Although I had passed easily through these barriers, this final checkpoint was the only one that mattered now. As the guard glanced up from my documents towards me, I flinched. Even if my pass looked genuine, I feared that my guilt would show. When he handed back our documents without a single comment, Young-min and I walked as calmly as we could out of Musan Station.

We had chosen to cross the border from Musan, as the Tumen River – which forms part of the border separating North Korea from China – is at its narrowest there. The distance of this crossing determined our fate. If we climbed higher into the mountains, there might be smaller streams that fed the river, which we could cross with less difficulty. But there was no transport that could take us that far. We had been able to find a direct train to Musan because it was home to a large mining industry, and this was the closest we could get to the border.

When cadres miss three days of work, they are registered missing and a search warrant is issued in case of desertion. Even when you are ill, you must notify the relevant authorities about your whereabouts, because someone will be sent to verify that you are where you say you are. This would be our fourth day away from work, longer than we'd planned because of the delay to our train. Pyongyang must have issued a search warrant by now. We were in a race against time, and we were already losing.

As soon as we left the station, we set off towards the Tumen River. Along the way, we got lost and had to ask a local for directions. We had no idea what lay one step ahead. Our plan was to reach the riverbank, then look for a suitable place to cross. Hiding ourselves in foliage, we would then wait for the path to clear, and sprint over the frozen surface of the river.

When we neared the Tumen River, I felt a surge of exhilaration. The river was frozen solid, and could not be more than sixty metres wide. Crossing the border would present no problem at all! But I panicked when I realised there was not a trace of surrounding vegetation. Where would we hide? There were ranges of hills all around us, just as I had seen on a map. But even the skeletal remnants of trees had been stripped of their bark, I presumed, by those who were starving to death. Even twigs had been gathered for fuel, and the hills were naked.

We had no choice but to continue along the riverbank, on an unpaved track, with nothing but our papers to rely on for protection. If we kept going, a forest might appear to screen our escape – or so we believed out of sheer desperation – and we walked for miles. We passed watchtower after watchtower, set one kilometre apart in the bare landscape along the riverbank.

Sometimes we saw soldiers' helmets bobbing about inside. Where there was no one in camouflage moving, signs fixed to the ground like abandoned rifles read: *No entry! Border area!* Or: *Stop! We will shoot you!* Wherever the width of the river was narrower, there was a garrison with a red flag and a checkpoint. Any vehicle or person wishing to pass through had to be questioned about their reason for travel, have their bags searched and pockets examined. But as soon as we showed our papers, the guards stopped thundering their orders and saluted us. Some even lowered their voices and pleaded for a cigarette.

On the road, in addition to border patrols, we encountered several militia guards who did not wear military uniform or badges of rank but were dressed in camouflage. Whenever we were stopped, we shoved our papers in their faces; and if we thought the confrontation might escalate, we offered cigarettes too.

By sunset, we had travelled almost thirty kilometres along the border. Around 10 p.m., when the darkness became absolute and we could no longer see ahead of us, we knew we had to cross. Young-min and I edged closer towards the frozen river.

'Hands up!'

A soldier's voice rang out of nowhere. Young-min gripped my arm so hard he made me jump. I considered punching the soldier rushing towards us and bunched my fists by my side, ready to strike. But he blew a whistle; completely to our surprise, countless lights lit up, their beams converging on us.

Given no chance to explain ourselves, we were brought to Guard Post No. 6, prodded in the back all the way by cold gun barrels. As we entered the small building, I saw the open door of a cell. Handcuffs hung from its bars.

A soldier addressed us. 'This is a border area. Why are you here at this time of night? Show me your identification documents and travel passes.' As he spoke, he signalled with a jerk of his head, and the heavy door thudded shut, trapping us inside the building. Young-min trembled visibly, suggesting that we had been caught in the act of defection.

'My friend here is feeling cold. Let us get warm first,' I said, struggling to keep my composure.

As I reached into the breast pocket of my shirt for our identification papers, I could feel my heart beating. My hand shook as it brushed against my jacket pocket, which held incriminating evidence of treason. I was carrying on my person the poems I had written in secret, having taken them out of my rucksack earlier.

When the first lieutenant reached for my identification papers and saw that they did not belong to an ordinary citizen, he stiffened and sprang out of his chair. Although he was an experienced soldier, he seemed never before to have seen identification papers displaying the gold insignia of a Central Party cadre, nor the blue stamp bearing the authority of the secretive United Front Department.

'Why have you come to the border area?' the first lieutenant asked again. Perhaps my youth seemed incongruous with the gravitas of the emblems, and he looked me up and down. His eyes seemed to ask, 'What do you have there in your other pocket?'

I took a deep breath. 'We were sent by the Party Committee. Our mission is to retrieve some documents from Musan KPA headquarters. But the night's turned cold. We came here in search of a guard post where we could stay the night.'

'No! I saw them trying to set foot on the ice!' one of the soldiers interrupted.

Well versed in the Party's ladder of petty seniorities, I instinctively adopted the demeanour of a cadre who had been provoked by an underling. 'You shit! How dare you point a gun at me? Do you know who I am? I want to punch your insolent face . . .'

Before I could finish, the first lieutenant cut in: 'Connect the phone to Musan KPA headquarters and find out if they're expecting two visitors from Pyongyang.'

I felt faint. Young-min, who had been warming his hands near the stove, shot me a look of despair. A soldier picked up the receiver and dialled. He waited, and then replaced the phone in its cradle. 'Comrade First Lieutenant, there's a power cut down the line. I can't get through.'

On hearing those words, my stubborn will to live was rekindled. I addressed the first lieutenant. 'Enough of this pissing about. You can have him try again in the morning. Give us some bedding, and do it now! Hurry up!'

I was desperate and blustering, but it seemed to work. Begging them to let us go would have been an admission of guilt, so instead I asked them to let us stay the night. The first lieutenant faltered and glanced down at my papers once more. He even offered me a chair.

As I sat down, the heavy door creaked open and a group of soldiers shuffled in. They were returning from patrol. Gathering round the first lieutenant, they peered alternately at me, at Young-min and at the identification papers.

A second lieutenant of the patrol came up to me and asked, 'Do you know Seo Jung-hwan?' I had never heard the name and felt like I was failing a test. But Young-min jumped up from his chair.

'Seo Jung-hwan from Kimchaek City? The boy whose father is the Party Secretary for Kimchaek?'

The second lieutenant became noticeably excited. 'Yes, that's him! Comrade First Lieutenant, he knows my old classmate Jung-hwan!'

I remained seated in a daze. The first lieutenant's face displayed an expression of contempt as he looked at the second lieutenant and Young-min, who had begun to chatter away like old friends. I mustered my courage once more and shouted, 'Hey! You really know Jung-hwan?'

'Yes, sir! We go back a long way.'

'How wonderful! An old friend of a dear friend, and so far from home. We've been looking for somewhere to stay for the night. Will you put us up?' Before anyone could protest, I took out a bottle of expensive Western cognac and six packets of Marlboro cigarettes. There is nothing more precious to a North Korean soldier than alcohol and cigarettes. While cash served well as a bribe, cigarettes were a more prestigious commodity, especially if they were a foreign brand. Besides personal items, I had packed my rucksack with three boxes of Marlboro cigarettes and two bottles of cognac, in preparation for just this kind of occasion. As the first lieutenant saw the alcohol and cigarettes, his eyes lit up.

Even the most basic rations for soldiers were intermittent, and not only that, foreign goods exuded an intoxicating aura: tokens of the Other World that exists beyond the borders. One of the soldiers exclaimed that this was the first time in his life that he would get to try Western liquor, and the first lieutenant proceeded to distribute the cigarettes to his men as if they were his own gifts.

Provided with prickly military blankets for the night, we lay awake listening to the snoring of soldiers, as well as to the change of patrols with each passing hour. As each group of soldiers set off, they took over the weapons of the previous shift and armed themselves with spare cartridges and hand grenades. The metallic noises screeched, *Death to the traitor!* I prodded Young-min lightly, and saw that he too was unable to sleep. Time crept by as we lay awake in the cold.

The next morning, we left the guard post with a letter from the second lieutenant addressed to Seo Jung-hwan. A group of soldiers waved goodbye and we reciprocated awkwardly. As soon as we were out of their sight, we high-fived each other and excitedly recounted moments from the night before, albeit in a low voice. But our footsteps soon turned heavy. The border area was much more tightly controlled and tense than the tranquil countryside we had imagined from Pyongyang.

Young-min spoke first. 'Should we go home?'

Facing each other, we slumped down onto a disused section of railway track that stretched along the Tumen River.

'It's too late for that now,' I reasoned. 'We've missed too many days of work already and they've probably put out a search warrant for us. You know the Party. We can't go back.'

'Then how do we cross?'

It was as if he wanted me to admit defeat on our behalf. Wearily, I looked at our surroundings. In the silence it seemed that we were the only people left on earth. The hills and river were white, covered with snow. Somewhere far away, a whistle blew three times – perhaps another arrest. Just over the river, on the other side of the border, we could hear the lowing of an ox. The sky seemed exceedingly blue and a bird flitted across that borderless space. We could see over the river, but we were helpless to cross it.

Young-min spoke again. 'We've come all the way here from Pyongyang. Just across this river – just there – is China. It's right in front of us. How on earth do we cross?'

As he'd pointed out, nothing much lay between us and China, and each side of the border looked alike. Our lands were covered with snow, and so were theirs; except that their mountains were covered with trees like balls of cotton, and ours were sheer and bare. In the summer, our hills would be hellish red and theirs green with foliage. To me, this confirmed that we had every reason to cross the river.

'Let's cross, now!' I was surprised by my own words. Until this moment, I had been focused on moving under cover of night. 'Now's the time – the soldiers keep watch at night, but now, it's bright as day, and we can see them before they see us. Let's cross!'

As if we had planned it, I glanced round on the North Korean side and Young-min checked the Chinese side. 'No one's around,' he said. 'Should we stand up?'

'Now?'

'Yes! Now!'

Although we spoke with confidence, neither of us stood up. What frightened us more than anything was that neither of us had the courage to act. We breathed deeply, and as our humiliating weakness of mind was laid bare, it was also cathartic. The silence recharged our resolve, and we reached for each other's hand to feel the heat of our bodies. We had walked to the edge of this cliff together, and would jump together.

We counted in unison.

'One …'

'Two …'

'Three!'

We leaped up and started sprinting across the frozen Tumen River. My heart pounded with every step, and the ice bellowed under our feet. Over ten metres, twenty metres? Someone started yelling.

'Hey! Get those bastards!'

I turned to look towards the noise. A group of soldiers stood with their rifles aimed. I saw the barrel, and heard the rifle cock. The roof of my skull seared with pain, where I knew the bullet would enter. I screamed but could not hear my own voice.

PART TWO

FUGITIVE

'YANBIAN LOOKS TO THE WORLD, THE WORLD TO YANBIAN!'

'**D**on't look back. Keep your eyes ahead,' I panted again and again as we sprinted across the ice.

The frozen surface of the river beneath our feet turned at last into land. We had stepped into China, and had committed an unredeemable act of treason. On the North Korean side, a soldier yelled, 'Shoot! Shoot!'

The shout sounded as if it was coming from very near. I heard no shots, but imagined a bullet grazing past me, lodging itself in a tree up ahead. I couldn't look back, because there was no way back.

Gritting our teeth, we kept going, heading for the nameless mountain ahead of us. Although my legs were moving, the mountain seemed to be getting further away. With almost every step I fell to the ground like jelly. The snow was ankle-deep, and my limbs were too weak to support my body. When one of us fell, the other pulled him back up. Fear pushed us on and kept us moving; fear prevented us from looking back to see who or what was behind us.

'Just a little further. We're almost there,' I gasped. Strangely, I found a rage surging from within, drowning out the terror that had been gripping me. Had this narrow stretch of frozen river been all that had condemned us? Still, we were not yet free. Terror lay not only in the guns behind us. Soldiers might appear somewhere ahead too.

I said to Young-min, 'Check around for patrols; you look right, I'll look left.'

Snow, fields, mountains. There were no soldiers in this landscape. We were relieved to hear each other's voice say the same words: 'No one on this side.' Even the urgent shouts of the North Korean soldiers had faded into silence. But this exposed us to the terrifying vacuum of China's vast emptiness, waiting to swallow us whole. China's soldiers might be waiting for their approaching prey, hiding in a future we could not see.

But as we continued towards the mountain, we saw no guns and heard no soldiers' whistles. As we neared its base, we saw no other living thing. Coming face to face with the base of the mountain was like coming to seek refuge in the arms of divinity. The countryside was covered with trees, so unlike the barren hills of North Korea. These trees would welcome and hide us. Only a few minutes before, we had looked on this place as if it were a distant planet, but now we were standing within that other world. Only now did we catch our breath, turning to look back towards North Korea. There were no soldiers on our trail.

We were seized by ecstasy. As we stood there, gawking at each other like fools, tears ran down Young-min's cheeks. When he wiped my face with the back of his hand, I realised that I was crying too. But it didn't matter, because crying at times like these was the mark of a true man. Instead of saying this out loud, I made a fist and punched Young-min's chest. He did the same to me. After two or three more punches, the punches became tickles, and we fell about laughing. We had experienced a miracle, and we were proud of our courage. I posed to aim an imaginary rifle at Young-min. He spread his arms wide and puffed out his chest, daring me to shoot. We fell into laughter once again, clutching our bellies and marvelling at how we could indulge in such play.

Young-min found a pebble on the ground and hurled it in the direction of North Korea. I felt the vanishing speck dislodge the anger knotted in my stomach and dissipate it. We had not merely freed ourselves from the grip of the regime, but hurled it away like the pebble Young-min had thrown. Nevertheless, the silence of the border was oppressive, and I cowered when I registered that ours were the only voices to be heard. But Young-min seemed to derive security from our isolation in this deep woodland, because he spread his arms again and fell backwards onto the snow.

'Let's rest here for a few days,' he said. 'If I freeze to death on this mountain, that won't be so bad.'

As he spoke, a bird flew across us from nowhere and, flapping its wings loudly, passed low over our heads. It felt like an omen, a warning that other living beings were near. Young-min didn't seem to notice. He was making snoring noises and giggling to himself. I wanted to roll about in the snow with him, but didn't have the heart and stood nervously fiddling with my rucksack. We had passed through so many obstacles to get here and, merely moments ago, had stared death in the face. I could think of nothing more wretched than being caught after managing to cross that border.

I said, 'We don't have time. North Korea will be alerting China. If we stay here, they'll find us. Let's go just a bit further, find a town.'

'How? We don't know where to go,' Young-min replied.

I stopped fiddling with my rucksack. As Young-min said, we had no way of knowing where to go under this new and foreign sky. Perhaps we should follow the Tumen River south.

Peering into the woods and hills deeper into China, I spotted what appeared to be a small village in the distance. I could even make out a woman wearing red. What if she had seen us? Would she have alerted the authorities? The colour red sent a shiver through me. Still, I saw no choice but to head towards the village.

'I'm going to check out the village. You stay here. I'll shout if I run into trouble,' I said.

I was high on the confidence of having outrun the North Korean border guards in broad daylight. My announcement woke Young-min from his trance and he seized my arm.

'Where on earth are you going? How do you know there won't be patrols there?'

I replied, 'You know how they say there are lots of South Korean tourists in China. I can pretend I'm one of them who's lost his way. Do you have a better idea?'

Young-min didn't approve and decided to stay where he was, but I made my way towards the village all the same. I walked quickly without looking round too much, as I didn't want to draw attention to myself. As I neared the woman in red, I saw that she appeared to be in her forties. She looked like an ordinary countrywoman, the sort that would be wary of strangers.

I approached her. 'I'm a South Korean tourist. Can I ask you for directions?'

Without saying a word, she hurried ahead of me and gestured towards a house. She spoke no Korean, but I assumed that she must be pointing to the house of an ethnic Korean.

Many ethnic Koreans live in the three north-eastern regions of China, near the border with North Korea. Korean settlers had moved north in large numbers at the beginning of the twentieth century, during the Japanese occupation of the Korean peninsula. The population of Koreans in this region of Manchuria quickly rose from about 700,000 in 1870 to 1.7 million by the end of Japan's colonial rule. Though Japan was defeated in the Second World War and its occupation had ended, chaos returned to Korea within five years in the form of the Korean War. According to the Chinese Communist Party's policy on minority groups, the Koreans were acknowledged as a Chinese ethnic minority and allowed to settle in the Yanbian Korean Autonomous Prefecture in north-eastern China.

By the year 2000, there were some two million ethnic Koreans living in China. Perhaps because all that separated them from their

fellow Koreans to the south was a political border, the house of the
ethnic Korean that I was led to did not look much different from
a country hut in my homeland. It didn't have a corrugated iron or
cement roof like many of the other buildings surrounding it. These
huts were called 'earth huts' in North Korea, because their shape
suggested that they had been raised from the earth.

The hut was shabby. One corner of the mud wall was crumbling,
and it had clearly not been looked after. Perhaps the only way it
differed from a country hut in North Korea was that it was a larger
building. I approached the gate and, when I tried to peer inside, a
white dog put its head out and began to bark. I jumped and felt cold
sweat trickle down my back. I worried that Young-min might think
I was in trouble.

'Who's there?' a middle-aged man shouted in Korean from a stable
to the left of the inner courtyard. His beetle-browed face was that of
a farmer, large, round and black like the lid of an iron cauldron. He
wore a black imitation leather jacket, but his trousers looked funny.
Perhaps he had borrowed those yellow trousers dotted with tiny pink
flowers from his wife? He wasn't wearing shoes. I knew it would be
a waste of time to try to fool a local, so I reached for my cash. I took
out seven US$100 bills from my pocket and showed them to him.

'We've just crossed over that river. Could you take us to the city?
Here's what I can offer.'

The man hastened towards me as if he were falling forward and
pulled me into the yard with the strength of an ox. I asked whether
we were far from the city, but he ignored me. There was a strong
smell of manure. When we went into the house, the heat made my
face flush. There was *ondol* heating just like in North Korea, where a
fire in the kitchen circulated the heat under the floor. When I took my
shoes off and followed him in, the floor was deliciously hot beneath
my feet. For wallpaper, there were sheets of Chinese newspaper glued
in a type of papier mâché, and I even spotted a portrait of Mao

Zedong amid this collage. If someone had done such a thing in North Korea, inadvertently recycling the portrait of Kim Il-sung or Kim Jong-il, he would have been sent to a gulag. When I had time to reflect on what I had seen, I wondered whether the reason that China had been able to reform and become more open while North Korea had not lay in the fact that, although the Chinese Communist Party had its own version of the Supreme Leader and even shared a history of leadership cultification similar in some ways to ours, in China the cultification of one man had ceased to be the overriding priority and *modus operandi* of the state.

But these thoughts came later. My immediate focus was on the man, who was searching for something in his wardrobe, which appeared to have metal ox-shoes for handles. There was a low table with an unfinished meal on it, and on the floor there was a pitchfork, caked with dirt. I realised why he had come out into the yard without his shoes.

'Here, I've found it,' he said. He took out a faux black leather jacket similar to his own along with some dark brown trousers, and thrust them at me.

'Put those on, quickly,' he said in a North Hamgyong accent, distinctive for its characteristic stress on final syllables. Hamgyong Province was in the northernmost part of North Korea, and perhaps the close geography and history of the area led to the shared accent.

'My clothes are made in Japan,' I replied. 'I was going to pass myself off as a tourist . . .' I had dressed especially in Japanese-made clothes because I didn't want to stand out in China with clothes that might give away my identity as a North Korean. My expensive coat was filled with down, and was good for keeping warm in the cold.

He shook his head. 'No, you have to dress like a local. If you stand out, they'll notice at the checkpoints. Don't complain, lad. Do as I say. Ah yes, and that money, is that $700 for me?'

I passed seven $100 bills to him without a word, in the hope that he would trust me. He hastily counted the notes. His fingernails too were caked with mud.

I said, 'I have a friend with me.'

Before recounting his money, the farmer looked up with eyes as wide as those of an ox that had just slipped on ice. 'What? How many?'

'One,' I replied.

'Well, what are you standing there for?' he asked. 'Bring him here.'

By the time I returned with Young-min, the farmer had changed into travelling clothes. The bus would arrive at the village in ten minutes, he explained. Impatiently, he helped us change into our new attire. Young-min looked at him in irritation. The black imitation leather jacket that I had put on wasn't too bad, but Young-min had to wear an orange-coloured one with prominent Chinese lettering on the back. I stuffed my old clothes into the rucksack, and tucked the manuscript of my poetry into my coat pocket.

We left the house and walked along the unpaved road for five minutes. The farmer, now wearing dark trousers instead of the yellow ones with pink flowers on them, looked much smarter than he did before. He introduced himself as Chang-yong. He looked more nervous than we were, and kept glancing around with suspicion in his eyes. He spoke quietly. 'Don't say a word when you get on the bus. There is a checkpoint on the way to Yanji. Sometimes they check, sometimes they don't. If someone tries to make conversation, just pretend you're deaf. If border guards come onto the bus, I'll speak on your behalf. Remember, lads: don't say a word! You'll be fine. There are ethnic Koreans here who don't speak Chinese. And if you have any more cash with you, give it to me. If you get caught, I can bribe the officers. How much more do you have?'

I pretended not to have heard his last question. I was not ready to entrust my life to a total stranger.

As we waited for the bus I wondered at the fact that there was a village so close to the border, and flinched nervously at the noise of a passing truck. On the North Korean side, apart from one or two military trucks on the road, the most common sight was a horse- or ox-drawn cart.

Just as farmer Chang-yong had promised, the bus soon arrived. Young-min and I looked at each other in amazement. It was nothing like the smirks we gave each other when the exceedingly late arrival of our delayed train in Musan was greeted with delighted cries from the passengers. In the capital of North Korea, buses never ran on time, but they seemed to do just that here, even in a rural Chinese border village. We found empty seats behind Chang-yong and sat down. When the bus door screeched shut, it was like being shut in a cell and I wished we had not boarded the vehicle. But seeing the Chinese around us in noisy conversation, carrying on with their daily routine, I relaxed a little and it seemed as though we had been welcomed into their world. Even though these were Chinese country folk, they seemed carefree in their prosperity. The men looked well fed and the women were as plump as the wives of Party cadres in North Korea. Some of them even wore gold jewellery. No one living in the North Korean countryside could make a display of personal wealth in that way because they would immediately become a target for thieves. Even in the bright colours of the clothes worn by these countryside Chinese, I felt I could glimpse an economic confidence.

When we looked out of the window, it was eerie to see the Tumen River and the North Korean lands beyond it. If we had hesitated instead of sprinting across the ice, we might still be standing there in desperation. The Chinese perhaps regarded the North Korean people with pity, as they gazed across at our hills bare of trees. Even we two, who had just crossed over from that country, cringed at the nakedness of the distant landscape. Although I did not understand a word of Chinese, it seemed to my ears that our fellow passengers would be swearing at the North Korean regime for stripping its country bare.

About half an hour after the bus had set off, Chang-yong turned towards us and blinked. I had been drifting off in a daydream and, as the bus jerked to a halt, was startled to see what lay ahead of us. There was a camouflage-patterned obstacle on the road, with armed soldiers standing guard. They were wearing grass-coloured military coats that came down to their knees, in sharp contrast to the dark-yellow uniform worn by North Korean soldiers. One of them raised a white-gloved hand to stop the bus.

I was certain that they had been sent to arrest us. I felt very conscious of my manuscript of poetry, as I had been at Guard Post No. 6. My legs shook uncontrollably even though I was sitting down. Chang-yong's still silhouette seemed to indicate his indifference, and I chided myself for so easily trusting a stranger. I looked around to see how we might escape from the bus if the soldiers came towards us. The only thing I could think of doing for now was to lean on Young-min's shoulder, pretending to be asleep. When I opened my eyes a little to check on Young-min, I saw that his eyelids were trembling, although they too were closed. In an attempt to reassure him, I made faint snoring noises, being careful not to attract unwanted attention.

I heard the doors of the bus swing open. In the heavy sound of the stomping military boots, I could feel the weight of the soldiers' rifles. One of them spoke, and the ring of his announcement in Chinese overwhelmed the chatter in the bus. I flinched, fearing he might be talking about us.

I heard the approach of boots and the murmuring of passengers. What would I see if I opened my eyes now? Was the soldier watching us? I sat there feeling the goose pimples rise along my arms and kept my eyes shut. The boots stomped away from us and I heard the door of the bus close again. I could not quite believe what was happening, but the wheels of the bus began to turn. When I finally dared to open my eyes, I saw that the bus was really moving again.

Turning to look behind us, I could see the backs of three soldiers as they signalled to the driver of an approaching truck. I shook Young-min, whose eyes remained closed. He began to laugh, still with his eyes shut and in time with the swaying of the bus.

Chang-yong quickly got out of his seat and turned to us with a broad grin. He whispered quickly, 'Well done, lads! Keep it up. The soldiers don't bother checking every vehicle thoroughly. Sometimes they come onto the bus and just look round once. They're here to look for North Korean refugees. They're easy to spot because they're underfed, have flaky skin, and look dirty after living rough. But your skin is like ours, so you don't stand out.'

I looked at Chang-yong's skin. It was dark, and clearly marked him out as a farmer who spent his days labouring under the sun.

He continued, 'Pyongyang people like you are obviously different. There's one more checkpoint. Just do the same thing again.'

We had listened happily to his explanation until he mentioned another checkpoint ahead. Once was lucky, but how could we risk our lives again on the basis of clean skin? I tried to get out of my seat, but Chang-yong gripped my knees and stopped me.

He said, 'If you walk, they'll suspect you even more. Many North Koreans don't have money for a bus so they go by mountain roads, and get caught by the border guards there. There's lots of traffic on the road today, I'm sure they won't inspect thoroughly. I'm telling you, take it easy.'

The local farmer's instinct turned out to be spot on. At the second checkpoint, our bus was let through without even being stopped. Nevertheless, I was soaked in sweat. I was no less on edge than when we had crossed the river.

As our bus entered wider avenues, Chang-yong came to sit across from us and told us that we were now safe. My panic finally began to subside. Just as he had described, the mountains that rose up around us disappeared to make way for open fields. There were private residences here and there. There were pedestrians, more people on motorcycles, and, finally, we saw red cars with TAXI written on them.

Young-min pointed to a huge sign that towered above the road like a gateway into a new world. It read 'Yanbian looks to the world, the world to Yanbian!' in large, red Korean script. It was surprising enough to find our writing in a foreign land, but I was astonished by the fact that even a provincial border town in China wanted to open itself to the world. In North Korea, we had slogans such as 'Let's install mosquito nets to keep out the winds of Capitalism!' or 'Let's install barred windows!' The openness of China moved me deeply. I had certainly made the right choice, to escape from a system that had kept us so deliberately isolated. Away from the border patrols, we would now hide ourselves among 1.3 billion Chinese. I could not shout out my exhilaration aloud, but my heart rang with it.

2 | FRAMED FOR MURDER

'HEY! Please stop for us here!' Chang-yong called out to the driver and the bus sputtered to a halt. When I stepped out I realised that although the road was wider, we were still very much in the countryside and it seemed that we had just been dumped in the middle of nowhere.

'Now, if you walk along this road, it'll take you just half an hour to get to Yanji's city centre. There're no more checkpoints. I guess I'm done here. Take care, lads, and good luck.' Chang-yong reached out to shake my hand.

I couldn't return his handshake. It was soon going to turn dark, and we didn't speak a word of Chinese. Where would we go from here? I shivered with the cold. I replied, 'I'm really sorry, but could you stay with us for a little bit longer? Would you please tell us what we should do next, and give us some idea of how to keep away from the authorities?'

Chang-yong seemed surprised. 'What? You don't know anyone in Yanji? But you told me you had to get here! You mean you crossed the river without a plan?'

Young-min stepped forward and said, 'We do have relatives here, but we don't know how to contact them.'

Chang-yong was at a loss, but he decided to take pity on us. Opening his mobile phone, he began to dial. 'It's me,' he said. 'I don't think I'll be coming home tonight. Yes, of course I've got my fee. We're near your mother's place and I was going to stop by anyway. Would you call her to say that two more are coming? It'll just be for the one night.'

After finishing the call to his wife, Chang-yong explained to us that his oxen had not been fed today. Tonight, we could stay at his mother-in-law's place, but he would have to leave us first thing in the morning to deal with the animals. As if on cue, a blizzard descended and buffeted us with snow as we walked. Chang-yong drew his short neck down into the collar of his jacket and began to grumble. He said others might have left us to our fate and that we were lucky to have met a simple farmer like him. When a taxi passed by with a loud honk, he swore in Chinese. That voice seemed to belong to another man.

'How far is your mother-in-law's?' Young-min asked.

'Fifteen minutes,' Chang-yong replied.

With those two words, he trudged ahead, as if to say it was up to us whether we followed him or not. He was huddled against the cold wind, but behind him, we couldn't contain our excitement: the soil beneath our feet was not patrolled by North Korean soldiers or by the Ministry's secret police. As if to reflect this difference, the snowstorm abruptly ceased, and there was the sunset, which seemed extraordinarily foreign and exotic. We were no longer at the end of yet another day lived in loyal obedience to Dear Leader and the Party; instead the sunset portended new days whose potential I could not begin to imagine, just like in my childhood memories. The marbled sky seemed majestic with these thoughts. Young-min too seemed intoxicated by our new environment. And by the time we had climbed the small hill to where Chang-yong's mother-in-law lived, the view was even better. There were hundreds of village houses spread out before us, all similar but each distinct. In the north, where the winters were long, narrow chimneys rose prominently above each homestead and the smoke that rose from them looked like the fluttering standards of an army gathered to confront Winter himself.

Chang-yong said he couldn't visit his mother-in-law empty-handed; especially not when he was bringing guests. We stopped by a shop where meat hung under the eaves outside, facing the street. It went against all the logic we knew from our lives in North Korea – there, the shopkeeper would be standing with his wares around him, and anything as precious as meat would be kept inside, away from potential thieves. We bought two pounds of beef and, as we walked the short distance to the apartment, darkness fell.

Chang-yong had warned us that although he owned several fields and oxen, his mother-in-law was very poor. Nevertheless, when we stepped over the threshold of her house, it was much nicer than a mid-ranking Party cadre's flat in Pyongyang. Back home, a refrigerator, a colour television and a sofa were signs of this class of prosperity. But here, in addition to those items, even the wardrobe and drawers seemed to be good-quality items too. The mother-in-law spoke in a northern Hamgyong accent just like Chang-yong's, asking anxiously whether we had hurt ourselves while crossing the river. Her concern for us was more heartening than the heating that warmed the room.

I was looking round, saying what a nice and spacious home she had, when my voice faltered as I noticed the calendar that hung beside the curtains: it showed a large photograph of a Western model clad only in a bikini. In North Korea, no matter how private your home, such a thing would be impossible. In fact, precisely because it *was* the intimate privacy of your home, it was a sanctified place in which you would of course hang portraits of Kim Il-sung and Kim Jong-il. There did exist calendars showing famous actresses, but they were to represent their loyalty to the Party through their art: it wasn't supposed to be about the women's celebrity or beauty or some product they were advertising. If any North Korean had hung such a calendar as this on their wall at home and it was discovered, that person would be found guilty beyond doubt of worshipping materialism and punished accordingly. Both Young-min and I found the calendar too shocking to bear and turned to sit facing away from it, as it appeared to our sheltered North Korean eyes like a public display of pornography.

Steam swirled wonderfully from the kitchen and, as Chang-yong's mother-in-law prepared the beef and chopped vegetables, I inhaled the strange, strong smell of what could only be Chinese spices. As we waited, we listened to Chang-yong explain how there were more than 100,000 North Korean refugees hiding in China. He told us that the Chinese authorities actively sought them out in an attempt to reduce the numbers. Then he proceeded to tell a horrible story about refugees being seized and handed over to the North Korean secret police.

'Why didn't the soldiers shoot as we crossed the river?' I wondered aloud. Chang-yong suggested that the North Korean soldiers did not have permission to fire towards China. He grinned and patted us both on the back for sprinting so well. He added that although he had met many North Koreans on the run, we were the only gentlemen to have given him the sum of $700. Apparently, it was enough to buy a cultivator, he said loudly enough for his mother-in-law to hear, and his face glowed with pleasure at the thought. He then frowned, saying that if he were found to have accepted money from us, the fine would be twenty times as great as the fee. He repeated several times that if we were caught, we must not tell anyone that we had given him any money.

As we listened, we realised that our escape was far from over. We had managed to run away from North Korean soldiers, but there were Chinese soldiers waiting for us here.

Suddenly, Chang-yong's mobile phone rang. He listened for a moment and then answered, 'Hey, I said I couldn't come home tonight. What? Say that again?'

His expression became serious. Although it appeared that the person at the other end had already hung up, he kept the phone clamped to his ear as he stuttered at us, 'Are … are you murderers?'

The question caught us both completely by surprise. The mother-in-law, who was still cooking in the kitchen, stopped what she was doing too and peered through to see what was going on.

Chang-yong said, 'That was my wife on the phone again. She says that border guards *and* armed police have been searching the village. The time, your clothes, your height, it all fits. According to the message from North Korea, you're murderers. They say you're armed and dangerous. The border areas have gone crazy.'

My chest tightened and my face flushed hot with anger. How could they possibly frame us for murder? Our worst crime was that we'd fled for the sake of our loved ones.

Chang-yong leaned in closer. 'I know you're not just ordinary folk,' he said, hesitantly. 'The defectors they're really desperate to catch – well, North Korea always frames them for murder. I know that much because I've lived here all my life. You have money and you've got good skin. You're from Pyongyang. You probably held important jobs. Who are you?'

We decided to trust this good man completely, as the Chinese authorities were on our trail now. I told him curtly that I was a member of the United Front Department and my friend worked for Section 5, and that both institutions were attached to the Central Party.

'Please, tell me so I can understand. I get the Party, but what's the United Front Department, and what's Section 5?'

While I hesitated to reveal our full identities, Chang-yong's large eyes grew wider with fear, and the fluorescent light above reflected brightly in his dark pupils.

'The United Front Department oversees policy and operations related to South Korea,' I explained. 'And Section 5 – how can I put it – it takes care of Kim Jong-il's personal needs, through entities such as the Joy Division.'

Chang-yong leapt up in surprise. I thought it was in reaction to my mentioning the United Front Department, so his next question threw me off completely.

'Joy Division?' he exclaimed. 'That thing where Kim Jong-il sleeps with girls? But your friend here is a man! You're not saying that Kim Jong-il sleeps with *men*?'

His heavy northern emphasis on the last syllable was even more pronounced, and both Young-min and I burst out laughing. Chang-yong's confused expression made us laugh even more. At this point, his mother-in-law came in carrying a small table laden with wine and beef stew. Chang-yong reached for the wine, but instead of pouring us all a glass, he asked agitatedly what we meant by Section 5.

Still grinning, Young-min explained, 'The most powerful entity in North Korea is the Organisation and Guidance Department of the Workers' Party. That's because our General, I mean Kim Jong-il, exercises all his powers through that Department. Under it falls the chain of command over every single Party, military or administrative entity in North Korea. Section 5 of the OGD oversees matters relating to Kim Jong-il's private life. Kim Jong-il's guesthouses, villas, health, food, hobbies and entertainment – all of this is the responsibility of Section 5. The girls you were thinking of, they're also employed by Section 5. That's why, in North Korea, we call pretty girls "Section 5 girls". We have staff in every county, city and district, and part of their duty is to go around girls' middle schools to hunt for the prettiest ones.

'They only pick thirteen-year-olds, which is also the age when many of them start menstruating. After selection at the age of thirteen, the girls undergo an annual physical inspection to check for disease and to make sure they're still virgins. At sixteen, when the girls finish middle school, the regional branches of Section 5 make a selection from among them. The ones who make it through to the final round are sent for a year's training and then dispatched throughout the country to Kim Jong-il's holiday homes or hunting grounds. They receive their assignments at seventeen and end their service at twenty-four. Most of them go into arranged marriages with Kim Jong-il's personal guards or senior cadres cleared to work in foreign affairs. Some even go on to become cadres themselves. Section 5 manages the whole operation.

'As for me,' Young-min went on, 'I served as a court musician. Kim Jong-il's longevity is not just about physical well-being, but emotional well-being too. I've been part of Kim Jong-il's personal entourage for ten years. And my friend here, he's a classmate of mine from music school. I majored in piano, then went on to study composition, while my friend finished his music studies and moved to work in literature. He studied at Kim Il-sung University, before starting work at the United Front Department.'

In his earnest desire to explain, I feared that Young-min was speaking much too honestly. But it was spilt milk, and we had nothing to lose, so I decided to chime in.

'My friend here is a highly respected composer in North Korea. He had the special trust of Kim Jong-il, who personally gave him a piano. His grandparents are mentioned in our textbooks as leading anti-Japanese resistance fighters, as well as in Kim Il-sung's own memoir, *With the Century*.'

Chang-yong and his mother-in-law made no response, but remained like stone, stunned by what they'd heard.

Young-min spoke: 'I wanted to ask you something.' He quickly rose and took a worn envelope from our rucksack. 'This is the address of my relative in China, from a few years back. I would be grateful if you could take us there.'

After peering at the address, Chang-yong raised his voice. 'What a rich relative you have! This neighbourhood, everyone in the region knows how expensive it is there. So you're thinking of settling there with your relative?'

It seemed that he finally trusted us, and he leaned over to fill our cups with wine.

'No, we're planning to head to South Korea.' We spoke almost in unison.

There was a moment of silence before Chang-yong raised his cup high. 'If you want to go to South Korea, leave it to me,' he said solemnly. 'My nephew, he's a professional. Defectors of your rank are guaranteed a comfortable journey to South Korea.' Then he bent forward and whispered, 'You know, my nephew – he speaks directly with South Korean spies.'

'Really?' We both spoke at once. Chang-yong nodded emphatically, and insisted that the South Korean spies would probably send out escorts for defectors of our stature. At this, we raised our cups and clinked them together. Chang-yong's mobile rang again. He looked shocked as he listened. 'What? Why on earth did you tell them? Stupid woman. What, they knew already? Why didn't you tell me earlier? OK, fine.'

Chang-yong leapt from his seat. 'Get up! The authorities are on their way! They asked my wife for her mother's address. I mean they checked it with her, because they already had it.'

We gathered our belongings and left the house quickly, to the scolding of Chang-yong's mother-in-law, whose careful preparation of dinner had been spoiled. We hurried after Chang-yong, blindly following whichever alleyway he chose to run down. The squeaking of snow under our feet and the barking of dogs all around made my panic worse. When it was brighter, the village with its multitude of chimneys had looked like a forest. But a couple of minutes running through alleys brought us to a dark and wild mountainside. Chang-yong stopped to catch his breath, like an ox that had come to a halt after being forced to do more work than its strength allowed. As he slumped to the ground, he grasped one of his ankles and moaned. I wondered if he might have sprained it.

I wanted to ask whether he was all right; I wanted to show my genuine concern, but it was all I could do to suppress a burst of absurd and pathetic laughter that was bubbling up inside me. We were running like this for our lives; but with our entry into his quiet life, for a sum of US$700, I could see the wretchedness we had brought on Chang-yong as clearly as I could visualise his yellow trousers with their pattern of pink flowers. I managed to compose myself as I examined his ankle, but then all three of us began to laugh.

As farmer Chang-yong finally caught his breath, he began to fume. 'Remember I asked you how you found my house, and you said a Chinese woman showed you the way? I bet it was her who told on us. That bitch must have reported you to the authorities. She's done it once before.'

Although it was dark, his breath was visible with every word.

'I swear I'll never help another one of you. I tell you, it's the money. I shouldn't have taken the $700 from you. In fact, other defectors are fine, but tangling with you two – it's too dangerous. You don't know how many times I've been interrogated already, living near that damned river. Anyway, where will you go now? It's dark.'

I despaired to hear him ask us the question we were about to ask him. The air was bitter and cold. Should we plead with him and offer $200 more? I put my hands into my pocket and was feeling for the money, when Chang-yong exclaimed, 'Hey! I know. Come on.'

He explained that his mother-in-law had an outbuilding across the street from her house. He would secure the door with a padlock after we had hidden inside.

'What? Soldiers are looking for us and you want us to hide near her house?' I retorted.

Young-min added in a trembling voice, 'I'd rather go deeper into the mountains. I don't care how far we have to go.'

Chang-yong interrupted him, saying, 'Just listen to me. You guys are murderers in the eyes of China. That's right, murderers! You won't be safe, even in the mountains. Besides, what are you going to do for food? And it's risky to be outdoors after dark. Anyone can be stopped by the night patrols for an identity check. If you get caught, that's it for me too. How are you going to explain how you got to Yanji? Are you prepared not to implicate me? How am I supposed to trust you two? You know the saying, "It's darkest under the torch"? However much they are feared, even soldiers can't enter someone else's locked shed. Do you hear what I'm saying? I'll bring you the rest of the beef stew and some blankets. And the wine too.'

We had no choice but to comply. The shed was actually a small shack that might once have been used as a home, although it looked to have been abandoned for years. There was a space where an old-fashioned kitchen fire had been. The smallest of the three 'rooms' in the shack had a hole in the roof and the stars could be seen in the open sky. It was not much better than being out in the cold, but at least we would be sheltered from the worst of the wind. In the kitchen area, there was a heap of dry pine needles for kindling.

Chang-yong took a long time to return to us, perhaps because he was arguing with his mother-in-law. Although this was technically part of Yanji city, it seemed as remote as the countryside. In our hut there was no sign of habitation, and certainly no heating or calendars depicting bikini-clad models, but the solitude of the place gave me hope that we might live here in hiding as long as we needed to.

My daydreaming was disturbed by the barking of dogs, and it sounded as if they were coming closer. The barking must have drowned out the sound of traffic, because I then heard engines being turned off and car doors opening. My hair stood on end.

There was a chaotic stamping of heavy military boots, and then the voices of several men. My worst fears were confirmed when I heard Chang-yong's voice among them, speaking in Chinese. The glow of the full moon shone down on us through one of the shack's dirty windows, like a spotlight intent on revealing a criminal's whereabouts, and we squatted in a dark corner away from the light. The rucksack was still on the other side of the hut. I was afraid that Chang-yong would be frightened into revealing our whereabouts to the authorities, and even the short dash over to the rucksack seemed too much to risk. We remained like this, on tenterhooks, for over half an hour.

Then all at once, the sound of heavy footsteps was followed by car doors being shut, of engines starting and of vehicles pulling away. I was so grateful for the silence at the end of it. But Young-min and I remained in our corner, stuck to the wall as if we were a part of it.

A few minutes later, I could hear Chang-yong muttering in the yard. The familiarity of his voice was welcome, but part of me feared that soldiers might secretly be following him. When the door to our shack opened, I was relieved to see that farmer Chang-yong was alone. He was carrying a large blanket and a package.

'I told you!' he exclaimed. 'I was right – it was that bitch who snitched on us. But I kept my mouth shut, said I didn't know anything about you. Fucking bitch!'

'Please, calm down.' As I waved my hand to quiet him, Young-min peered outside to check that no one else was there.

But Chang-yong spoke even more loudly than before. 'Don't worry, they've gone. They were looking for you, saying you're a pair of murderers. They even showed me photographs of you.' He put the package on the ground. 'Here. Some dumplings. Eat this and stay here till morning. I already called my nephew – you know, the one who knows South Korean spies. He says he's some distance away, and he asked me to look after you for five more days. He says there'll be a large reward if I hide you well! What a good lad. Anyway, I'll bring you a day's worth of food every day. Just sit tight and everything will be fine.'

Torn between our fear at the thought of our photos in the hands of the authorities, who were parading us as murderers on the run, and the hope that Chang-yong's nephew would come to our rescue, we waited one day, then another, each day stretching before us like a decade. Chang-yong continued to bring us food each night.

Once or twice, after the loud barking of dogs at dawn, Chang-yong circled our shack to check the area, and then disappeared again. Young-min, saying he would probably die of a heart attack before we were caught, asked several times a day whether it would be better for us to go straight to his relative's house. Each time, I shook my head. Finally, I lost my temper and raised my voice.

'Think about it,' I snapped. 'We've already been caught once by the border guards in North Korea. That's why the Chinese authorities have our photographs. We've been in China for a few days, and by now the authorities here must have been sent more evidence from North Korea. These soldiers were able to track us down to Chang-yong's mother-in-law. Do you not think they would know about your relatives? They've probably got the place surrounded. So forget it. We're going to wait for Chang-yong's nephew.'

Even in his sleep, Young-min let out big sighs and managed to get on my nerves. I had to muster all my patience to keep myself quiet. If I complained, it might provoke him even more and I didn't want an argument to betray us.

On the third night, I fell asleep quite early after drinking the wine Chang-yong had brought us; he had told us it might be the coldest night of the winter. Young-min shook me and I awoke to his terrified face and the sound of barking all around us. The night before, a cow had wandered in the yard and its shadow had frightened me so much that I'd curled into a ball and had kept shaking for an hour afterwards. Although I mumbled that it might be the animal again, I jumped up when, through the crack in the door, I spotted someone outside shining a torch over our shack. We leapt back to the corner behind the padlocked door. Every time a beam of light seeped through the cracks in the door and wall, I flinched as if it were a blade that could cut through my skin.

The light was coming closer and growing brighter. I pulled the blanket close to me and crouched in the corner. There was the sound of footsteps, which then stopped at the door. The lock on the door rattled viciously, and the sound clawed at my chest. I thought the intruder might give up and go away, but the door finally swung open to reveal a large soldier. He grimaced when my eyes met his. After the short moment it took for the soldier to register that there were two of us, he started yelling something in Chinese and rushed out. I slapped Young-min's back to get his attention. He was bent over, frantically looking for something on the ground.

'What on earth are you doing?' I hissed. Then we ran into the dark.

I don't know how I managed to climb over the high wall across from the shack. I had often stared at it through the dirty window of our shelter, thinking I could never scramble over it even if our lives depended on it. Tumbling onto the other side, I sprinted after the shape running ahead of me. I muttered to myself again and again, 'I'm going to live, I'm going to live.'

I stumbled through the dark, but came to a halt when I realised that the shape I was chasing was not Young-min, but a calf. I turned to look behind me, but there was no one there. I bent double and retraced my steps to look for Young-min, ending up in a large empty plot with a line of sight to our shack. I counted four torches, then another eight. There were twelve torch lights altogether.

Still bent double, I crept down the alleyways in search of Young-min. Sudden footsteps made me jump, and I realised that one of the torch lights was beaming from somewhere close. In the glow of light, I could even see a red star on the soldier's cap. In only a few seconds, we would come face to face. But then a miracle occurred. A cow appeared next to me, out of nowhere. Perhaps it was the mother of the calf I had seen earlier. I quickly hid myself behind it. The distance between the soldier and me must have been less than five metres, and if he turned there was every chance that he would see my legs below the creature's belly.

But the cow registered my presence before the soldier did. It shifted nervously a few paces, and then started to move more quickly. Forced to run in the same direction as the cow, and doing my best to stay hidden behind its bulk, my clothes were torn by tangles of thorns in the hedgerows. When we reached a dark place far from any source of light, I pushed against the cow and ran ahead with the last of my strength until I reached the bottom of the mountain.

There, I sank to the ground and pressed my palm against my tight chest to still the pounding of my heart as I caught my breath. My surroundings looked familiar, and I realised I must be in the area we had run to on the first night when, led by Chang-yong after the phone call, we fled from his mother-in-law's house. Perhaps this was the only road in the neighbourhood! If so, Young-min might be nearby too.

'Young-min?' I called out. 'Young-min? Are you there?' I called a little louder.

The mountain did not respond, as if it had turned its back on me and piled a wall of darkness between us. Only then did I realise that my feet, numb and beyond pain, were bare. I sank into the snow and rubbed my frozen soles. They were like stone, not flesh. Cold winds stabbed at my cheeks and ears like needles. I heard a crunching sound, similar to footsteps on snow. Had the border guards followed me up all the way here? At the thought, I was furious, because I had lost the will to run any further with these frozen and unprotected feet. But unexpectedly, a voice called to me.

'Hey, it's me! Over here!'

I looked towards the noise, and saw some branches moving. The snow reflected enough light for me to see Young-min smiling and waving his hand, poking his head out between the branches of a bush. The bastard was alive! I ran towards him, and as soon as I got close, I punched him.

'How can you smile? You selfish bastard, you abandoned your friend to save your own life!'

Young-min received my punches to his chest without complaint. Only when I had finished my scolding did he tell me he had come here thinking I was right behind him. Then he took out something from an inside pocket and handed it to me. It was the manuscript of my poetry that I had brought from Pyongyang. That was what he had been searching for on the ground in the shack before we fled. Even in that desperate situation, confronted by soldiers, he had done the best thing a friend could do. I felt a pang in my heart at the thought. Then I noticed Young-min wasn't wearing shoes either.

'Stupid boy, you should have put your shoes on too,' I said, attempting a joke.

Fortunately, we had not taken anything else off, so the rest of our bodies were relatively warm. To be safer, we climbed a little higher up the hill. As soon as sat down, we put our feet on each other's bellies to warm them. We could see the whole village down below, and could even count the individual torches in the alleyways beneath us. Near where we had been hiding, two vehicles had their lights on although their engines were switched off. Chang-yong's mother-in-law was perhaps sleeping through it, as there were no lights on in her house at all.

We did not have to wait too long before the sky had begun to lighten and gain some colour. The order must have been given to withdraw, because the torches all moved towards the vehicles, which then drove off out of the village.

'Should we go back down?' Young-min asked first. I found the cold difficult to bear any longer, and we cautiously made our way back down to the village. Having confirmed our presence in this village, I had thought that the border guards might have left some men behind. But we had seen each of the torches disappear into the vehicles and, more than anything else, the greatest threat to our lives at the moment was the cold. As we picked our way down the hill, we had no feeling left in our feet at all and we stumbled several times.

When we reached the house of Chang-yong's mother-in-law, we knocked but there was no response. But as soon as we called Chang-yong's name a light came on inside and, instead of a spoken response, he rushed out to let us in. As he opened the door, we could hear his mother-in-law shouting something in Chinese.

'Unbelievable,' he said to us. 'You weren't caught after all! You lads are amazing.'

Those words made me feel very proud. But what we needed more than praise at that moment was heat. When Chang-yong noticed our exposed feet, he took a sharp intake of breath but didn't say a word. He went to find us some shoes, and returned to us bearing socks and rubber slip-ons, apologising that these were all he had. When I put mine on, they were surprisingly warming for my feet. Farmer Chang-yong said that if we had been captured, he too would have had to live a life on the run. He told us that we were therefore greater men than Kim Jong-il. Whatever his reasons for being relieved at our safety, I was happy that he shared our relief, and at that moment he felt like an uncle to me.

'The soldiers took your rucksack,' Chang-yong said. 'What was inside?'

When I replied that it was just books and a change of clothes, he asked me to confirm that there hadn't been any money in the bag. Young-min, who was standing to Chang-yong's side, went pale at the word 'money'. Before he could speak, I answered, 'Luckily, we had the money on us.'

As Young-min signalled to me with his eyes to check whether I was telling the truth, Chang-yong's mother-in-law called from inside, and he went into the house.

'You really have the money? Is it in your pocket?' Young-min asked half expectantly, half suspiciously.

I took him to the corner of the yard and said, 'Listen, we have nothing, we have absolutely nothing. Everything was in the rucksack. But we have to pretend we have money. That man can abandon us if he wants, but we can't do anything without him.'

Farmer Chang-yong came out of the house with another package. He complained as if to let his mother-in-law hear, handed us a bottle of wine, and reassured us of his nephew's promise. We would have to wait just two more days. He added that we should take care not to freeze to death in the mountains. But we must not light a fire, he warned us. He said that one of the reasons that Chinese authorities actively searched for North Korean refugees hiding in the mountains was because of the frequent mountain fires they started.

'Go now, up near that rock over there. I'll follow with bread and more blankets.' As he pushed Young-min onwards, he grabbed my arm. He explained that his mother-in-law was angry with him for keeping us at her house longer than she'd expected, and putting her in danger. The only way to calm her down, he said, was to give her money.

I put on a stern face, saying, 'We trusted your instructions in coming here, but we were almost caught. I'll think about more money when your nephew arrives. We don't know what else might happen, so please understand our situation.'

With that, Young-min and I headed into the mountains. An hour later, Chang-yong came to give us an old blanket and a package of food. He waved his fist at the cold and said that we would be better off on the hillside than on flat ground that couldn't shield us from any direction; then he made his way back down the slope. A little while later, he reappeared, saying that we must not fall asleep, because the temperature could fall to −30°C in the night. He stressed several times that we must keep ourselves awake at all costs.

We thanked him and saw him off again. We found a spot that was a little less steep, and dug away the snow until we could see earth, clearing a space just big enough to fit two people sitting down. We sat there huddled together with the blanket over us. The bottle of wine we shared was emptied far too quickly. But the alcohol spread heat through my body, which felt comforting. We also had a hot water bottle each, and I felt even warmer knowing that Chang-yong was on our side.

Young-min said, 'Let's each pretend the other one is a woman.'

Both of us burst out laughing at those unexpected words. Having been cooped up in a locked shack for the last few days, suspicious of even our own breathing, it felt wonderful to laugh again. The thought of having evaded the border guards in such a close call felt like a triumph too.

As the night grew darker, the mountain came alive. I remembered, back in North Korea, being captivated one quiet night by the never-ending sound of waves crashing onto the coast in South Hamgyong Province. I think I was seven years old. I had not seen the ocean before, and as that vast expanse lapped restlessly, it seemed to be a living being. That night, I ran on the sand barefoot, saying that I would wake the sea from its twitchy slumber.

'Hello, sea! It's me! Wake up and come play with me!'

As I shouted at the waves, and as if the sea were waking with a stretch, lightning flashed in the distant dark of the sky.

Like the sea that night, the mountain whispered and pulsated in the dark, as if it were teeming with spirits. A distant sound coming from the peak of the mountain grew louder and, as it swelled into the valley, we imitated the noise, letting our voices rise with it. When the cold wind blew past us and away as if it were a visible being, I could feel the deep energy of the mountain as it readied another wind to sweep down from its peak.

That night, Young-min and I shared our deepest secrets with each other like lovers. Our first crushes, recollections from childhood, the family we had left behind; as if painting the sky above with the colours of our memories, even the smallest recollection held significance. As the conversation turned to our loved ones, Young-min and I could do nothing but be there in silent solidarity, each for the other. Even after swallowing a fistful of snow, my throat burned with raw emotion.

The conversation turned to the North Korean regime. Ours was a system that would rather have us convicted as murderers and killed than permit us to abandon it, let alone stand in its way. The taste of bile from the pit of my stomach that made me realise, until now, I had not merely spent my life living within the borders of North Korea, but been imprisoned behind them.

ANNALS OF THE KIM DYNASTY | 3

IN the autumn of 1999, I was appointed to work on the compilation of the *Annals of the Kim Dynasty* as a state historian. Following my composition of the epic poem to Kim Jong-il that had so pleased him in May, and my subsequent elevation as one of his Admitted, I had become a rising star in the UFD and received an urgent summons to the office of First Deputy Director Im Tong-ok. There I found myself in the company of seven colleagues I knew from various sections within the UFD.

I'd barely taken a seat when Director Im said, 'Please stand up.' He looked down at the sheets of paper in front of him on his desk. 'I am instructed to deliver the General's orders, as follows: "Even the ruinous five hundred years of the Lee dynasty during the Chosun period was recorded in the form of the *Annals of the Lee Dynasty*. It is a grave failing that we have no *Annals of the Kim Dynasty* to record the great rule of Kim Il-sung and Kim Jong-il. The UFD must therefore bring together the best minds in the country and urgently accomplish the completion of this work."'

The *Annals of the Lee Dynasty* is a history of the Chosun era, spanning the half millennium between AD 1392 and 1893 on the Korean peninsula. However, it seemed paradoxical to emulate those ancient volumes when we lived in a Socialist system that was strongly critical of that feudal dynasty. And although my appointment to such a team was a great honour, I was even more surprised that the carefully selected members of the group were writers, not historians, a signal that history came second to the cultification of the Supreme Leader.

The eight of us lived and worked in the Munsu Guesthouse, inaccessible to any outsider. Such guesthouses were independently operated by Central Party departments to provide exclusive facilities where vetted cadres could work in strict secrecy. The premises were extremely well furnished and were smaller versions of the sort of guesthouses used as accommodation for state-level visitors to North Korea.

The UFD operates several guesthouses, such as Ui-Am and Soonan. Among these, the Munsu Guesthouse had previously been used for those defecting to the North. Situated as it was in the residential area of No. 3 Chungryu-dong in the wealthy Daedong River District of East Pyongyang, not even the local residents knew that this L-shaped building was used for classified UFD operations. The interior of the high-walled compound was extravagantly appointed and, in order to ease recent defectors into collaboration, it had been decorated with luxurious foreign furnishings and materials, including expensive pieces made by South Korea's leading furniture companies. Until then, I had engaged in 'Localisation' only through reading materials and consumer goods, but when I entered an entire building that that had been Localised, it blew me away. In recent years, defections to North Korea had ceased, and the villa was now designated for internal UFD use. We were the first North Korean guests to live in the premises.

The task that had been entrusted to us was the brainchild of Kim Jong-il. The first step had been taken on the third anniversary of Kim Il-sung's death, in July 1997, when Kim Jong-il used the date of his father's birth (15 April 1912) to mark the beginning of a new *Juche* calendar. With the birth of Kim Il-sung at year zero, the history of Korea had begun anew. Kim Jong-il had defined the ethnic identity of North Koreans as 'Kim Il-sung's People' and he now needed to legitimise this. His plan was to establish a history of Kim Il-sung that would consolidate and underpin the basis of Korean identity as an identification with the legacy of Kim Il-sung, rather than with a shared race, language or culture. In order to emphasise that North Korea was the legitimate Korea, he wanted to create a history that would include Koreans not only in the North, but also in the South and overseas. None of the relevant archival records could be released to anyone without a UFD clearance. But above all, Kim Jong-il could trust no one outside a handpicked circle with the Supreme Leader's unvarnished secret history. We would need to master that secret history before we could reshape – or distort – it to achieve Kim Jong-il's purpose.

North Korea asserts that Japan's defeat in 1945 was the direct result of Kim Il-sung's achievement as a guerrilla leader in the anti-Japanese resistance. The Korean War, which was actually suspended by an armistice, is declared to have been Kim Il-sung's outright victory over US imperialism. Even the history of the Cold War is taught in North Korea as a Communist history that revolved around the efforts of Kim Il-sung. The international section of the Central Party became active in setting up *Juche* Research Institutes overseas, in an attempt to encourage foreigners to sympathise with North Korea's worldview and version of history.

One reason why North Korea is unable to pursue reform and open itself more to the world is that this would risk exposing core dogmas of the state as mere fabrications. Kim Jong-il decided that under no circumstances should any potentially harmful source material relating to Kim Il-sung's past be made available to the public. He had therefore assigned the task of creating the history to UFD cadres, who already held the highest security clearances in the nation owing to the sensitive nature of their policy and intelligence work.

Even so, there was a further level of atomisation built in, with each of us in the group responsible for a specific theme or decade in the history of North Korea. Before our work began, we signed a contract confirming that we would pay a severe penalty if we overstepped the limits of our remit in conducting our research. We carried out our work in separate studies. I was put in charge of the history of Kim Jong-il's activities relating to and stemming from his role in the Propaganda and Agitation Department, including his artistic achievements, from the mid 1960s up to the present day.

We were not allowed to enter anyone else's study. But since the eight of us – segregated in turn from the rest of North Korean society – lived communally at the Munsu Guesthouse for the period of our task, the boundaries of secrecy gradually eroded and we formed deep bonds with each other.

Of the eight of us, I thought that the writer in charge of Kim Il-sung's early years had the most challenging task. He often chain-smoked after dinner.

'How are things going?' I asked cautiously, not long after we had begun our stay. Instead of responding, he lit another cigarette. But he eventually turned to ask me a question.

'You're the youngest here. Let me ask you something. Our Supreme Leader was born on 15 April 1912. It's such a significant day that there's plenty to say about it. But what did he do the next day? I could refer to his mother's milk as a revolutionary nutrient. But what did the Supreme Leader himself do? In all honesty, what else could a baby at that age do but piss and shit? And how am I going to describe the two years after that? If you were in my position, how would you approach the problem?'

Another writer, who was working on the history of North Korea in the 1980s, shared his dilemma with me. He said he had found in one of our Supreme Leader's personal memos a mention of his attending a performance in North Pyongan Province in 1972. He asked me to help with finding source materials on similar events, with which he was going to fill three days' worth of history in the decade that he was supposed to be writing about. In this way, our contract of secrecy became nothing more than a piece of paper as the continuation of our mutual safety came to depend on mutual trust. We spent increasing periods of time in conversation with one another rather than in our segregated studies. And as I encountered more and more historical records, I grew ever more disturbed at the picture that began to emerge from the source materials.

Our group had been entrusted with the originals of documents relating to Kim Il-sung and Kim Jong-il from the archives. Compartmentalisation prevented any one person from seeing a comprehensive overview of the nation's history, but when the pieces came together, the shape of the overall picture was clear and definite: Kim Jong-il's authority had not, as the official narrative of hereditary succession stated, been passed on to him by Kim Il-sung, even though this was what he claimed as the basis of his legitimacy. Rather, the son had usurped the father.

The old saying that power cannot be shared between fathers and sons suggests some kind of universal and inevitable fate. The seeds of Kim Jong-il's vicious struggle for power against his father Kim Il-sung were unintentionally sown when the boy was abandoned by his father at the age of eight, after the death of his natural mother, Kim Jong-suk. One year after her death, on 25 June 1950, Kim Il-sung invaded the South. Kim Jong-il spent three years separated from his father, as he was sent away from the fighting. After the armistice, he returned to Pyongyang, but father and son grew no closer. By 1954, he had gained a half-brother in Kim Pyong-il, whose mother was Kim Sung-ae, a secretary who had become inseparable from Kim Il-sung.

Kim Jong-il entered Kim Il-sung University for his studies, and graduated in 1964. As the eldest son of Kim Il-sung and the bearer of his father's line, if there were to be a hereditary transfer of power at all, Kim Jong-il would have been expected to be awarded some responsibility or title, in line with Korean custom. But one year before Kim Jong-il's graduation, in 1963, Kim Il-sung married Kim Sung-ae, and this served to cement the exclusion of Kim Jong-il from the prospect of leadership.

As the Cultural Revolution got under way in China, during which time Mao's wife and first lady, Jiang Qing, held great sway, there was a parallel development in North Korea. Kim Sung-ae, as first lady, gained considerable authority at this time, with North Korea's political elite lining up behind her as if she were a North Korean mirror of Jiang Qing. Because Kim Sung-ae's son Kim Pyong-il – and not her stepson Kim Jong-il – was being prepared for succession by Kim Il-sung's associates, Kim Jong-il now found himself in a situation where his father's supporters had turned into his political enemies. To this day, the mere mention of Kim Pyong-il's role in events leading to Kim Jong-il's succession remains a blasphemously taboo subject in North Korea.

Although North Korea states officially that Kim Jong-il began his career in the Party's Organisation and Guidance Department, this is not the case. It's a deliberate distortion to provide a fitting start to the career of the future Dear Leader. At this stage, with North Korea's power elite firmly behind Kim Sung-ae, and with even Kim Il-sung's younger brother Kim Yong-ju pitted against him, Kim Jong-il had been placed well away from the centres of power, relegated to a post in the Propaganda and Agitation Department.

Kim Jong-il did not show signs of turning against his father at that time. In fact, in his work in the PAD, he contributed to the cultification of Kim Il-sung and the glorification of the anti-Japanese activities of his father's guerrilla comrades. His activities were so expansive that a monthly magazine called *Recollections of the Anti-Japanese Fighters*, established under his direction, came to be considered as compulsory reading nationwide. Many statues of Kim Il-sung and anti-Japanese fighters appeared during this time too. Ultimately, Kim Jong-il's early years in the PAD provided him with a crucial set of cultural and ideological tools that he would grow to depend on when he eventually came to rule through his dictatorship of the mind.

Even by the end of the 1960s, Kim Il-sung had not yet been established as a godhead. At the end of 1968, Minister of National Security Kim Chang-bong attempted an armed coup against Kim Il-sung. In January 1969, after Kim Il-sung had officially purged Kim Chang-bong and his faction, he appointed General Choi Hyon as a replacement. In gratitude, Choi Hyun pledged loyalty to the absolute rule of the Supreme Leader. But he was a strict conservative who believed in the hereditary transfer of power through an elder son, and it was he who secured for Kim Jong-il a place in the OGD through a closed Party meeting in the summer of 1969. In turn, Kim Jong-il kept Choi Hyon's son, Choi Ryong-hae, as his right-hand man for the rest of his life.

Kim Sung-ae's factional power, however, was not to be easily overcome. Her elder brother Kim Kwang-hop was the Vice Prime Minister, and enjoyed the support of Kim Il-sung's younger brother, Kim Yong-ju. Among themselves, Kim Il-sung's own supporters openly referred to his son Kim Pyong-il as the successor to the Supreme Leader.

However, Kim Jong-il found a way of ridding himself of these forces in the Three Great Revolutionary Goals, which imitated the structure of the Red Guards of China's Cultural Revolution. While China's Red Guards aimed to eliminate Capitalist and revisionist elements, the three revolutionary goals for North Korea were ideology, industry and culture. In the manner of the Red Guards, units made up of youths about to finish their education were set up all over the country to implement the Three Revolutionary Goals. Their main enemy was the 'abuse of power and corruption of provincial bureaucrats'. As Central Party cadres with ties to regional forces were eliminated one by one, Kim Jong-il's power grew centrally, as well as through building on solid regional support.

His father Kim Il-sung's authority at this time was channelled through the government, which had ruling powers. In this climate, Kim Jong-il was seen as no great threat to the power of his father and his supporters because he was merely an employee of the Workers' Party, which was just one of many bureaucratic institutions. Apart from Choi Hyun, no other minister even considered him as a potential successor to Kim Il-sung. But as Kim Jong-il's power base was the Workers' Party, it was the only means at his command to expand his influence and confront the government. He found the pivot he needed in the philosophy of *Juche*.

Juche was based on a focus on the person, and as such was a humanist philosophy. Kim Jong-il oversaw a change to this philosophy, according to which a person now had to be part of an institution to progress, and those who were brought into such an institution could triumph only under the excellent guidance of a Supreme Leader (*Suryong*). *Juche* thus became a '*Suryong*-ist' ideology centred not on the individual person, but on one individual alone: his father, Kim Il-sung. (The original author of *Juche*, Hwang Jang-yop, who was the Party's international secretary, eventually fled from the creation he had spawned to seek exile in South Korea in 1997.)

By 1973, 'Kimilsungism', which asserted that the Supreme Leader guided the Party and the Party led the people, had become the omnipotent weapon of the Party. It was from this time that Kimilsungism became the people's ideology, and loyal obedience to the cult of Kim became the moral conscience of every Party member. Anyone seen to be challenging this moral conscience, in however slight a way, would be sent with three generations of his or her family to a gulag where the family line would come to an end. It was also during this time that surveillance institutions, formerly under the remit of the Ministry of Social Security, were given independence in the form of the newly created Ministry of State Security, which reported directly to the OGD.

Kim Jong-il elevated the authority of the OGD and PAD, which were his bases of power, by emphasising society's need for the Party's organisation, guidance and propaganda if Kimilsungism was to be realised. In this way, he found a means to accommodate the cultification of Kim Il-sung within his Party-based powers, or rather, have the abstract cultification of the Supreme Leader *support* his own Party-based powers.

When Jiang Qing was purged in China in 1976, her fall reflected badly on her North Korean 'mirror', Kim Sung-ae, who became isolated and fell from favour. After his stepmother Kim Sung-ae lost her position as head of the Women's Committee and her key to outside relations, Kim Jong-il's position was strengthened.

To consolidate the Party's claim to 'upholding' the Supreme Leader's guidance, powers to appoint personnel were removed from the government, and Kim Jong-il's political enemies were vigilantly watched under the pretext of ideological surveillance by the OGD's section for Party guidance. The North Korean state, previously founded on the twin powers of the Workers' Party and the government, came to be entirely dependent on the Party. By Kim Jong-il's time, the Party had replaced all the functions of government, which had become no more than a hollow shell and a historical remnant.

But why did Kim Il-sung stand by and do nothing about his son's consolidation of Party-based power? The answer is: because he saw only the cultification of himself, as did the outside world. Kim Jong-il's consolidation of Party power was clothed in a moral upholding of 'Kimilsungism' and advertised itself through the language and ideology of the Supreme Leader's legacy. But while Kim Jong-il appeared to remain loyal to his father on the surface and in public perception, behind the scenes he was steadily reducing old guard powers, preparing the system for the time when one man – he himself – would have absolute and concentrated power to determine the future of North Korea.

In the beginning, it started innocently enough with the replacement of direct proposals to Kim Il-sung with cassette recordings, under the pretext of lightening his father's duties. The recording of proposals on tape effectively routed all proposals for Kim Il-sung's ratification through Kim Jong-il, who controlled the technology. Eventually, every single proposal was routed through the OGD, so that only the selected and redacted ones would be sent up for Kim Il-sung's approval. By 1980, Kim Jong-il had already completed a system whereby all real powers were vested in one man, himself, as the OGD Party Secretary, while on the surface authority appeared to rest with Kim Il-sung as the Supreme Leader.

Kim Jong-il consolidated his absolute Party-based power through the OGD by monopolising five spheres of influence.

The first was the OGD's exclusive right to allocate positions of departmental director level and above in the core institutions. Also, in the military, generals in the key regiments were directly appointed by the OGD.

The second was the OGD's absolute right to 'Party guidance', which allowed it to intervene in every administrative task carried out at any level. It did this by strictly monitoring regional and departmental Party Secretaries, and through a network of isolated cell-like structures. The result was that its military arm could summon any of North Korea's highest-ranking generals to grovel and be humiliated, while its foreign affairs arm exercised the same authority over cadres who maintained contact with the outside world, such as diplomats or businessmen.

The third was the OGD's absolute surveillance powers, which allowed it to monitor, purge or banish any cadre. The structure of this section was extremely compartmentalised yet centralised, designed to uphold and facilitate Kim Jong-il's rule by terror. North Korea's secret police, the Ministry of State Security, reported directly to this section of the OGD.

The fourth was the Department's absolute right to ratify and sanction policies. All institutions in North Korea had to route their proposals through the OGD's reporting section in order to be authorised by Kim Jong-il before they became valid.

The fifth was the OGD's responsibility for the protection of and catering for Kim Il-sung and Kim Jong-il. This meant overseeing *all* concerns pertaining to the Kims, as well as the procurement of luxury goods and operation of the Guards Command.

Somewhat ironically, the source materials for the process of this meticulous consolidation of power are preserved in the Party's History and Literature Institute, categorised under the factional fighting that occurred in the process of hereditary succession.

In the course of my research for the *Annals of the Kim Dynasty*, any questions that I had were answered efficiently by employees at the Institute. They were very helpful, often going out of their way to send me additional and related supporting materials. But even in this archive, which was supposed to contain all the secrets of North Korean history, there existed no single document that summed up the fierce rivalry which existed between the factions of Kim Il-sung and Kim Jong-il. Although we reached our conclusion reluctantly, the overwhelming evidence that demonstrated the enmity and power struggles between the son and the father (including documents showing how father and son had announced directly opposing policies at the same time) left us with no alternative. We had to concede that, while Kim Jong-il's legitimacy might have been based on hereditary succession from father to son in terms of the official narrative, in reality it had involved usurpation by the son of the father. Kim Jong-il had consolidated power by wresting it *away from* his father instead of receiving it *from* him.

I became terrified by the knowledge that Dear Leader was neither compassionate nor divine, and had acquired his power by acts of terror, betrayal and revenge. Once, while drinking tea with one of the writers in our group whom I trusted most, I made a confession. 'I want out,' I said. 'The secrets are too much for me to bear. I don't think I can ever have a free conscience again, knowing the truths behind the lies.'

He replied, 'Don't be stupid. There's no way you can stop now. The best you can do is to keep it all shut inside you, and don't mention anything to the others, okay?'

To my great relief, I was released from completing the full duration of my duty to the *Annals* when the order came from Director Im to compose the UFD's epic poem for the year 2000 as a tribute to Kim Jong-il. But although I returned to my familiar bed in my family home, I didn't feel I'd returned to a familiar world. I knew my past as a secret historian of Kim Jong-il would haunt me forever, like a watching shadow of suspicion. What frightened me more than anything was that I had forbidden knowledge about the Leader, and I would never be free of it.

The most troubling aspect for me at the time was Kim Jong-il's merciless rule by purging, which did not spare members of his own family. As soon as Kim Jong-il had consolidated his power, he used the 'side-branch' notion to designate members of his family as the side-branches of a tree that must be pruned for it to grow tall and strong. To begin with, his uncle Kim Yong-ju and stepmother Kim Sung-ae were placed under house arrest; and in 1981 he ordered that the children of Kim Il-sung's supporters should not be accepted into the Central Party. This became fixed as an internal regulation in the OGD.

Kim Il-sung's associates began to disappear one by one, and those who remained grew increasingly disgruntled by the fact that their children were being relegated to provincial postings, dead-end government positions or military ranks outside the power structure of the Party. The disaffected supporters of Kim Il-sung confronted the issue by going as a group to the Mount Keumsu assembly hall (also known as the Palace of the Supreme Leader) on 15 April 1982, Kim Il-sung's birthday, to discuss the issue with the Supreme Leader himself.

By this time, however, Kim Il-sung was merely a figurehead. All power in the state had been meticulously routed to Kim Jong-il through the OGD's tentacled reach, with positions of real authority occupied by Kim Jong-il's classmates from Kim Il-sung University. Kim Jong-il's power over the Supreme Leader himself was absolute: Kim Il-sung had to request permission from the Party's OGD before he could meet up with any of his supporters or old comrades. His own powers were restricted to those that would continue to make him appear powerful to North Koreans and outsiders alike, such as on-site inspections and diplomatic authority. Even Section 1 of the Guards Command, the personal bodyguards of Kim Il-sung, now answered directly to the Party's OGD. In this way, a leader who had once received close protection from a loyal cohort of guards lived out his last days under the close surveillance of a cohort loyal to Kim Jong-il.

This is also the reason why there was not a single General Meeting of the Workers' Party for over twenty years between the sixth General Meeting of October 1980 and my crossing of the Tumen River in 2004. Kim Jong-il had so weakened the Politburo itself, which came under the authority of the Party's General Secretary, Kim Il-sung, that it was powerless even to call meetings.

As Kim Jong-il consolidated his authority, just as the father was the public power-holder while the son was the actual power-holder, a dual structure came into being whereby real power depended on the level of trust Kim Jong-il placed in one, rather than on one's official position. This made it impossible for outsiders to analyse the workings of North Korea, as the revealed hierarchy was a sop to the old guard and actual power was held by trusted individuals beyond public scrutiny.

In other words, supporters of Kim Il-sung might be given prestigious official posts, but actual powers were restricted to Kim Jong-il's own associates. A cross-shaped system with two power structures emerged, whereby publicly high-ranking positions and Kim Jong-il's delegation of actual power were never vested in a single person. For example, Park Ui-chun, the Foreign Minister, was nothing but a straw man, while First Deputy Minister Kang Sok-ju held the real power in international affairs. This discrepancy between the hidden and surface structures allowed Kim Jong-il to maintain a system of control that could not be understood or manipulated by any outsider.

In the process of consolidating his authority, Kim Jong-il did not hold back from humiliating his father, and the following incident demonstrates the Supreme Leader's impotence in the face of his son and his son's OGD.

As one of the eight writers of the *Annals*, I was vested with the authority to summon for interview any of the surviving official witnesses of North Korean history relevant to my area of study, including the nation's most senior generals. Through one of them, I discovered the real reason for the revolutionary re-education of Kim Du-nam, who had been Kim Il-sung's military adviser.

'Revolutionary re-education' encompasses all the Party's warnings and penalties related to ideological sessions, forced labour, expulsion from the Party, loss of post or banishment. In fact, among North Korea's senior cadres, there aren't many who haven't received such a 're-education', because it is seen as a kind of vaccination against a full-blown greed for power. There are even senior cadres who are former inmates of North Korea's infamous Yodok camp. Unlike other prison camps, where you can only leave as a corpse, going to Yodok is not the end of your life or career if you choose to endure forced labour and indoctrination obediently. It is a brutal ideological training camp, where you re-learn the only truth that matters in North Korea: that loyalty to Dear Leader buys renown, and disobedience brings death.

The person from whom I first began to understand the events relating to Kim Du-nam was a general whose father had lost his authority as a consequence of Kim Il-sung's unseen fall from power. Although it was he who told me the story, he too seemed to fear Yodok.

'No stranger must know this story. Don't write it down: just know about it. Better still, hear it to understand it, and then erase it from your memory.'

This is the story he told me.

In the mid 1980s, a high-ranking military group from the USSR visited North Korea. Kim Il-sung wanted to enquire about the hospitality being offered to them, and ordered his military adviser Kim Du-nam, a four-star general, to request their schedule from the military's Foreign Affairs Bureau. When Kim Il-sung discovered that the visitors were staying at a guesthouse belonging to the Ministry of People's Armed Forces, he phoned his son Kim Jong-il to ask whether it might be more suitable to accord them the level of hospitality more appropriate to a head of state, suggesting the Baekhwa-won Guesthouse as a possibility.

Kim Jong-il immediately ordered the OGD to reveal who had notified Kim Il-sung's office about the arrangements for the USSR delegation. The next day, he fired the Director of Foreign Affairs of the Ministry of People's Armed Forces, and sentenced Kim Il-sung's military adviser, Kim Du-nam, to 'revolutionary re-education' for six months.

Among many further indignities, Kim Il-sung had to offer up a personal ode of praise on his son's fiftieth birthday, on 16 February 1992.

In this way, Kim Il-sung lived out his final years as the leading character in his own cult, which was, however, controlled by the son who had effectively usurped him and who would now succeed him.

But Kim Jong-il was careful to keep up the pretence that father and son got along well. In 1994, after Kim Il-sung's death, the

North Korean state publicised artefacts associated with the Supreme Leader's office. Among them was a speech handwritten by Kim Il-sung before his death, in which he proposed a summit to discuss unification with South Korea. This manuscript was even publicly displayed in the Mount Keumsu Memorial Palace for propaganda purposes in support of the ideology of federal unification of the two Koreas.

It seemed that Kim Jong-il supported his father's pursuit of peaceful unification. But in reality and behind the scenes, he fiercely opposed it. In 1994, alarmed by the threat of pre-emptive strikes made by the US, Kim Jong-il permitted former US president Jimmy Carter to visit Pyongyang. Kim Il-sung took the opportunity to declare publicly his approval for an inter-Korean summit, and many in the international community noted optimistically that North Korea's leader had reached out to the world. They perhaps did not realise that Kim Il-sung was no longer in control, nor that Kim Jong-il – who did hold power – was pitted against his father.

Among the source materials I saw during the course of my work on the *Annals of the Kim Dynasty*, there was one document in particular that illustrated the contrast between what Kim Jong-il projected through propaganda and his actual intentions. The document in question is the minutes of a Party meeting that took place in early July 1994, organised by Kim Jong-il himself. According to these minutes, the meeting was titled 'Today's climate calls for practical developmental policies for protecting Socialism, not policies for unification of the homeland'. It called on cadres to discredit all thoughts of unification associated with the inter-Korean summit that his father had proposed, going so far as to state that his suggestions were indicators of senility. In fact, the conversation records a meeting that was held among Kim Jong-il's closest associates not only to criticise Kim Il-sung's proposal, but to obstruct it.

Why then did Kim Il-sung stubbornly pursue the summit in the face of Kim Jong-il's opposition? Authority to talk to the outside world, which he had as the apparent leader of North Korea, was the last remaining power he held. Putting unification on an agenda that was so publicly and irrevocably in view of the world was perhaps a final attempt to have his say on the future of Korea in a way that his son could not merely ignore and recast.

Kim Jong-il refused to fulfil even one of his father's simplest last requests. Kim Il-sung had said that when he died, he wanted to be buried alongside his fallen comrades at the Mount Daesung Revolutionary Martyrs' Memorial. After his death, his ex-guerrilla comrades even signed a group petition for this wish to be carried out. But Kim Jong-il thought that if Kim Il-sung's body were laid to rest at this location, the authority of his father's revolutionary comrades would be seen to be reasserted, which might in turn threaten his own power because he had once taken away theirs.

As if to reflect his anxiety over this divisive and delicate balance, at the same time as he refused the Mount Daesung burial, he announced to the world through the Workers' Party newspaper *Rodong Sinmun* that 'It is the most righteous and moral thing to respect the first generation of revolutionaries', referring to the very group who were his enemies. Meanwhile, Kim Il-sung, denied his last wish of being buried next to his supporters, was mummified in the Mount Keumsu Memorial Palace – spending his afterlife as a propaganda icon used to legitimise Kim Jong-il's hereditary succession.

Given the subterfuge and machinations performed by Kim Jong-il against his father, it was no easy task for me and my seven colleagues at the UFD to write the *Annals of the Kim Dynasty*, between 1999 and 2000. That said, they continue to be broadcast daily on North Korean state television under the title *Uncovering the Revolutionary Annals of Comrade Kim Il-sung*.

4 | CRIMINAL OPERATIONS

T HOSE who simply cross the river out of hunger are punished relatively leniently for their defection, spending a few months in a hard labour camp. But the higher one's position, the more treacherous the defection is considered to be, and the punishment is correspondingly greater. The knowledge of this and our fear of the possible consequences for our loved ones weighed heavily on our hearts.

In the hope that it would get a little warmer on the mountain after the sun rose, Young-min and I stayed up all night talking. But a stronger blizzard came just before dawn. Weak after shivering all night and unable to stretch my legs, I thought I would pass out. I felt as if we had come to a cliff's edge, confronting the reality that we must spend another twenty-four hours in these freezing conditions. At least we still had the thermos of warm tea and the bread that Chang-yong had given us, which afforded us a little consolation.

When Chang-yong finally returned, he brought with him a new blanket and a hatchet. Our old blanket was like corrugated iron, frozen stiff, so Chang-yong had to carry it on his head down the hill. Before he left, he grumbled that Pyongyang boys might have money, but they didn't know how to survive; he chopped small logs and gathered branches from nearby to make us a shelter. Inside, we were shielded from the worst of the bone-chilling wind.

But the respite didn't last long. As the sunlight couldn't penetrate it, the shelter was like a freezer and the air inside was bitterly cold. It felt as though I had my feet in iced water, in spite of my wearing rubber shoes. In an effort to keep warm, we ran to the top of the hill and back down several times during the day.

At night, the blizzard worsened. Farmer Chang-yong had given us two bottles of wine, and when I put one down to drink from the other, the bottle frosted during the few moments it was resting on the ground. Yet, even if misery was all that there was left to look forward to, every second I survived in that mountainside shelter reminded me of the preciousness of human life.

The morning promised by Chang-yong finally arrived. After the sun had passed its midday mark, he reappeared with a man of about our own age. The young man was wearing blue jeans and an expensive-looking beige leather jacket. He was fit and agile, and our first impression was that he did indeed seem like someone who might have connections with South Korea's spy agency. His eyes were small and gave the impression that he did not trust anyone easily, yet he was full of quiet confidence. He was the kind of man who only spoke when absolutely necessary, and his greeting was as short as he could make it. But his slight smile did not leave his face throughout our meeting.

'My name is Shin Gwang-ho,' he said.

He was certainly Chang-yong's nephew in that he shared his heavy northern accent, reminiscent of North Hamgyong Province. He looked us up and down, pausing as he noticed our rubber shoes. When he finally offered his hand for us to shake, it was soft and warm. But after shaking our hands, he furtively wiped his own on his jeans.

He asked us for our identification documents, saying it was just a routine precaution. I noted his professionalism in recognising and checking the dates, stamps and quality of our papers, and I felt somehow that I could trust this man. Although Chang-yong was on edge, fidgeting at the sound of barking dogs in the distance, Mr Shin didn't seem to notice and focused on his task.

Apparently satisfied, he looked up at us. 'Would you please wait a moment?'

This time, I wondered if he was speaking in South Korean. This was because he said 'Would you please' before the request. I had learned at the UFD that there were three types of politeness markers in South Korean. The first was to refer to oneself in a lower register than the listener; the second was to add something like 'would you' (requests ending with *yo*) as a general marker of respect; and the third was similar to a military manner of speaking: 'Sir, would you please' (requests ending with *sipnika*). In North Korea, there exist the first and third types of politeness markers, but not the second. Instead of subtleties of distinction for different situations, there were only two distinctions, the one for ordering and the other for complying, so the senior person in this sort of scenario would say 'Wait!' and the junior party would comply.

However, in North Korea, there was another politeness marker that not even the most senior cadres could use, which was the marker reserved only for the ruling Kim. This works most typically in a *siut* addition to the verb conjugation. For example, the people are said to have 'done' something (*hada*), but the Supreme Leader 'did do' something (*ha*-siut-*da*). This distinction was strictly observed not only in everyday life, but also in all forms of the written word. In this way, although Mr Shin spoke to us in a standard polite register (a request ending with *yo*), he had added the *siut* conjugation reserved only for Kim Il-sung and Kim Jong-il in North Korea. This seemed to us at the time to be a significant marker of respect. He turned away to make a call on his mobile phone. After speaking quietly for a few moments, he hung up and we stood waiting in the snow, hunched against the cold. A short while later, a four-wheel drive appeared and stopped halfway up the slope. As Chang-yong had implied, his nephew's resourcefulness was at a very different level from that of his farmer uncle, for whom the greatest imaginable excitement was the prospect of buying a new cultivator. When Mr Shin told us to hurry, we quickly hugged Chang-yong, who was waiting for our embrace with his arms open wide, and said goodbye. Not only did he not ask for more money, but as we clasped each other he whispered into my ear that I should not tell his nephew about the $700 we had given him. As we climbed into the Jeep, we thanked him once again and promised to come back and visit him after we'd made it to South Korea.

The Jeep was as powerful and agile as Mr Shin. Listening to Korean pop music on the radio as we bounced along the road, I felt we could ride this Jeep all the way to Seoul. Instead, we arrived back in Yanji, this time in a central and modernised area. There, right in the middle of the city, Mr Shin brought the Jeep to a halt, opened the door and asked us to get out. Having been so far from the bustle of ordinary life, we found the busy crowd overwhelming. Mr Shin didn't seem to notice. He just shouted, 'Hurry up!' and we followed him.

We went into a shopping mall, where I was startled to see a group of armed police on patrol. Yet Mr Shin dared to call my name out loud. His apparent carelessness put me on edge, but Young-min and I did as we were told as he beckoned impatiently to us from outside a clothing store.

After putting on the new clothes he'd chosen, I looked in the mirror, pleased at first, but then shocked to see my easily recognisable face staring back. What was I doing, standing in such a public place with my face displayed for all to see? I quickly asked for a pair of sunglasses instead of new clothes. Mr Shin said that would arouse suspicion, but Young-min pleaded likewise. He even explained at length how we had lost our sunglasses in the rucksack we had been forced to abandon. Mr Shin was reluctant to make the purchase, saying it might make us stand out, but in the end he gave in to Young-min.

From then on, we wore our new clothes and sunglasses. I felt I could stand tall, safely disguised by the dark glasses. Young-min grinned at me from behind his shades, although I could not see his eyes. I felt a pang of sadness, thinking that this is how I must have looked to my parents when they saw me for the last time.

When we went back to the car, Mr Shin was waiting with a camera. He said he had to provide evidence to his superiors of how he had used their money. If we had not bought the sunglasses, I don't think I could have let myself be photographed in public. After we'd finished with the photographs, I noticed some more police officers standing behind us, completely oblivious.

That was the first day I felt we were really able to appreciate the impact of reforms in China. Just like the North Korean saying that 'Even viewing Mount Keumgang should be done after eating' (meaning that even gazing at the best views on earth ought to be done on a full stomach), we headed first to have lunch. Mr Shin took us to an expensive restaurant that specialised in smoked duck served whole on a large plate. Mr Shin boasted that this was a favourite dish of such illustrious figures as Emperor Qianlong, Empress Cixi, Mao Zedong and Deng Xiaoping, but our delight in the dish was pleasure enough without these sorts of associations. After stuffing ourselves with duck, we went – for the first time in our lives – to a Korean-style sauna open to both men and women. I asked why it was referred to as Korean-style, and Mr Shin explained that, in South Korea, you could take a bath, have a sauna and stay the night all in one establishment.

When I plunged up to my neck into a large hot tub, washing off the dirt I'd accumulated since we'd left Pyongyang, it seemed as though all my suffering was being washed away too. Even the hot water overflowing from the tub was miraculous. By 1994, when the central heating system of Pyongyang had all but collapsed, hot water had become a rare privilege. In November 1998, just before the start of winter, the Party finally acknowledged this through a public order, stating that each household must sort out its own heating problems.

At the time, Pyongyang residents openly stated that they were happy to forgo hot water, if only they could be provided with a decent supply of drinking water.

The only residential area in Pyongyang that provided a hot water supply to its residents was Changgwang-dong of Joongu Area, where Central Party cadres lived. Even there, the supply was only provided twice a day for two hours at a time, between six and eight in the morning and seven and nine in the evening, when people were preparing to go to work and arriving home. With the situation so dire even for the most privileged people in the nation, the places foreigners frequented, such as Koryo Hotel, and facilities set up for foreigners, such as saunas, became established as the social gathering places of the North Korean elite.

Until I left Pyongyang in 2004, the price of one kilo of rice in the markets was 1000 won. At the exchange rate of the time, this was the equivalent of 50 US cents. At a time when many couldn't afford to pay even such a small sum for essentials and sometimes went without food for days, a fee of US$5 or US$8 for one entry to a foreigners' bath or sauna represented an inconceivable extravagance. Instead, the middle class of Pyongyang, who didn't have enough foreign currency purchasing power to afford this luxury, frequented the boiler rooms at foreign embassies, restaurants or central state institutions. If you paid a bribe, the staff would allow you to have some of the hot water from the overflow pipe. You could sometimes see foreigners at these locations, but there would always be surveillance around and no one dared to get too friendly with the visitors.

Even today, the vast majority of the North Korean population, which struggles with many of the basics of day-to-day living, relies on vinyl bathing 'greenhouses' imported from China. These come in single and double sizes. If you hang this vinyl encasement from the ceiling, it reaches to the floor. In effect, it is a large plastic bag. If you enter it carrying a bucket full of boiling water, the steam rises and the plastic bag swells like a balloon. You wash yourself by mixing cold and boiling water, and you're kept warm by the sauna effect.

In contrast to all this, China seemed to me paradise on earth. The hot water that filled my tub was much more than that to me. It was yet another example of how reform had transformed Chinese society to the extent that the enjoyment of the most luxurious privilege, by North Korean standards, was available even to ordinary people. On hearing our description of the 'greenhouse' baths, Mr Shin said that there were rural places in China where they still washed themselves using a similar method. Ironically, it was due to Chinese reforms that these 'Korean-style' saunas had appeared. Seemingly proud of this, he leapt out of the bath, declaring that he would give us North Korean hillbillies a real taste of Chinese-style reform.

He took us to a room furnished with beds, where a man stood in a white bathrobe. Mr Shin said he was the back-scrubber, who would scrub our backs for a few coins. I couldn't understand why on earth anyone would stoop to scrub another man's back, even for money. We were made to lie down to see for ourselves what it was like. The man went to work energetically, but I felt so embarrassed that I couldn't enjoy the experience. Coming from a country where ideology dictated that no ordinary individual was permitted to benefit from the personal service of any other individual, this back-scrubbing experience made me feel that I was overdosing on the worst excesses of Capitalist exploitation.

Changing into bathrobes, we followed Mr Shin into the main hall, where we were profoundly shocked once again. This time, it was at the sight of men and women in the same room wearing only bathrobes, despite being complete strangers. When a woman wearing shorts that revealed her knees approached and plonked herself down next to us, Young-min and I jumped up from our seats. In North Korea, only a madwoman would behave in such an unguarded manner in the presence of men. While we stared in amazement as she nonchalantly peeled a tangerine, Mr Shin laughed.

After the sauna, we went to a karaoke bar. Mr Shin probably thought that we would find the karaoke more astonishing than the back-scrubbing services, but he was wrong. In fact, we had sung more karaoke than Mr Shin.

Pyongyang has karaoke bars too. The main difference between them and this one in China was that back home you had to pay an entrance fee of US$10 per person and you didn't have time in one session to sing as many songs as you could here. Instead, you would receive a special token in exchange for a US dollar, which allowed you to sing one song. But for a country where millions were on the starvation line, karaoke, like hot water, was an extravagant luxury.

In Pyongyang's karaoke bars, the play lists are filled with songs of praise for Kim Il-sung and Kim Jong-il, but no one in his right mind would have paid precious foreign currency to sing such common fare. Nevertheless, even being drunk in a karaoke bar with friends might not exempt a person from being accused of subversion if he messed up the lyrics while singing a song of praise for Dear Leader. So the most popular songs in these establishments were songs such as 'Whistling' or 'Nice to Meet You': popular melodies considered relatively free from political implications, yet whose lyrics had been adapted to comply with the Party.

In a country where the arts were explicitly political, there were not too many songs to choose from. Whenever Young-min and I went to a karaoke bar in Pyongyang, we sang 'Morning Dew' over and over again. The song was actually South Korean, one of the anthems of the South Korean democratic movement that rose against that country's military dictatorship in the 1970s. But the Party had edited the lyrics to suggest that South Korean citizens looked towards Kim Il-sung as the force that would unify the Korean peninsula, and so the song was sanctioned for karaoke use.

When Young-min and I now took turns to sing 'Morning Dew' in perfect tune, Mr Shin was astonished at how we hit all the right notes. He gave us a thumbs up and said that we were clearly different from ordinary refugees who had never seen a microphone before. Whenever we heard his compliments ringing through the sound system, we felt embarrassed and waved our hands to quiet him, but Mr Shin went on to shout drunkenly, 'Here in this land, there is no Kim Jong-il!'

The evening passed quickly, and it was past ten by the time we stumbled outside. When we got into a cab, Mr Shin told us that we would be staying at his place for a few days. The cab dropped us off in front of a decrepit building, where there were no lights in the stairwell. Mr Shin led the way up to his third-floor apartment with a cigarette lighter, warning us that the stairs were slippery.

We stopped at a door with a small plaque that read 302. When Mr Shin rang the doorbell, a woman in her mid-twenties opened the front door. She was wearing a hooded purple sweatshirt and matching bottoms. Whether it was because of her rolled-up sleeves or her pursed lips, I felt I could sense in her a certain inner strength. But her face remained impassive and all she said was 'Yes,' or 'No,' in a Spartan way.

'This is my wife.' Mr Shin gave his curt introduction, but the impact of those words was deep for me. The muscles in my body, which had been tense and rigid with chill and fear of death since crossing the Tumen River, relaxed a little. I felt there was no more comforting word in the world than 'wife', with its domestic connotations.

The inside of Mr Shin's flat looked not much different from an average flat in North Korea's capital city. The kitchen doubled as a bathroom, with a tap and toilet next to each other in the confined space. This was also where we took our shoes off to enter the rest of Mr Shin's home. There were two rooms in addition to the kitchen-bathroom, where Mr Shin ate and slept on the heated floor in true

North Korean style. In the bigger room of the two, there were three wardrobes. Apart from those items and a loud whirring fan heater on the floor, there were no furnishings.

In the smaller room, there were some blankets folded up in a corner. Gesturing towards them, Mr Shin said, 'You can use this room. It's warmer than the other one because it's smaller. Goodnight then.' With those words, he left us alone. Young-min and I both stretched our limbs. Hearing the cracking noises in my joints gave me pleasure, because I feared they had withered in the terror and cold of the last few days. There was more that gave me new reason to hope. Tonight we were no longer hiding out in a shed or on a frozen mountainside, I thought, but in a real home. After switching off the light, I snuggled under the blankets in our warm room.

As I lay in the dark, images of the dangers and close calls we'd experienced over the last few days began to play over and over in my head like scenes in a film on repeat. They were mere memories, but nevertheless my heart thumped; my mind fell prey to doubts about whether we would make it through the night, and I wondered how much longer we could remain on the run. The faintest sound of a motor vehicle outside sent shivers through me and, when it was quiet, I held my breath in anticipation of the next potential threat. Although this pattern continued without any real danger materialising, my restless mind didn't tire of the routine. My finer feelings and emotions had evaporated after these days spent so close to death, and now I was relying solely on my animal instincts, desiring and imagining nothing but survival. Although I recognised and wanted to reject this response, I couldn't. And I felt dismayed and hollow at how weak I had become.

Young-min slept with his back to me, but whenever he breathed really loudly, I could sense his inner torment. There might not be any soldiers knocking at our door, but they were already in our heads, and we had to do battle with them throughout the night.

In the morning, someone knocked on the door of our room.

'Are you up yet?' Mr Shin asked. He had in his hand some paper and a pen. We had been up and awake for an hour, had folded our blankets, and were peering through the window at Yanji. 'I'll show you around Yanji as much as you want, but now isn't the time. I need both of you to write me a statement before we can eat breakfast.'

He passed us the paper and pen and asked us to write 'carefully' a statement detailing our family relations, what intelligence we had to pass on to the South Korean government, and the reason for our defection. He emphasised the importance of intelligence, but said that since he himself must not know about the details, we should just summarise it in bullet points. The way he spoke suggested that he was practised in this routine. But what did we have to offer that would count as intelligence? All the same, the request felt professional, as if he were directly representing South Korea.

I don't think I'd ever taken such care with every single word of a piece of writing as I did that morning. Young-min too made a great effort, as if writing a letter to the South Korean president himself. We worked for over an hour and showed the results to Mr Shin. He said that even though we were writing in bullet points, we should explain enough to make sure we could be trusted. He suggested, for example, that I should hint at what the Seed-bearing Strategy referred to. I felt that in order to persuade the South Korean intelligence of our credentials, I needed first to gain the trust of Mr Shin, and told him that the strategy referred to a kidnapping operation practised by North Korean agents.

I first learned of this immense criminal operation when I was a student at Pyongyang Arts School. Among my classmates there was a girl called Ri Hyun-suk. We had just finished eating our packed lunches and had started to peel some tangerines to share between us when she confessed to me, 'I'm actually Japanese.'

I choked on a soft segment of fruit. I'd known her for several years:

how could she possibly be a foreigner? All citizens of North Korea had to be Korean. I laughed awkwardly. Hyun-suk began to cry and then she left the room. A few days later, after going on a date together, I had the opportunity to see her home.

She lived alone with her mother in a very luxurious private mansion. Not only her house, but all the other houses in that walled compound were mansions. Before we parted, she told me, as if letting me in on a top secret, that all the residents of that walled compound were involved in 'Localisation' schemes. When I asked what she meant, she said this was where female North Korean agents who had been made pregnant by foreign husbands lived with their children. It was part of a plan to establish North Korean family ties for foreigners, to make them sympathetic towards North Korea. Her father, she said, was the most important figure in the Japanese Socialist Party.

I did not believe everything she told me then, not until the second time I encountered the 'Localisation' strategy after my admittance into the United Front Department. There, I learned first-hand that there were others like Hyun-suk who had foreign blood in them and were brought up not knowing their own fathers. This was 1999, when the Japanese government had raised the kidnapping of Japanese citizens by the DPRK as an issue, and was demanding their return.

At that time, I was working on a book of poetry commissioned by Director Im Tong-ok and was staying at Ui-am Guesthouse. Although, as head of the UFD, he was in charge of any espionage, policy or diplomacy related to South Korea, he needed to maintain his literary credentials because the UFD relied on tools of psychological warfare that encompassed the arts. Moreover, Director Im was caught up in a power struggle at the very top that required him to offer Kim Jong-il a book of poetry. OGD Deputy Director Hwang Byong-seo, having upset Kim Jong-il and been banished to the provinces, had offered his apology to Kim by dedicating a book of poems to him. When Kim Jong-il reinstated the man on the grounds that the dedication was proof of his absolute loyalty in the face of adversity, North Korea's most powerful men became pitted against each other in a battle to the death to please Kim Jong-il with their own 'literary offerings'.

The Ui-am Guesthouse, in the Daedong River Area of Pyongyang, belonged to Director Im Tong-ok. A very limited number were permitted to go inside, and those allowed entry were being afforded a special show of trust by him. For this reason, conversation on classified state secrets was allowed to take place there to a certain extent. One day, when head of UFD policy-making Chae Chang-guk visited the guesthouse, I asked about our department's need for Japanese citizens.

'You'll hurt yourself if you know too much,' he responded with a hearty laugh, instead of answering my query. But that evening, as we dined with other cadres in the compound, the very same subject came up again in the context of diplomacy with Japan. Chae Chang-guk didn't seem to be concerned that I was part of the conversation, and I understood tacitly that while he couldn't tell me directly, it was something I was allowed to know. That evening marked my true induction into the nature and scale of international crimes perpetrated by the North Korean regime.

The history of North Korea's kidnappings began in the 1970s. Until the end of the 1960s, North Korea was effectively ruled by the military. Following the end of the Korean War in 1953, Kim Il-sung built up the authority of the military in order to consolidate domestic politics on the basis of anti-South Korean sentiment, and to entrench his power. But for Kim Jong-il, who had been preparing the ground for his succession to the throne since the early 1970s, the military was a threatening entity: as long as it could influence policy-making, it effectively held power. Under the guise of forming a state based on single Party rule, Kim Jong-il took away the inter-Korean diplomatic and business privileges of the military and transferred them to the Workers' Party.

The military had to consent to Kim Jong-il's proposals because of the nature of Kim Il-sung's Koryo Confederation strategy, according to which there would be two political systems on the Korean peninsula initially, until such time as the two Koreas could be united under a federal government. For this to work in Kim Il-sung's favour, what was required was not merely military might, but the dissolution of South Korea's military leadership. This was to be accomplished through infiltrating South Korea's democratic movements, which were increasingly rising up in protest against their military dictator.

This is what led to the creation of the United Front Department, the Strategic Command, Office 35, and the Foreign Investigations Bureau (the precursor to the Foreign Affairs Bureau), all of which were to be controlled by the Workers' Party. In order to showcase the superiority of the Party over the military in activities in the inter-Korean sphere, in 1972 Kim Jong-il instigated an ambitious project called 'Localisation'.

While the military's Reconnaissance Bureau produced spies by training those who had defected to the North, the new departments of the Workers' Party were more proactive in how they acquired 'Localised' knowledge: they chose to kidnap citizens of the country that would be spied on. Eventually, the military became restricted to gathering tactical intelligence in the inter-Korean sphere. While the Workers' Party also conducted espionage in the inter-Korean sphere, its remit was extended to the promotion of Korean reunification (on DPRK terms) at the international level by means of cultivating pro-North sympathisers worldwide and engaging in counter-intelligence and psychological warfare initiatives.

There were three main reasons put forward by cadres working on these operations to justify Kim Jong-il's strategy of kidnapping foreign citizens. First, to recruit teachers who would provide 'localised' knowledge of their country and thus aid in the training of North Korean spies. Second, it helped accomplish identity fraud and allowed North Korean spies to acquire genuine foreign identities. Third, depending on the individual circumstances of adaptation and loyalty, kidnapped children could be trained and returned to their country of birth as North Korean agents.

In 1977, Yokota Megumi, a Japanese girl who is one of the most well-known victims of North Korean kidnapping, was captured for the third reason when she was only thirteen years old. While she was fully foreign, her youth meant she could be persuaded to feel loyalty to the DPRK – or so it was thought. The following year, sixteen-year-old South Korean student Kim Young-nam was kidnapped in Gunsan, in Cheonbuk, South Korea, along with dozens of other teenagers from around the world.

Nevertheless, Japanese citizens made up the greatest number of foreign kidnap victims. This was because the Party's inter-Korean operatives had an outpost in the Jochongryon, the Association of Chosun People in Japan, and there were political and geographical advantages in mounting operations against the South from a base in Japan.

However, no matter how thorough the reach of Kim Jong-il's dictatorship of the mind, it didn't win the genuine loyalty of the kidnapped. I think the kidnapped teenagers were able to resist ideological brainwashing because of their vivid memories of the lives they had known and the trauma of being separated from their parents.

In the mid 1980s, Kim Jong-il therefore proposed the Seed-bearing Strategy as a solution to the problem. The idea was to create spies who looked foreign, but who were North Koreans born and bred. In order to accomplish this task, the Party's inter-Korean operatives pursued a two-fold tactic that involved kidnapping foreign women, and sending attractive North Korean women abroad to become pregnant with men who had white, black or brown skin. Their children are born in North Korea with different-coloured skin from the rest of their countrymen, and the rest of their lives are spent in strict apartheid. Their health is looked after by Office 915 of the Party's Strategic Command, which treats only inter-Korean operatives. Everything else they need in life is arranged directly by the most powerful entity in North Korea, the Party's Organisation and Guidance Department.

My classmate Ri Hyun-suk, however, had spent her life in relative freedom, and was integrated into society to a certain extent. This was because her mere presence as a hostage in Pyongyang provided leverage against her father, giving him a greater incentive to encourage foreign aid to North Korea and advocate for engagement strategies favourable to the DPRK.

The scale of Kim Jong-il's international crimes, which extended to kidnappings as he established his succession from Kim Il-sung, were first revealed to the world at the time of the 2002 summit with the then Japanese Prime Minister Koizumi. Before this time, even the Japanese were sceptical of the notion that the DPRK might be kidnapping their citizens. But at the summit, Kim Jong-il acknowledged the kidnapping of Megumi and others. He issued an apology, saying he had only found out about these incidents after the event, and that special departments had carried out the kidnappings out of heroic and nationalistic fervour. Not only Japan, but the rest of the world was shocked.

The gross miscalculation by Kim Jong-il had its roots in North Korea's anticipation of US$11.4 billion of aid from Japan, and the following events unfolded behind the scenes. Just before Koizumi arrived in Pyongyang, the DPRK Foreign Ministry's final agenda for the summit was to be provided to the UFD for viewing. As we waited throughout the morning for the agenda to arrive, the atmosphere was grave: we had submitted an unambiguous warning to Kim Jong-il earlier, saying that if the kidnapping issue had already been included in the agenda for the North Korea–Japan summit, there was a serious risk that it might attract international attention through the interference of South Korean or Japanese civilians. This would put North Korea in a very difficult position, and someone on our side would surely have to meet a grisly end following the summit.

After receiving a summons from Supervisor Park Chul to appear at an emergency meeting, I joined other colleagues in the meeting room. On the table lay the agenda, a packet of documents printed on white paper.

'This agenda must be confirmed by Office 101 and returned to headquarters before the end of the day. We have thirty minutes to complete the task. There's not enough time to contribute individually, so I suggest we nominate someone to read the agenda out loud to the group.' Normally, any UFD employee was permitted to view documents sent to the Department by Kim Jong-il. But if there was a departmental meeting to discuss them, the documents had to be sealed again and returned to their source.

As we had suspected, the agenda looked unfavourable. Above all, the tone of the Japanese response to North Korea's proposal that they pay US$40 billion in war reparations was alarming. North Korea had argued that the war damage and interest accrued since the time of the Japanese occupation amounted to US$40 billion. Japan responded by saying that North Korea owed money to Japan for the use of factories, railroads and other infrastructure built by Japan, and subsequently not dismantled, in the period following the Japanese withdrawal from Korea. But the most pertinent card they played was that Japan could not pay in cash, because if they did it would afford opportunities to the US to meddle under the pretext of inspecting funds related to nuclear issues. In the end, North Korea had settled for a proposal of US$11.4 billion in material aid.

When Koizumi arrived, Kim Jong-il found himself entangled from the start in a discussion that centred on Japan's seeking of a state-level apology for North Korea's kidnapping of Japanese citizens. Just as the UFD had warned, Kim Jong-il had walked into a trap whereby he was obliged to engage in a 'constructive' dialogue that required real – rather than strategically feigned – give-and-take.

From Kim Jong-il's perspective, the worst of it occurred after the first morning session. The Japanese delegation's room had been bugged and during the break one of their team was heard to object strongly to North Korea's unwillingness to negotiate a state apology for the kidnappings, and to recommend that Koizumi leave Pyongyang without participating in another session. The conversation was reported to Kim Jong-il, who then must have feared that the foreign currency aid package he so desperately wanted could be at risk. What happened next was shocking.

In the afternoon session that followed, Kim Jong-il made an off-the-cuff apology for the kidnappings. It was the only time in his life that he made a public apology. No one on the North Korean side had ever seen Kim Jong-il speaking on impulse like that, and it would never happen again. In an attempt to limit the damage, the Party's Propaganda and Agitation Department immediately released the news that Kim Jong-il had 'acknowledged' the kidnappings. But it could not control the Japanese media, which duly reported that Kim Jong-il had 'offered an apology' for the kidnappings.

In Korean, there is a saying that goes, 'The man with cake has no intention of sharing it, but the other man has already begun to set the cutlery.' Kim Jong-il dreamed of modernising the country with a two-track railway as a central part of his economic reconstruction plan, because he hated the single-track railway laid by the Japanese and wanted to be 'liberated' from that particular reminder of Japan's colonial rule. At the same time, the Propaganda and Agitation Department had ramped up anti-Japanese propaganda through all media outlets, emphasising the suffering of the Korean people under Japanese occupation.

Such was the background to Kim Jong-il's ignoring of the UFD's advice. To make his point, he had sent us the Foreign Ministry's summit agenda at the last minute, as a token reprimand for our arrogance in criticising him. This was received as a clear warning, because by default Kim Jong-il usually trusted the UFD on every aspect of North Korea's engagement and diplomacy with the outside world. Emerging from tense give-and-take games sustained for decades, the UFD was in fact a peerless, finely tuned organisation, whose mission was to create the best possible circumstances and context for ensuring that all kinds of 'diplomacy' and 'engagement' were conducted in a way favourable to the Party. In the context of our special relationship of trust, it had been humiliating for the UFD to have to refer to an agenda prepared by the Foreign Ministry. Nevertheless, we had been concerned that the prospect of US$11.4 billion of aid would blind Kim Jong-il to the long-term implications.

In the end, the summit of September 2002 that culminated in Kim Jong-il's apology was a disaster for him in every way possible. As the extraordinary news spread throughout Japan and beyond, both the US$11.4 billion in aid, and the Jochongryon, which functioned as an outpost and foreign currency safe in Japan for North Korea, came to be at risk. Kim Jong-il allowed five kidnapped Japanese to visit their homeland as a gesture of goodwill, but that didn't help. Adding insult to injury, the five refused to return to North Korea. Kim Jong-il was enraged, and insisted that there would be no further summits with Japan during his lifetime unless Japan paid him the foreign currency he demanded. He reaffirmed the rule that 'Diplomacy is a counter-intelligence operation' and removed from the Foreign Ministry the right to diplomatic involvement on any issue connected with the kidnappings, returning control of these matters to the UFD.

Bʏ the time I had finished outlining the Seed-bearing Strategy, Mr Shin was leaning forward, listening intently. He had kept a somewhat condescending distance from us since our first meeting, but seemed to soften after my account. As if to introduce himself to us for the first time, he told us that he was thirty-two and that he had been born in Yanji. He had worked for five years as a broker helping North Korean refugees escape from China, and boasted that he had contacts in the intelligence agency in South Korea. He added that anyone working with North Korean refugees was monitored by the Chinese authorities, and that he had already had to move house several times.

He glanced over at his wife as he told us this. The many moves explained why the apartment was so devoid of personal belongings even though they were newlyweds building a new life together. He now wanted to settle in South Korea and have some stability, even if it meant doing menial jobs there. He sighed as he spoke, and I felt that we still weren't safe in his hands. However, on learning that Mr Shin's wife was from North Korea's North Hamgyong Province, my trust in him increased, though Young-min did not yet seem convinced.

'Breakfast is ready!' Mrs Shin declared from the other room.

As soon as we joined her, I exclaimed that it was wonderful to meet another North Korean, and Young-min and I both asked eagerly about her story and her hometown. But her face remained blank, as if to ask why we were making such a fuss about her past. She spoke only to tell us to tuck into our food, and we fell silent.

She brought out steaming rice and a tofu stew with red chilli oil floating on it. The chopsticks and spoon were carefully placed next to our food. Even if she was a bit unfriendly on the outside, she was clearly a warm-hearted woman. This was the first proper sit-down home-cooked meal we'd been able to enjoy since crossing the river, so I immediately picked up my spoon. Then I realised that the low table was too small for four adults, and that only three places had been set. I noticed a bowl and chopsticks placed on the floor in the kitchen area and saw that she had already sat down beside them. Before I could ask her to join us, she put a spoonful of rice into her mouth.

'Come, let's all eat together out here,' Young-min called out. She lowered her eyes and turned away from us. North Korea is a patriarchal society, which went straight from feudal Confucianism to Kim dynastic rule. The plight of women becomes much worse the further north you venture from Pyongyang, and the cold and harsh climate only makes their domestic work harder. But to witness such an example of North Korean provincialism in a foreign land embarrassed me. Mr Shin sighed too, saying they needed to buy a bigger table. To cover the awkwardness, he explained at length that when there were guests, there wasn't enough room. But I felt grateful that this man had married a poor North Korean woman for love, and this made me respect him more.

Mr Shin finished eating first, rose and put on his coat. Slipping our statements and photographs and copies of our identification documents into an envelope, he said, 'The Chinese authorities sometimes check the post. That's why I'm going to give this directly to a boatman who will sail to Incheon port in South Korea. Within five days, we will get a call or a visit from the South Koreans. Then you'll be able to make your way to Seoul.'

Before he left the house, he turned and told us that South Koreans would on such occasions of uncertain hope shout *Pa-ee-ting!* – which means 'Fighting!' in Korean. Young-min and I looked at each other and shouted '*Pa-ee-ting!*' and gave each other a high-five. We were going to shout it again, but Mr Shin's wife spoke first. 'Be careful!' she warned him.

About three hours later, the doorbell rang. Mr Shin had not yet returned, and any unexpected sound made us jump. Mrs Shin peered through the peephole before opening the door. Even this precaution made us nervous and, as she undid the bolt, I was concerned that she might be about to let trouble into the house. When the door was opened, there was a loud racket as several women kicked off their shoes and walked in. It looked like they had all bought their clothes cheaply in the same shop, and they were wearing flimsy coats, one with a tacky yellow zipper. One of the women had a baby on her back. Speaking in a heavy northern accent very similar to Mrs Shin's, they asked her to shut the door quickly, saying that there were police everywhere today, and that they had almost been stopped.

When they noticed us, the women fell silent. As she bolted the door, Mrs Shin called out from behind them, 'Don't worry, they're North Koreans too, friends of my husband's.' I was a little worried that she might be carelessly giving away our identity.

With the arrival of the women and their conversations, Young-min and I withdrew into our smaller room and closed the door. I was curious to hear what they were saying, but with their heavy accents and Chinese words mixed in here and there, it was almost unintelligible.

Mr Shin returned an hour later. He seemed to know the women well, because the gathering burst into life when he came in, but he left them immediately and came to see us in our room and return our documents.

'How did it go? Were you able to send our papers?' I asked as soon as he came in.

'Yes, I've sent copies of everything,' he answered.

More than the words he said, his confident smile was reassuring. I asked who the women in the other room were, and Mr Shin checked to see if the door was closed behind him before answering. He then leaned in and spoke in a low voice.

'They're victims of human trafficking who have managed to escape.'

'Human trafficking? What's that?' Young-min asked, and I was just as curious.

Mr Shin replied, 'In China there are fewer women than men and some villages have no women at all. These men, they can't get married unless they have money. And Chinese women are said to be quite daunting. Remember Empress Cixi who ruled this place a century ago? She was very fierce. Anyway, there are quite a few men who specialise in kidnapping North Korean women as soon as they cross the border into China. Lots of people who speak Korean in the border area have connections with criminal organisations.'

'But not Chang-yong?' Young-min asked, hoping that the answer would be no.

Mr Shin replied, 'I'm not saying this because he's my uncle but, really, he's just a simple farmer who only knows about his cattle and his crops. People like him will never get on in life,' he added bluntly. 'You two are really lucky. If you had met the wrong kind of people, you might have been held hostage until the South Korean spies could produce enough ransom money.'

I remembered Chang-yong's face on the way to his mother-in-law's house, when he'd told us how lucky we were to have met a simple farmer like him. Mr Shin slid closer to us as we sat on the floor. He continued, 'Do you know what they call North Korean women over here?'

We shook our heads.

'Pigs. In the Chinese countryside, pigs are valuable, so people call the women pigs. They're graded according to their age and appearance. A grade one 'pig' fetches around 200,000 won; grade two goes for 150,000 won; and a grade three will bring in 100,000 won. The brokers, who act as middlemen, take half the selling price as their fee. Grade one is equivalent to about US$1500. If you get sold for that amount, at least you go to a better house.

'Below that amount, the women get taken to very remote farms or are married to disabled men who can't find wives. They spend the rest of their lives rotting – the countryside here is a miserable place. Some women are shackled at night so they can't run away. Think about it – a farmer who has bought a woman has made a big investment, and these North Korean women are already risk-takers who've crossed the border. Do you think they'd not run away? Well, they do keep running away, and because everyone knows this, they're kept in chains, at least until they've had their first baby.

'While most North Korean women get sold on, the North Korean men end up in one of two ways. Either they get caught sleeping rough and are sent back to North Korea; or, if they have enough money and meet a decent broker, they eventually make it to South Korea. But in the eyes of traffickers, the women here are worth at least 150,000 won each.'

Even as I listened, I doubted what I was hearing, and could not believe it was true. Perhaps it was better to be sold into marriage than starve to death in North Korea, but for human beings to be priced like pigs was obscene. And to think that these 'wives' were kept shackled – I was shaken by the idea that foreign men could treat our women in this way. I was even angrier at the brokers who made money from this. But most of all, I felt disgust for Kim Jong-il, who didn't seem to be humiliated at all by what he had reduced his nation's women to, or to care enough to intervene.

Young-min was shocked too. He seemed at a loss for words, and looked restless as he lay down on the floor, and then sat up again. He asked how many women were trapped in this network, and Mr

Shin said that all he knew was that there were some 100,000 North Koreans caught in limbo in China. I couldn't believe that no one in Pyongyang talked about a situation as grave as this.

Then the door opened a crack and a woman with dyed brown hair poked her head round. 'Are you from Pyongyang?' she asked. 'My friend just said you were.' Then she went back behind the door and whispered, 'You say it – I can't.'

I didn't know what they wanted, but they seemed to be nudging each other. Mr Shin asked in a loud voice, 'Alcohol? Do you want a drink?'

'Yes!' came the chorus of replies, and we ended up having a boozy lunch together. In Mr Shin's small Chinese flat, there were now five North Koreans and we started by introducing ourselves in turn. The woman who had first opened the door to our room said she was from Chongjin; the woman next to her was from Hamheung. We added Sariwon, Pyongyang and Yanji in turn, and then we lifted our cups to toast all our homes. We drank three bottles of strong Chinese alcohol, eating only pickled cabbage and leftover tofu, but it made for a wonderful and rich feast when enjoyed in their company.

Perhaps because we were all North Koreans and shared our fugitive status, the topic of conversation soon turned to how we'd kept out of sight and evaded the Chinese authorities. The women all seemed to agree on the importance of dyeing their hair. In North Korea, since the idea of pure ethnic identity was strong, everyone's hair was black, and the first thing women did after crossing the border was to dye their hair another colour. This helped them feel like someone from the outside world and not conspicuous as a North Korean on the run. That was when I realised that all the women had indeed dyed their hair different shades of brown. The woman who had the baby on her back returned after putting her baby to sleep, and her hair was brown too. When Young-min said they looked like Westerners with their light-coloured hair, the women smiled, delighted with their disguise.

For refugees, there is often more pain caused by the things we can't take with us than by the things we are running away from. So when the conversation turned to talk of home, everyone spoke and listened solemnly. After each person's story had ended, we toasted the memory of loved ones left behind. Then it became the turn of the youngest of the women to speak, the one with the baby. She hadn't yet spoken and Young-min, perhaps wanting to make it easier, asked a question.

'We missed you when we took turns to talk. How old are you?'

'Sixteen,' came the quiet reply.

In fact, Young-min had suspected that she was young, and had been urging her not to drink too much. But she kept sipping at her cup, and now her cheeks were bright pink.

'You're lucky to have got out with your little sister,' he said. 'Where's your mother?' I'm sure Young-min spoke without thinking. But the girl narrowed her eyes, shot Young-min a sharp look and tutted angrily. Then she filled her plastic cup with soju and downed it in one go.

Young-min tried to apologise, 'Sorry, I realise your mother didn't manage to cross with you. I hope you'll be able to see her again . . .'

Before he could finish, the girl threw the empty plastic cup across the room.

'Shut up, you arsehole!' she shouted.

Our jaws dropped. What had Young-min done to provoke such a response? What confused us even more was that, apart from Young-min and me, the others remained silent and looked away.

As Young-min glanced around, wondering what on earth was the matter, the girl screamed at him again. 'I am the mother! Does that make you feel better? And the baby, she isn't my sister – she's my daughter. So what's the problem? Am I a freak? Is my little girl a freak?'

Young-min's chopsticks fell from his fingers. She probably needed a mother's love, yet she was a mother herself with a baby to care for, and on the run at only sixteen. As if she pitied herself for this very reason, the girl suddenly grasped Mrs Shin's hand and started to cry. 'What am I going to do?' she sobbed. 'I went to the hospital yesterday. A friend took me there. Do you know what the doctor said? I don't know what to do . . .'

She couldn't finish her sentence, and beat her chest twice. Mrs Shin poured her a cup of water; she gulped it down and spoke again. 'My little Jung-hyun, they can't fix her eyes. She's got to live the rest of her life blind. And do you know what else they said? They asked if something had happened when I was pregnant, if I'd ever knocked my womb or had a fall.'

I looked into the girl's eyes, which were now clear and bright from her tears. Her trembling lips were a pale pink. This time it was I who handed her water. As if she'd lost awareness of her surroundings, she looked up and said to the ceiling, 'I passed out. When that bastard bought me, I was fourteen. I didn't know anything. He started to pull off my clothes. That middle-aged monster. Do you know what happened that day? I started to cry because I was scared. Then his mother and sister came into the room, those witches. They held my arms and legs down, and pulled my knickers off.'

The girl started shaking, and clutched Mrs Shin's arm as she wailed. 'Then, you know what, the so-called mother-in-law, sister-in-law, as they held me down, that old monster, he – you know – right in front of them.'

With her lips pursed and her eyes wet with tears, Mrs Shin held the child tight.

The girl whimpered, 'Then I passed out. Afterwards, my poor Jung-hyun, my Jung-hyun was born blind. Because of that fucking monster.'

I tried to blink back the tears that filled my eyes. And then I could no longer hold them back. Young-min downed his cup of soju, and could no longer restrain himself either. Mrs Shin led the teenage mother into the room we had slept in, and the only sound was of the other women sobbing. That child was only sixteen. How many more like her were there out there, forgotten by the world? How wretched their lives were. As the other women began to open up and tell their own stories, my chest tightened even more.

'At least she was able to run away,' said the woman from Chongjin who had introduced herself first. 'One girl I knew from back home escaped over the river too. She was sold into a Chinese village family where she was locked up and used by all the men in the family. One day the father-in-law would be the aggressor, the next the brother-in-law, all sleeping with her. So she doesn't even know who the father of her baby boy is, whether it's the husband or the father-in-law or the brother-in-law. In the end, they pimped her out to other men in the village, and pocketed the money. Luckily, there was one decent man who helped her escape.

'There are many "dark children" here in China, babies abandoned by North Korean women. Because their mothers are North Korean, they have no rights and their births aren't recognised by China. They can't go to school or anything like that, and they live on the streets. That's why they're called "dark children".'

The woman from Hamheung, who'd seemed to be lost in pain until then, took a deep breath, as if she still couldn't quite believe that the story she had to tell was one she herself had lived through.

'I wasn't going to bring up my own experience, but before I was sold, I was kept prisoner by a broker. There were sixteen other women there apart from me. He said that we could earn money by working on computers, but it turned out to be sex chatting. We were forced to be naked on camera. When I resisted, he threatened to report me to the authorities. When I still resisted, he beat me. From morning to evening we were made to do sex chatting. But six months of this work only added up to around a hundred dollars in payment for us. He said it was expensive to feed us. Besides, as North Koreans without legitimate identities, we can't open bank accounts here. So the broker said he was keeping our wages in the bank, and that he would return it all with interest. But, in the end, I never saw any of it, not even the one hundred. He said he'd lost it in a deal. After profiting from us for around a year, he was planning to sell us off as if we were new refugees who had just crossed over. He said he would kill us if we didn't comply. And, really, I knew he'd have just killed me. That knowledge gave me the determination to escape, and then I met my friends here on the streets. We're going to Tianjin to see if we can work in a restaurant. They say there are lots of Koreans there. Maybe we'll meet someone who can help us get to South Korea.'

Young-min was red-eyed and visibly agitated by a combination of drink and anger, and suggested that returning home might be a better option than enduring such humiliation in China.

'Are you *really* North Korean?' one woman asked in astonishment, adding that although she could perhaps endure the hunger, she could never stomach returning to that cruel country. Others joined in, clicking their tongues in disapproval.

The woman from Hamheung, who I had thought was the most withdrawn, started cracking her knuckles nervously and said agitatedly, 'A lot of the refugees in China have experienced repatriation. Those of us who have been sent back, knowing what the world is like over the border, usually have another go at escaping. Do you know what happens during repatriation? Even the handcuffs are different. Here in China, the handcuffs are shiny and new, but as soon as you cross the Friendship Bridge over the Yalu River and into North Korea, they change your handcuffs. North Korean handcuffs are rusty and disgusting. Besides, even though they're foreigners, the Chinese are more humane than our own people. Before my repatriation, one of the Chinese officers even apologised, and gave me 100 yuan. But in North Korea, they're merciless.

'They got all of us women together, took off our clothes and groped inside our vaginas with their fingers. You know, looking for hidden money and stuff. Pregnant women are treated like animals. There was a woman who was seven months pregnant among us when I was caught. Saying that she had bastard Chinese seed in her, the North Korean officers kicked her on the stomach over and over until she passed out. She died.

'And when you go to prison after processing, that's when you really want to kill yourself. They keep you awake for days and beat you, and interrogate you to find out whether you might have intended to go to South Korea or the US. If they suspect you of either, you're sent to a proper prison camp, instead of being sent to an ordinary labour camp to serve a three-year sentence. But even there, it's hard to make it through without suffering permanent disability. I couldn't bear the thought of going to either place. Seeing that ahead of me, I couldn't face it. So I swallowed a hairpin to kill myself. The bastards took me to the hospital, where I overheard somebody say that someone as strong-willed as me would definitely have had South Korea as my destination and, as soon as I recovered, I should be sent for a six-month pre-trial confinement.

'At night, when the surveillance was slack, I managed to escape and cross the river again. Even now, I can't believe it. They had cut my stomach open to take the hairpin out and sewed it back up, and although the wound opened again, I didn't feel any pain. Really, no pain at all.'

As I listened to their stories, I could see every scene vividly and imagined myself being taken away and repatriated. The woman who had just told us her story then asked me a question.

'So you're a cadre from Pyŏngyang. Why would you leave?' As she spoke, all eyes in the room turned to us. It seemed that each gaze was saying, *I left because I had no choice, but what hardship could you have had?*

I could not think of anything to say. Young-min spoke first. 'You're all North Korean,' he said. 'You've heard of the Scrutiny, right?'

'Yes,' came the replies.

'Well, the administrative director for that was my father.'

The woman from Chongjin froze in the middle of pouring herself another cup of soju. It was as if even the liquid had turned to ice. As everyone stared at Young-min, their faces didn't just register their shock. There was suddenly a distancing from him, as if he was an object of grotesque terror.

All over North Korea, the mere mention of the Scrutiny would be enough to silence any crying child. Every North Korean who was alive then knows about Kim Jong-il's Scrutiny which began in August 1997, and the bloody massacre that followed.

One sweltering summer's day in Pyongyang, an execution took place. Several hundred thousand spectators were gathered to watch it. The condemned man was a foreign spy, it was declared. But in fact, standing against the upright wooden plank – his limbs and torso bound with rope – the accused was none other than the Party's Agricultural Secretary, Seo Gwan-hui. As the man in charge of the nation's food supply, he had become Kim Jong-il's scapegoat for the widespread famine that had followed the collapse of the Public Distribution System in the mid 1990s.

Seo Gwan-hui had been charged with spying for the Americans and the South Koreans. It was alleged that he had been assigned by them to systematically undermine North Korea's principle of 'Self-reliance' in the sphere of agriculture. As a result, the crops had failed year after year. Accused of causing deaths among the people by starvation, he was not executed by firing squad. Instead, the crowd, whipped into hysteria, stoned him to death.

Capitalising on the widespread frenzy that followed Seo Gwan-hui's conviction for spying, a mass purge was instigated, and war declared against The Spies Within. The campaign was to draw on the same apparatus that had been used to condemn Seo. Back then, one of the main responsibilities of the now defunct Ministry of Social Security was to oversee recordkeeping for North Koreans. Every North Korean is assigned an identification booklet at birth. This is a life-long report card that records any change of circumstances throughout his or her years of education, contributions to the workplace and efforts in the local Party branch. Even if a person is unemployed, the officer in charge of their residential area and an officer from the Ministry will jointly assign him or her a grade for behaviour; so blank years are never an option.

In order to 'prove' the disgraced Agricultural Secretary's collusion with foreign intelligence agencies, the Ministry of Social Security argued that the blank spaces in Seo's identification booklet demonstrated that he had left the country to receive secret training in America. In fact, the three blank months in question reflected an unrecorded period in his life that occurred during the chaos of the Korean War in the early 1950s.

As the evidence for the crime had been obtained by scrutinising his identification booklet, an aptly named campaign – the Scrutiny – was launched. This process was escalated to a level whereby everyone who held an identification booklet dating to the Korean War was to be scrutinised. With its headquarters in the Ministry of Social Security, local bureaux of the ministry established dedicated Offices of Scrutiny throughout the country. Young-min's father Hwang Jin-thaek, who headed the Ministry of Social Security, was appointed as the administrative director of the Scrutiny. Choe Mun-deok was appointed as its political director.

To consolidate the powers of the Ministry of Social Security, and to provide the distraction Kim Jong-il needed in the instability that followed from Kim Il-sung's death and the years of mass starvation, he gave overall command of the campaign of the Scrutiny to his brother-in-law Jang Song-thaek, who was then Deputy Director of the Party's Administrative Department. Kim Jong-il's intention was to lend weight to the Ministry of Social Security, which had until then ranked beneath the Ministry of State Security and the military in its surveillance powers. As Kim Jong-il's word served as the law, and because there was no man in North Korea more powerful than himself, he effectively gave hegemony over surveillance to the Ministry of Social Security by declaring, 'I'm first in line for your campaign of scrutiny.' Consequently, the Ministry of Social Security rose to dominate both the military and the Ministry of State Security.

Moon Sung-sul, the General Secretary of the Workers' Party HQ and the third most senior man in the country after Kim Il-sung and Kim Jong-il according to the Party's hierarchy, became the first victim of the Scrutiny as sanctioned by Kim Jong-il. As head of the Workers' Party HQ, Moon Sung-sul also served as the First Deputy Director of the Party's OGD and held sway over the nation's most powerful men, for all of them reported ultimately to that entity. Nevertheless, he found himself the first in line to be charged with espionage by Jang Song-thaek, because he had been responsible for putting Jang Song-thaek under surveillance by the OGD and restricting his influence on the grounds that he was a 'side-branch' of the Kim family who posed the greatest factional threat.

Jang Song-thaek took the opportunity to seek revenge by having Moon Sung-sul tortured and beaten to death. However, this move was much more than a mere act of personal vengeance on the part of Jang Song-thaek; it was a clear warning to the OGD leadership that they too were not immune from destruction if they fell out of Kim Jong-il's favour.

The Ministry of State Security received the same warning. In 1998, the Ministry's First Deputy Director Kim Yong-ryong shot himself when agents from the Ministry of Social Security burst into his room to arrest him during the Scrutiny.

It was at this time that Young-min's father, Hwang Jin-thaek, was also arrested. He had raised questions about the attack against Moon Sung-sul, and Jang Song-thaek was able to obtain approval from Kim Jong-il to bring anti-revolutionary charges against Hwang.

Following Jang Song-thaek's lead of reprisal, the Scrutiny's political director Choe Mun-deok prosecuted Seo Yoon-seok, the Party Secretary for Pyongyang, on suspicion of espionage. Choe Mun-deok was exacting revenge for Seo's having previously dismissed him from his post. The poisoned water seeped downwards as others, in turn, inspired by the example set by their superiors, sought to resolve their personal grudges in a similar way. Through widespread abuse of the surveillance powers offered by the Scrutiny, which relied on gaps in the entries of records from the Korean War, a bloodbath washed over the nation. Nearly 20,000 cadres, military figures and security agents, as well as retired scholars, artists and athletes, were executed or sent to prison camps – and that was only according to the number released through official Workers' Party lectures. The actual impact was far greater because of the principle of guilt-by-association, whereby relatives and close associates were all purged alongside the 'criminal'.

As both cadres and ordinary North Koreans alike reacted with increasing unrest and discontent, Kim Jong-il decided to turn down the heat by redirecting blame towards the campaign of Scrutiny itself. According to him, the early prosecutor Choe Mun-deok's abuse of his office had sown the treacherous seeds of 'greed for power' in the Scrutiny. Choe Mun-deok alone bore the brunt of Kim Jong-il and Jang Song-thaek's responsibilities and was publicly executed in February 2000. The six thousand officials who had worked directly under him were summarily stripped of rank.

At this time, Young-min's father was reinstated and his reputation restored as far as the Party was concerned, but he died in hospital two weeks after his release from prison. Young-min said that when he looked into his father's open but lifeless eyes, he cried not in mourning, but because of the injustice of it all. His father had shown only loyalty to the Party; yet in his final moments, he had to fix his eyes on a blank ceiling, unable to gaze at his loved ones. As Young-min closed his father's eyes, the trembling of his hand was the only visible trace of emotion that he could allow to escape from his heart.

As Young-min finished telling his story, the North Korean women, who knew the Scrutiny well, were silent for a moment. Only Mr Shin, who had always lived in China, was incredulous: 'So you're telling me that these violent mass purges went on in 2000? In today's world, and not in some history book? I really can't believe it.'

The women from Hamheung and Chongjin both described how the Scrutiny had devastated their own hometowns like a tsunami. Fear and suspicion became so pervasive across the whole of North Korea that even the sight of a truck routinely delivering goods would be mistaken for a vehicle transporting another relative of a Scrutiny victim to a prison camp. Mrs Shin described the violence and social anarchy that followed in her town in the wake of the Scrutiny's bloodbath. After Kim Jong-il publicly denounced the campaign, the officer responsible for her town was beaten to death in the dark of night.

When incidents such as this began to occur all over the country, and not only beatings but also the murder of Social Security agents, Kim Jong-il ordered the Workers' Party to prepare a series of compulsory lectures to be delivered nationwide. According to the reading materials for these lectures, the Ministry of Social Security would change its name to the Ministry of People's Security because it ought to 'maintain security for the people, rather than oppress society'. It was claimed that Kim Jong-il pencilled in the new name for the ministry with his own hand out of love for his people. In this way, he thought, the negative connotations of a ministry associated with the Scrutiny's brutal violence might be erased.

Kim Jong-il's use of political theatre in dealing with the issue did not end there. Through the authority of the Supreme Commander, he ordered the release of victims of the Scrutiny held in prison camps, in order to 'bring justice' to the many who had been convicted on false charges. In order to maximise the effect of their joy when they found they had regained their lives, he ordered that prisoners should not be informed of their release until they were in a Party lecture hall where an audience could witness their genuine joy. But this tactic backfired appallingly, and the Party halls became instead public courts testifying against despotism. Wretched prisoners were brought by truck from the camps and pushed into the hall; and even when Supreme Commander Kim Jong-il's release order was read out, they thought it might be a cruel prelude to execution. One person pleaded for his life; another coughed blood and passed out, thinking that he was going to be killed. Several were actually executed because they cursed Kim Jong-il before the audience in the Party hall.

There were other respects in which the tragedy experienced by the victims of the Scrutiny could not be reversed by mere words. Some spouses, who had escaped condemnation when their husband or wife was sentenced but were forcibly divorced, had already re-married; others had committed suicide. Some victims returned to find their homes and possessions re-assigned to others and ended up on the streets. Kim Jong-il then issued an order for regional Party Committees to provide temporary housing for them, and also to offer rice and cooking oil. The Party's Propaganda and Agitation Department used this as evidence to instigate mass propaganda campaigns describing Kim Jong-il's leadership as 'all-embracing of the people, like the heavens', moving on from the previous slogan of 'strong leadership'.

6 | AT A LOSS

WE spent only one afternoon with the North Korean women, but even though it was only a short time together, it was also a most crucial time. We compressed into those hours each of our individual experiences of life in North Korea, shared among us and no longer kept to ourselves. Above all, our time with the women confirmed for Young-min and me that the falsehoods on which Kim Jong-il's tyranny depended could not remain immune from scrutiny forever. While we were inside the system, his command of absolute authority seemed to be the sole and most powerful manifestation of truth in the world. But how vicious and perverse that power was, which pursued us even after we had left its borders.

It was only then, looking back from the outside, that I realised this power could not belong to a strong man. It was the tantrum of a defeated man, a man who had been abandoned not only by Young-min and me, but by the very people he would have perceived as worthless and weak, such as these women who had endured the worst of humiliations.

Another important lesson I learned from the women was one of courage. The escape that Young-min and I had planned was born out of desperation, and we had only gone so far as to promise to commit suicide if we failed. But these women were driven by a powerful resolve and would keep on trying to escape, even after being captured and returned to North Korea. For them, this resolve had led to their decision to take action and cross China to Tianjin. We were not alone in our fate.

The problem was that, although Mr Shin had taught us to cry *Pa-ee-ting!* at uncertain times such as this, there were not yet signs that the miracle we hoped for would become a reality. Even after the women had gone on their way and the house had been empty of their voices for a week, we had still received no response from South Korea. Mr Shin, too, sighed as the days went by. I kept my doubts to myself for as long as I could, but in the end I had to ask him what was going on. How much longer would we have to continue to wait in hiding?

He asked his wife to go out and get some wine. Then he sat down with a serious expression on his face and said, 'There's this South Korean I know quite well. He's very interested in North Korean refugees, and I think he works for South Korea's spy agency.'

'What – you *think* he works for the agency? So you're not certain?' I asked.

'What spy would admit to being a spy? I've met him several times and he knows a lot about North Korea. He always speaks carefully, that's for sure. He's given me a retainer several times and asked me to contact him if I happened to come across a defector from Pyongyang. Just a few days ago, he was checking up on how you guys were doing. The clothes I bought you, food, all my expenses so far – it's all his money. That's why I took pictures after we went shopping and sent them to him along with copies of your papers. But it's odd that I can't get through to him any more. When I dial his mobile, it says the number doesn't exist.'

All my hopes faded in an instant. The man we'd put our trust in, Mr Shin's contact and our saviour, might be nothing more than a mirage. Mr Shin wasn't even sure about the man's identity, and there was no guarantee that he worked for South Korea at all. We had been waiting for a miracle from some unknown person. I regretted even asking – not knowing would have been better than this new uncertainty. Not only the future, but even the miracles that had blessed us until now, all this seemed meaningless.

Was there no other way forward? Why was it so difficult to get to the country where our fellow Koreans lived? Mr Shin explained that there were other ways of getting to South Korea through Vietnam, Mongolia or Thailand, but this only made us feel worse. We had already had several near misses just coming from the border to Yanji – how could we possibly go so far and cross so many more borders? In the end, the problem was money. Mr Shin reminded us that staying here any longer required money, and setting off anywhere required more money.

Young-min excused himself and went to our room. He returned carrying the envelope that held the note with the address of his relative. As Mr Shin read the note's contents, his eyes lit up. With a wide-eyed expression that reminded me of his uncle Chang-yong, he exclaimed that the relative must be very rich. Immediately, he got out his phone and dialled a number. He spoke in Chinese, which I couldn't understand, but it was clear from his face that the call went well. As he hung up, he turned to us and could hardly contain his excitement as he began to explain.

'I have a friend who is a reporter at Yanbian Broadcasting, and he says that if these people really are your relatives, there should be no problem getting you to South Korea. In fact, I think I've heard of this name too. This lady, she comes up in textbooks in the Chinese schools here as an anti-Japanese heroine. And her children have land in Shenyang too. Is she really family?'

Kim Il-sung's anti-Japanese experience is hugely exaggerated and religiously indoctrinated into every North Korean mind. Moreover, all famous ethnic Korean anti-Japanese fighters are alleged to have been loyal to Kim Il-sung. In Chinese textbooks, where Koreans are recognised as an ethnic minority, they are praised as ethnic Korean-Chinese 'anti-Japanese heroes', whereas in North Korean textbooks, they are acclaimed as 'Kim Il-sung's loyal comrades' who followed in Kim Il-sung's anti-Japanese footsteps.

I replied that even in North Korean textbooks, Young-min's grandmother was known as a key historical figure. That being so, Mr Shin said we could definitely make it to South Korea from here. He was more excited by our connections than even his humble uncle Chang-yong had been, and went so far as to ask us to take him and his wife with us to South Korea. That's when I learned that after being recognised as the legal spouse of a North Korean refugee, an ethnic Korean from China could qualify for South Korean citizenship. Mr Shin, far more optimistic about the possibilities than we were, said that we should visit Young-min's family that very night.

Young-min eagerly put his coat on, but I couldn't feel quite as positive. It was certain that by now there would be police watching the relative's house every minute of the day. Young-min argued that there had been no response from the South Korean contact for ten days, and the number was now out of order – we had no other choice. At least we had Mr Shin to look out for us, and so we decided to give it a go.

Mr Shin insisted we get an expensive cab, so that any police watching the house would be less suspicious. After a half-hour journey we arrived at a private residence that was more palatial and impressive than anything I could have imagined. The problem was that the surrounding area was very brightly lit. There was also a suspicious-looking private car with its sidelights on and engine running opposite the front gate. I said we should drive round the block. But however carefully we checked out the area, it appeared impossible to get close to the building safely on foot.

We decided in the end to wait in the taxi in a nearby alley while Mr Shin went to the house. He was to arrange a place and time to meet, and if the family didn't believe that he had come on behalf of Young-min, he would bring one of them to the alley where we would be waiting. As he walked off, Young-min and I waited anxiously. In spite of the cold, my palms were sweating. It was sheer torment once Mr Shin was out of sight. Young-min wanted us to go round the block once more, but neither of us could speak to the driver in Chinese.

Perhaps fifteen minutes later, Mr Shin came running in an obvious panic, his arms and legs flailing. As soon as he got in the cab, he waved at the driver, urging him to set off. With fear in his eyes, he turned to see if anyone was following us. Young-min and I asked several times what had happened, but each time he replied curtly that he would tell us once we were out of the cab. Instead of stopping the cab near his house, we got out several few blocks further on.

As soon as the cab left, he turned to us angrily. 'A lot of people here in Yanji speak Korean! Even some of the Chinese cab drivers understand Korean, so what am I supposed to say if you keep asking what happened?'

He was trembling, and lit himself a cigarette with shaking hands. After inhaling deeply, he calmed a little and offered one to each of us. I didn't want to accept. He obviously had some bad news to tell us.

'Now listen,' he said, and his tone was ominous. 'Even after we separate, don't even think about going to that house. It's not just surrounded by police. There are even some North Korean agents on standby, a Prosecution Squad from the Ministry of State Security.'

As soon as we heard about the Ministry's Prosecution Squad, I could feel their shadows upon us.

'When I pressed the doorbell, a man came out and said he was the son. I told him Young-min from Pyongyang sent me, and do you know what he said? He said he didn't want to know about his cousin, and anyway he has no connection to you following the death of your grandparents. He said how dare a murderer come to his house – that you were wasting police time, and that he and his family had had to deal with the constant surveillance of North Korean agents; and he said don't ever show up again if you want to live. I tried as hard as

I could to persuade him to meet you, but you know that car parked opposite the mansion? Two men got out of it and started walking towards me. If I hadn't seen them, I'd be in an interrogation room right now.'

Just hearing him speak sent a shiver through my body. What would have happened if we had gone ourselves, or if Mr Shin had been captured? The possibilities made my heart pound and I feared the car might have followed us. I told Mr Shin that we should get back inside the apartment block and turned to walk, but froze in my tracks when Young-min collapsed in an alleyway, and began to whimper piteously.

Back in the flat, we tried to console Young-min. Even his family outside North Korea now regarded him as a murderer, and I pitied him for how small and alone he looked. Mr Shin said that the cousin had taken his phone number and that he might possibly change his mind and call back. Even though Mr Shin did his best to sympathise, I felt that his words lacked conviction. Young-min's despair was obvious, and he didn't even bother to take off his coat as he slid down the wall and sat with his head on his knees.

Mrs Shin was scolding her husband in the other room.

'What? You left them your number? What if they hand it over to the North Koreans? What on earth were you thinking? Switch the phone off and take out the chip!'

Young-min looked up at the noise, but sank back into his depression. I spent an unbearably long night, first trying to calm Young-min, then drifting in and out of nightmares in which North Korean agents had already thrown me into a cell.

The next morning we left Mr Shin's house early. It was too dangerous for us to stay there any longer – not only for Mr Shin, but also for his wife who, like us, was a North Korean in China who might be repatriated if her identity were discovered. Mr Shin made us memorise his number, saying that we should keep in frequent contact as the South Koreans might come back with a response. He also put 100 yuan in my hand – about US$15. He apologised for the small amount, but it was as if he had given us all he had. Without that 100 yuan, we would have been lost as soon as we stepped out of the building, foreigners wandering without a penny in a land whose language we didn't understand.

More than the value of the money, the fact that we had any money at all lightened our hearts a little. Mr Shin saw us off and walked with us for a while, advising us to look for churches. He said that these places sometimes gave money, food and shelter to North Korean refugees, and a missionary might even help us get to South Korea. But, he said, we must be careful to insist that we'd fled the country because of hunger: if they found out that we had been accused of murder, it might scare them off. He also warned us that some churches were fronts for the Chinese authorities and might turn us in, so we must be careful not to trust anyone too easily.

'I can't believe there exists a religion that would give money and food for free to a stranger,' said Young-min and he smiled for the first time in days. I was very grateful for that smile. While he'd tossed and turned the night before, hurt by his cousin's rejection of him, I had lain awake worrying about how heavy his steps would be today. I deliberately gave Young-min a loud high-five, and whispered, 'Pa-ee-ting!' beneath the sound of our slapping hands. As if to lift a weight from his chest, Young-min strained so hard that the veins on his neck began to show, and he exclaimed in a whisper, 'Pa-ee-ting!' Fighting!

We automatically reached for our sunglasses, and burst into hysterical laughter when we realised we were both doing the same thing. It was not only funny, but pathetic – only seconds after we had summoned up our courage, here we were, hiding ourselves behind dark lenses. One of us remarked how Mr Shin's gift of the sunglasses was even greater than the food, help and shelter he had given us.

Wearing sunglasses and following the advice Mr Shin had given us, Young-min and I walked to the outskirts of Yanji, looking for any building with a cross on it.

'What should we say to a pastor when we meet one?' Young-min asked eagerly; and I as enthusiastically replied that we should answer each question with, 'Amen', and everything would work out. As I said this, my chest puffed with pride at my own pearl of wisdom.

As a former member of the UFD, I thought I knew all about religion. Even in North Korea, there is such a thing. More specifically, North Korea has a number of religious institutions that are controlled by the United Front Department. But in practice, North Korea is a one-religion state, where only the worship of the Leader is allowed. The UFD's religious institutions exist in order that North Korea may *claim* that it is a pluralistic society, and thereby appear to comply with the values of those who wish to give it aid or engage with the North through Track II, or 'informal', channels.

All of North Korea's religious institutions are staffed by UFD 'Track II diplomacy' operatives and include the Chosun Buddhist Association, the Chosun Christian Association, the Chosun Catholic Association and the Chosun Catholic Central Committee. I was aware that, in dealing with the outside world, the UFD used the names of the different religious institutions. Internally, it was illegal to use these, so they were referred to by numbers. Although a cadre might be a monk or priest as far as the outside world was concerned, in the UFD they were all faithful followers of the Kim cult.

If you are in Pyongyang and go to Jangchun-dong in Dongdaewon Area, or Palgol-dong in Mangyongdae Area, you will see buildings with crosses on their roofs. The priests who worship in these buildings sing authentic Christian hymns, in the same way that people outside North Korea do in ordinary churches. But the congregations are composed exclusively of UFD operatives and their family members, who are obliged to attend out of duty to the Party. No ordinary North Korean could even begin to consider worshipping in these buildings, as they are in operational zones where entry is restricted to UFD personnel and foreigners.

But, in 2000, the following incident occurred. Once, in order to welcome an international religious organisation to North Korea, the UFD conspicuously opened the doors of Jangchun Church in Pyongyang to the public. An old man in his eighties walked in carrying a Bible that he had kept hidden all his life. He said that he had believed in Jesus before the Korean War, but after losing his family to an American bombardment, he had converted and become instead a fervent believer in the Supreme Leader, Kim Il-sung. He even explained that at his age, old memories became important, and he had come to the church because he'd been delighted to hear hymns from his childhood. The old man was reported by the UFD operative in priestly garb and arrested on the spot by secret police.

That cadre was subsequently awarded a First Class medal, reserved for the most loyal to Kim, for the achievement of exposing a religious element who had succeeded in keeping his subversive beliefs secret until now. I was there sitting in the audience, applauding as the cadre received his medal. The old man was sent to a prison camp, and the very same Bible is used to this day by the UFD as a prop to boast about the history of North Korea's religious tolerance.

These religious activities only helped UFD cadres enjoy more luxuries that were not available to ordinary North Koreans. North Korea is technically still at war with the US, so internally, all humanitarian aid from outside is referred to as 'spoils of war'. Because the North Korean system associates itself with the ideology of *Juche*, it prohibits the word 'aid', which is regarded as a threat to 'self-reliance'. As a result, gifts received every month by employees of the UFD included 'spoils of war' donated by various South Korean and international religious organisations as humanitarian aid.

For example, on 15 April 2001 (Kim Il-sung's birthday), bicycles supplied by a South Korean Buddhist NGO were given to the UFD, and there were enough for all of us to have one. The next month, nappies and milk powder donated by a South Korean Christian NGO were distributed among staff. I knew from first-hand experience how great was the influence of the UFD, because it controlled how North Korea was presented to outsiders. And this was also how I knew that 'Amen' was a powerful word that could move Christians to come to our aid, if we could only find a church here in Yanji.

But although Young-min and I walked for a whole day, we didn't come across a single church in which we could say our Amens. Any building with a cross on it was either abandoned or locked. Once, a security guard opened the door, but as soon as we said we were North Korean refugees, he became furious and chased us off as if we were stray dogs. I learned the hard way how we North Koreans were hated outside our country, though the Party had taught us to see ourselves as 'the most glorious people on earth, Kim Il-sung's people'. Every time we were turned away, we joked haplessly about the Kim dynasty, which had made the world shun us as the scum of the earth.

When it started to turn dark, I felt strangely elated, perhaps because I had been frightened by the brightness of the day. I felt as if my body could float up into the darkness like a balloon. Taking my sunglasses off, I could see even more clearly than in daylight. All around us was countryside, and there were no other pedestrians. Even the fact that I could breathe freely and speak openly to Young-min without feeling paranoid made me feel like I was a pioneer in a new world.

The icy winds of January didn't worry us, and we weren't concerned about spending a wintry night outdoors. After all, we'd already made it through several nights on a frozen mountain. Under the heavy winter sky, in the middle of nowhere in China, we ran down an endless country lane shouting at the top of our lungs.

We ended up in a small village called Longjing. Not that we had intended to go there – we had just wandered along, aimlessly looking for churches, and this was the first village we had come to as we followed random roads. We decided to stay the night there and then take off again in the morning.

Fortunately, we found an empty stable. It would at least keep out the bitter winds. The floor too was thickly padded with straw. Before falling asleep, we held the 100-yuan note in our hands, holding up one side each, and gazed at it for several minutes. What would we be looking at now if we didn't have this? How hopeless we would be without it. Back home in North Korea, I had pitied the corpses of children starved to death, but had looked away from the adult bodies, shaking my head and thinking, *Why didn't they try harder to survive?* Why were they so stupid as to starve to death, with no sense of responsibility to themselves or anyone else? They could at least have stolen food and carried on. But that night I could see the end of my own life not far away. After we had used up the money and had not eaten for a few days, I might sit down and close my eyes to rest, let consciousness slip away, and not even realise I was dying. Stunned by these thoughts, I wanted to test out my voice to see if it was still there.

'I'm sure it'll work out. We'll get to South Korea before the money's gone.' Even as I said these words, I did not believe them.

As if he did not believe them either, and as if the 100 yuan would not be opening up our path, Young-min let go of his end of the note and dropped his hand. We were silent for a while. I wanted to sleep. But for tomorrow morning's sake, I didn't want to end the day like this. What else could I say? The thought of talking made my lips numb. Eventually, I put them together, and began to whistle a folk song from back home, 'Spring of My Hometown'. As I finished the first verse and began to whistle the second, Young-min joined me in a lower harmony.

Our hunger and despair lifted a little, and I was reminded of a performance we had given at music school. The students of Western music had borrowed brass instruments to put on a spectacular show that got the audience roaring with laughter. It was not unusual to see brass instruments, but the way they did it was the clincher: the trumpet played wittily, to the slow and low answer of a tuba that did not get the joke. After the silence that followed the applause, the composition students, both male and female, performed as a whistling choir. The audience went wild, and we had the whole school whistling for weeks.

As our whistling performance in the stable approached the last few notes, a mischievous grin formed on Young-min's face, and he went on for a second with a dissonant note. I prolonged my last note on purpose, and Young-min fell back into harmony, and we finished on a beautiful double note.

Young-min whispered first, '*Pa-ee-ting!*'

I responded, '*Pa-ee-ting!*' and found my tense muscles loosen. That was probably why I was able to fall asleep. Until that night, even the rustling of leaves had terrified me. That was the first night in China I was able to forget that border guards and North Korean agents might be lurking in the shadows of every building, bush and tree.

7 | FAREWELL, YOUNG-MIN

WE woke to the lowing of cattle. When I opened my eyes, something large and brown stirred next to me, and I started. An immense ox, as if annoyed by the intruders in his home, gave us a long look through the narrowed slits of his eyes and snorted loudly. Instinctively, I patted my pockets in case the ox had stolen the money from me. Seeing the red 100-yuan note tucked in among my poems brought me a sigh of relief.

Young-min sat up too. He looked at me and then at the ox and was about to speak; but then he lowered his gaze and began to pick miserably at the straw. We both realised that our faces and clothes were stained and that the look of a fugitive, which Chang-yong had said would give us away as North Koreans on the run, had crept up on us. If we continued our journey looking like this, there was no doubt that someone would report us to the authorities. We rubbed our faces with the white snow piled outside the barn, but it just smeared the dirt and made it worse.

We went to the nearest house and knocked on the courtyard door. Instead of cement or bricks, the fence was made of tightly joined planks. The chimney straggled above a dark-orange tin roof, which lacked the Korean roof tiles we had seen on some houses. We waited anxiously, feeling vulnerable with our dirty faces exposed to whoever might answer the door. There was some movement, and a moment later the door opened a little to reveal an old man peering out at us. He was wearing a worn black coat, but the buttons were shiny and new, and he didn't look like a farmer. He might have been very old, but his face looked more youthful than ancient. He could probably tell right away that we were North Koreans on the run, because he was about to close the door on us.

I bowed deeply. 'Sir, may we please use your soap to wash our faces?'

Instead of closing the door, the old man put his head out of the gap again and looked us up and down. We thought he might not have understood our Korean, but to our great surprise he opened the door fully and spoke to us in our own language, so welcome to our ears.

'Come in.'

The old man's yard was neat and tidy, unlike Chang-yong's house, whose walls were crumbling. There were three apple trees in one corner, straw wrapped round their trunks to keep them from freezing. The old man left us shivering in the yard and went into the house.

A few moments later he returned from the kitchen with a large brass washbowl full of steaming hot water. We rushed to help him with it and carried it to the corner of the yard opposite the apple trees. As Young-min and I politely told each other to go first, the old man shuffled towards us, lit a cigarette, and asked, 'Have you come from across the river?'

Young-min hesitated for a moment, then answered, 'Yes.'

The old man sucked deeply on his cigarette and blew out smoke that looked eerily white in the winter morning air. 'I've had no end of refugees knocking on my door for food,' he said. 'There's even been some who've stolen things and thrown rocks at me. But you! In all my life, I don't think I've ever had someone ask to wash!' He shook his head in disbelief. 'Have you eaten yet?'

When he saw that we couldn't answer with an immediate yes, he stamped out his half-smoked cigarette and asked us to come inside after we had washed. He shouted again from the kitchen, 'Come on in when you're clean!'

When we'd finished, we tipped out the soapy water and propped the bowl against the side of the house to drain. We made our way to the kitchen and pushed open the door to the room from which the voice had spoken. The old man was spooning out rice. The smell of it, so different from the outside air, flooded my lungs with warmth. At that moment, a feeling of bliss rushed through me that made my chest pound. It was a sublime moment of transcendence, the like of which I had never experienced before. The smell of cooking rice confirmed that the world had not yet abandoned us.

The rice was generously served in big bowls, steaming fresh from the stove. It was so chewy that, with each spoonful, there were grains sticking to the underside of the spoon as well as heaped in its bowl. The warmth of the grains in my throat as I swallowed comforted me. While we ate, the old man criticised Kim Jong-il emphatically. He said that in this modern age it was disgusting that our leader should starve his whole country, and insisted that Kim Jong-il's pot belly was clear evidence of his selfishness and greed.

I was grateful for the rice, but even more for his sympathy. It felt like support for our plight, especially as everywhere else the refugees were spat on.

The old man asked, 'Where are you heading? And how did you get into this state?'

'We want to go to South Korea,' Young-min replied.

'The authorities must be after you, then. You must be on the run.'

'Yes, we were nearly caught by the authorities,' I replied.

'Did you cross the river together?'

'Yes, we're friends.'

We answered his questions earnestly, wanting to show appreciation for his interest. But what he said next left us speechless.

'You're from Pyongyang,' he declared, 'and you're accused of murder.'

We didn't know what to say.

'This village is close to Yanji city centre,' the old man continued, 'and a lot of refugees pass through. There isn't a day without one of them. So the authorities keep an eye on this place. In fact, the day before yesterday, they searched every house, looking for two defectors from Pyongyang who escaped over the river after committing murder.'

My ears were ringing and the rice sat heavy in my stomach. When we left Mr Shin's house, we had taken some comfort in the knowledge that China is a large country. Yet in this village that seemed so remote, an old man we'd never met before knew exactly who we were. It felt as if there were nowhere on this earth where we could hide, and that North Korea's framing of us for murder would follow us to the ends of the earth.

'We're not murderers!' Young-min blurted out desperately, but the old man waved his words away.

'Look,' he said. 'I've lived for seventy years. I can tell by looking at you that you're not murderers. I also know that the North Korean bastards like to frame people for murder. Neither the Chinese authorities nor any of the locals here believe a word they say.'

We had been tense and nervous, and ready to leave at once, but this brought us some relief.

'So don't go everywhere together,' the old man advised us. 'Walk separately, and be careful.'

'Thank you, sir.' I found myself bowing deeply once again.

Young-min, as if he wanted to repay the debt, took the empty bowls and spoons back into the kitchen. He insisted on doing the dishes too, but the old man managed to call him back to the main room, and found some paper and a pen. He explained that there was a Korean church in Yanji that he knew quite well, and he would write us a letter of introduction to the pastor there. He said the pastor could help us get to South Korea. Young-min and I could not believe it, and could hardly contain our excitement.

The old man drew us a map showing how to get to the church from Yanji bus terminal, to be sure that we wouldn't get lost. He marked the church with a cross, and went over it several times to make it stand out. After repeating the directions, he tested us several times to make sure we hadn't forgotten anything. 'What building is this?' he asked. 'What road is that?' He checked everything thoroughly. We answered his questions like two eager students.

As we said farewell, he said to us, 'When you get to South Korea, settle in Seoul instead of in the provinces.'

After we'd heard these words, even our footsteps seemed lighter as we left the old man's house. The letter of introduction and map that the old man had drawn so carefully seemed like a passport that would take us all the way to South Korea. We felt confident, and didn't even put on our sunglasses. But we took care to follow the old man's advice about staying apart.

Whenever we reached a road where there were people, we pretended not to know each other. It was actually exciting. Sometimes Young-min led the way and I fell back, and in the end we fought over who would get to walk in front. Once, when I was leading, I hid in an alley for a joke, and I watched Young-min turn white and search frantically for me up and down the road. A long journey that would have taken over an hour by bus passed by quickly as we playfully made our way.

The old man's directions were so thorough that we very easily found Yanji Church in the busy city centre. Unlike other churches that stood out with prominent crosses, this church merely occupied some office space in a commercial building.

Before we knocked on the door, I glanced at the wooden sign that read 'Yanji Church' in black letters. Inside, I knew there would be South Koreans, and my heart swelled at the thought of falling into the embrace of my countrymen. Young-min too was verging on tears, as if we had come to the threshold of South Korea itself. I asked him to knock. Sure enough, a voice answered in Korean, and when we entered there were three middle-aged men inside. One of them, wearing glasses, flushed on seeing us. His eyes, peering behind thick lenses, seemed unusually small.

'How did you find us?' he asked. 'Come in, come in.'

The interior of the church was as spacious as the Revolutionary Study Rooms of Comrades Kim Il-sung and Kim Jong-il that were attached to all workplaces in North Korea. In the central part of the wall, where we expected portraits of the Kims to hang, there hung a cross instead. But the atmosphere of the room was just as solemn as the Revolutionary Study Rooms. Above the cross was a wooden slogan that read 'Let's be saved by saying Amen'. There were perhaps twenty wooden pews, and a desk near the door.

'We want to meet the pastor,' I said in reply. However, I didn't realise at the time that I had left out the honorific suffix *nim* that South Koreans must add when using a title such as 'pastor' or 'teacher'. In North Korea, the suffix *nim* may only be used for a member of the ruling Kim family – or for a teacher, because one of the titles of Kim Jong-il was Teacher Dear Leader. In this way, although we had come here to seek our saviour, we had not shown even the most basic respect for Him, and the eyes of the bespectacled man narrowed further.

'Where have you come from?' he growled.

'We can only tell the pastor.'

'He's in South Korea at the moment. You can tell me. I'm standing in for him while he's gone.'

My heart fluttered. If the pastor could go to South Korea from here, so might we! As I took the letter of introduction out from my pocket to give to the man, my hands shook. While he read the letter, Young-min looked curiously at the cross and Bible on the table, as if they were strange alien artefacts. To see these objects here in an ordinary setting, objects that you could see in North Korea only in the UFD's operational zones, made me feel like I had already stepped into South Korean territory. I couldn't stop grinning.

Suddenly, the man took his glasses off and screamed at the top of his voice. 'Get out of here at once!'

I stood there speechless.

'Hey! Throw these guys out, they're defectors!'

I felt as though I had just been knocked out. Before I could bring myself to consider that he might be joking, the two other men approached us and began to shove us out. Young-min didn't bother to struggle, but instead, fell to his knees at the doorway.

'We came here because we heard you were South Korean,' he cried. 'We risked our lives and crossed the border so that we could go to South Korea. We will die on the streets if you throw us out.'

'What, you think you're the only ones? Our pastor was arrested once because of you lot. The church will have to close down because of you. Get out! Get out, you bastards!'

I was astonished. Were these men from the country where we longed to seek refuge? When I saw the bespectacled man start to hit Young-min on the head, I felt my blood rush. He slapped Young-min in the face as he pleaded tearfully with them. I lost my temper and found myself screaming. I dragged the bespectacled man off Young-min and picked up the cross on the desk like a weapon.

'Do you call yourselves human? We risked our lives to come here!' I shouted.

'Hurry up! Call the authorities! Report them!'

I had been about to give them a piece of my mind, but when I heard those two words of terror – 'authorities' and 'report' – in a single sentence, I seized Young-min's arm and ran out of the church. It was a long way back to the entrance and we stumbled as we fled.

When we finally reached the street, the cars rushing past us sounded like sirens and I was filled with panic. Young-min led the way, but when he came to a fork in the road, he could not decide which way to turn and I crashed into him, sending both of us tumbling onto the street.

Only when we found ourselves in a remote neighbourhood in the outskirts of the city could we think of looking behind us. As I caught my breath, a vast emptiness filled my soul. Even the South Korean church had turned us away and there was nowhere else to turn. As if to demonstrate that we had tried everything and there was nothing left, Young-min took out the map the old man had drawn so carefully and tore it to shreds. Every shred of it, as it fell to the ground, was a fragment of our shattered lives. We sat for a while in silence.

Young-min tapped my arm as I stared up at the sky, and asked, 'Shall we spend some of that money today? Let's get ourselves a drink.'

I remembered our final night back in Pyongyang, when we'd decided to escape after a drink, but ignored him. Then I said, 'I'd rather look for a place to spend the night.'

I stood up and turned to go, but Young-min blocked my way.

'Why? Why should we?' he asked. 'You think we can make it to South Korea after what we've just seen? They were going to report us! You and I, we're neither North nor South Korean! Do you understand? We belong nowhere!'

I didn't answer. I didn't know what to say. We wanted to settle in a free Korea, but it didn't exist anywhere on earth. Although my body was physically here, it seemed as if my spirit had departed because I was too numb to perceive anything. If I had killed myself in North Korea, at least I would have been buried in the land of my family and friends. Here we could only wander like dogs until the rigour of death set in, and we would eventually disappear, unknown and unmourned, into the dust of these foreign roads. The thought of this tragic end to my existence convinced me that this was my last day on earth.

Young-min dragged me off to a drinks stall in the market. Bottles of alcohol, differently priced, were on display. He pointed to a small bottle of wine at 12 yuan, and then at a single empty glass, which would cost 5 yuan to fill. When I realised it was a powerful Chinese soju, it was obvious that we would pass out on the streets if we drank this on an empty stomach, and we'd be exposed to the authorities. What could we eat to prevent this? As I did the sums in my head, I put the glass back down.

'Look, we only have one hundred yuan. I won't drink. You can have one, though.'

Young-min's eyelids trembled as he looked at me in desperation. The dark eyes that I knew so well, usually full of loyalty and friendship and the spark of musical genius, were empty. His bloodshot gaze was tainted only with disappointment and spite. What else could I do? I stood my ground, because I felt the 100-yuan note was the only thing we had to hold on to. I was also exhausted and on edge, and if we lost even one yuan out of that hundred, it would destroy me. So instead of the drink, we ended up exchanging the 100 yuan for two 50-yuan notes. I was more fearful of losing Young-min than of meeting soldiers who would seize me. If we split the money, at least one of us might make it. Young-min sighed as I handed him his 50-yuan note.

'Okay,' he said. 'Let's get drunk out of our heads when we get to South Korea. But you keep the money, it's better for one person to look after it.'

I made him keep it, but took the opportunity to tease him. 'Don't think it's your money just because I'm giving it to you. It's not to spend, it's to let you think, "I've got money to buy food!" when you feel hungry.'

'Bastard. So that's why you've been so full of energy, because you've been holding the money!'

'That's right,' I smiled. 'And I should have said this earlier: you know when we ran in a panic out of the church? Well, we might have to do that again, so whenever there's a fork in the road, just take the one on the right. That way, you won't have to stop to think, and we'll be less likely to lose each other. Look, I can't and won't make it without you. You've got Mr Shin's number in your head, right? That's the only number we have to share if we split.'

The first 3 yuan we spent was on a small bar of soap. Our hunger was our own concern, but if we didn't keep up appearances, we would arouse suspicion.

We gave up on churches and decided to look for South Korean businesses, as that seemed to be the only other open door into a network of South Koreans. We looked out for anything we might recognise, such as Samsung, Hyundai or LG. Once, we went into a shop with an imitation 'Samsong' logo outside, and were chased out with insults in Chinese. At night, we'd sleep near a source of water such as a public fountain. We skipped breakfast, but around eleven in the morning we'd buy some bread for 2 yuan and share it again in the evening.

After four days on the streets, our money and stamina both ran out. On the fifth day, we didn't have anything to eat, and I felt very weak. We came to a dumpling stall, and I asked Young-min for his last 10 yuan so we could buy some food.

'What 10 yuan?' Young-min asked.

'You've 10 yuan left. Come on, let's buy some food.'

'I don't have any money!' Young-min grumbled at my insistence, and showed me his empty pockets.

Although it was a small amount of money, or perhaps because it was all we had, I had been very careful with the sums. I pulled him into an alley and added up everything to show him he was wrong. I repeated my calculations again and again, and it was clear he should still have 10 yuan left.

'So you're going to keep lying? What are you hiding from me? Did you eat without telling me?' Young-min avoided my gaze, picked a weed and began to tear its stalk into long shreds. I despised the very sight of his fingers as he plucked at it. 'Tell me!' I demanded. 'Look at me: if you've eaten, tell me straight!'

Young-min hurled the remains of the stalk to the ground and dusted the dirt off his hands. 'Yes, I used the 10 yuan,' he said. 'I used it for something really important. So what are you going to do about it?'

I shot back, 'Don't make excuses about things being "really important". If you've eaten, just confess to it like a man.'

'All right! Yes, I did do something without telling you. I bought a blade.'

Young-min took a razor from the side pocket of his jacket. I was about to shout, 'Why?' but the word stuck in my throat. When we were worried enough about our next meal, why would he buy a blade? Why would Young-min buy a blade without telling me?

His eyes welled with tears as he continued, 'We won't ever make it to South Korea. We were stupid even to think of it. I believed meeting a South Korean would solve everything, but that's not true. We've been on the street for days, and they'll definitely catch us soon. And then what? I don't care for my own life, but the Party will destroy my family too if they take us back and make us confess. So I bought this blade to kill myself with, so those bastards won't get what they want.'

His words rang in my ears, and the ringing would not stop. Seeing that blade on his palm, I was overcome with an impulse to kill myself first, out of rage. At the thought of such a blade in the hand of my only source of strength, I was helpless. Having no hope was far worse than having no money.

Seeing my despair, Young-min said, 'No, let's not be like this. Should we try my cousin one more time? Maybe if he sees me face to face, things will be different.'

His eyes were bloodshot and he spoke rapidly, as if possessed. I was frustrated that besides his thoughts of suicide, he still clung to the hope that his cousin might help, and realised that this was what must be making him weak. 'You heard as clearly as I did,' I said. 'He doesn't consider you to be family any more.'

'He probably panicked with the police around. If I explain in my own words that I didn't murder anyone, he'll get it. Even Mr Shin said that if he gets involved, we'll have no problem making it to South Korea. Come on, let's try one more time.' I turned to walk away, but Young-min continued, 'There's nothing else! It's the only hope left for us now.'

I decided that it would be impossible to persuade him otherwise, so I turned round again and said that we could think about it after finding a place to stay the night in the countryside. Young-min stared ahead but didn't say no, and we headed out towards the fields.

By the time we reached the first village it was dark. My legs kept wobbling and I had to make a real effort to stop myself from collapsing on the spot and giving up. We knocked on a few doors, but didn't have the courage to speak. When yet another household slammed the door on us, Young-min slid down onto the ice, right there on the threshold.

'It's because there's two of us,' he reasoned. 'Maybe it would be all right during the day, but no one would welcome two strange men into their home at night. They might even suspect us of being the two wanted murderers and report us.'

We sat in silence for a while. The one streetlamp in the village shone a spotlight on our solitude. The night sky seemed unusually low, and I could sense a snowstorm coming.

Young-min mustered all his strength to rise to his feet again. He said, 'How about this: we separate and each finds somewhere to stay. That might be easier on our hosts too. And we'll meet up under that tree over there in the morning.'

I asked, 'What if we don't find anyone who'll put us up for the night?'

'Then we keep on trying. At least the tree won't be going anywhere.'

I looked where Young-min was pointing. About twenty metres away, a large tree stood alone, the guardian of the village. We said goodbye. Young-min stayed behind in the village to try more houses, while I headed on to the next. I felt uneasy as Young-min earnestly waved me off, but his smile allowed me to turn and walk away.

PART THREE
FREEDOM

FROM YANJI TO SHENYANG | 1

WITHOUT Young-min, walking along the road was not just lonely, but terrifying. This was the first stretch of unbroken silence I'd experienced since crossing the Tumen River, and every step I took unsettled me further. Every now and then, I forced a cough to reassure myself that I was still alive. Sometimes I glanced behind me, mistaking the sound of my own footsteps for that of a stranger in pursuit. Perhaps because I had no food inside me, every time a gust of wind blew, my whole body seemed to sway with it. When I didn't have the stamina to hold my arms up, I stopped trying to cover my ears with my hands, leaving them exposed to the wind. At first, they were sore. Then they began to lose feeling, and finally they became itchy, a sign that they were freezing. I had to put my hands back on them to warm them up, but it was so cold that as soon I took my hands out of my pockets, they hurt as if they were breaking off from my arms.

When I arrived near homesteads the dogs were more vicious than the cold. Every time I approached the gate of a farmhouse, a dog would greet me with a growl, lips curled back to bare its teeth. As I plucked up the courage to knock on a front door, the dogs of the village shouted to their masters, 'Here is the murderer you're looking for!'

I wandered the neighbouring village for more than hour, realising that Young-min had been naïve to think that he or I would be let into a home more readily on account of being a single stranger instead of one of a pair. I remembered Chang-yong, who had brought us dumplings while we hid in the mountains; Mr Shin, who had given us 100 yuan and called it mere 'pocket money'; and the old man at Longjing, who had fed us rice when all we asked for was water to wash our faces. While I was immensely grateful for their kindness, I despaired that I would not meet with such good luck again. With a new sense of urgency, I decided to turn around and set off back towards the village with the tree under which we'd promised to meet.

Although I noticed a few stables on the way, I wasn't brave enough to spend the night outdoors on my own. If we had to spend another night under the freezing sky, I reasoned that it would be more comforting for us to do so together. I hoped that Young-min had come to the same conclusion and would be waiting for me beneath the tree. Even if he hadn't managed to find shelter, he might have found some food to surprise me with.

But when I arrived under the tree, Young-min wasn't there. Perhaps he had been fortunate enough to find a warm room for the night. As the darkness deepened, I had no choice but to spend the night alone, that tree my only companion. It was unbearably cold. Huddled beneath the tree, I counted the seconds out loud and waited for sunrise. As the winds changed, I shuffled round the tree to find better shelter. Icy tears trickled down my cheeks.

As blue gradually seeped through the night sky and morning approached, my vigil became more desperate. I endured the cold by mumbling Young-min's name over and over again, blowing on my hands with my breath. Yet long after the allotted time had passed, Young-min did not appear. When heavy snow began to fall from milky clouds, I could not bear the cold any longer. I stumbled into a small building not far from the tree. It contained some machinery connected to a pipe that seemed to disappear beneath the hills, and I guessed that the building housed a pump.

Wind buffeted into the pump house through the small glassless windows, but I was grateful that my clothes remained dry and free from melting snow. This comfort was momentary, however, as the space was cold as a tomb, its four walls like sheets of ice. When I decided I could not stand the cold any longer, I ran back outside. Sitting under the tree once more, I actually felt warmer, but my whole body was shaking. I bit my lips to keep my mouth shut, but my teeth clattered and I was unable to stop them.

More frightening than the cold was the thought of another night spent alone and in the open. I looked up at the sky, in the fear that it might be turning dark again soon. Suddenly, that wide sky shook as I teetered on the verge of collapse. I had to throw up although there was nothing in my stomach. When I sat down, I felt that my body was sinking further into the ground; and when I stood up, it seemed to sway from side to side as if I were on a swing.

As hard as I tried to decide on my next move, my brain would not focus on the decision. Despite my determination to gather my thoughts, my mind remained blank. The thought of not having eaten for several days was too painful to consider, until I was possessed by a sudden desire to find a stable and chew on hay. When I became conscious of this strange impulse, one of my poems floated into my mind. It was based on a story told to me by a beggar girl back home in North Korea. I was walking in Pyongyang when I saw her on the street. I knew that there was a food stall not too far away, so I asked what she most wanted to eat, something that she might share with her siblings. As we walked to the stall, she sobbed and told me her story.

THE MOST DELICIOUS THING IN THE WORLD

Three months ago, my brother said
The most delicious thing in the world
Was a warm corncob;

Two months ago, my brother said
The most delicious thing in the world
Was a roasted grasshopper;

One month ago, my brother said
The most delicious thing in the world
Was the dream he ate last night.

If my brother were alive today
What would he say this month, and next, was
The most delicious thing in the world?

When I wrote that poem, I had my table lamp switched off and I was crying. Even if I couldn't see it with my own eyes, the terror in the child's eyes and her hopes were too pitiful to face as words on the page. I hated the reality of hunger for that girl and her brother, and I had felt ashamed of myself. But when I came to find myself in the state of the poem's protagonist, it wasn't emotional in the way it had been when I had written it. It was distant and impotent. It seemed that my senses, once attuned to the faintest sound of rustling leaves, had shrivelled and been shattered by the cold winds. There was no poetry in hunger. North Korea was a nation without poetry. With only these last thoughts remaining, my body felt even heavier. I sat down in exhaustion and stared blankly at the sky.

An old woman passed by and startled me. 'If you've crossed over from North Korea, don't stay around here,' she said. 'Yesterday, the authorities swept through this village.'

It took me a while to comprehend her words, because my dulled senses were wandering aimlessly in the narrow confines of desperation. As I struggled to gather my mind into focus, one word stood out. Yesterday – wasn't that the night Young-min had stayed in this village? Had he been caught? Yet the old woman made no mention of anyone being arrested. Young-min would have fled without a single glance behind him. Maybe he had run too far, become lost, and was looking for a way back. Or perhaps he had gone to find Mr Shin. Yanji city centre was not too far from here.

I decided that I had to call Mr Shin as he was the only point of contact we shared. In some corner of my mind there was a nagging suggestion that I knew something relevant. To awaken my senses, I bit my tongue. Out of the throbbing pain, an image gradually formed in my mind: the house of the old man at Longjing, who not only gave us water to wash our faces, but a meal as well. He would surely help me one more time.

I hurriedly tried to raise myself from the ground, anxious to arrive at the old man's house before dark. But I took a step before I was able to balance myself and fell forward. My legs were unstable, and my feet were no longer under my control. When I picked myself up again, my legs swayed as if trying to hold up the heavens. The distance between each of my steps wasn't measured by my will. Whether it was because of the dark of night, or because the earth's gravity had lost its grip, it felt at times like I was sprinting, at others like I was walking on the spot.

In spite of my worries during that three-hour walk, I was able to find the old man's house without much difficulty. Driven by the belief that I had to knock on his door before he turned in for the night, I staggered to the doorway, where I collapsed in exhaustion.

'Sir!' My hands, pounding on the hard, thick plank at the base of the door, had no feeling left in them.

From somewhere inside the house, a small chime sounded. When the old man came to the door and found me on the ground, he bent down to lift me up and support me into his home. It felt like an embrace.

'Your friend? Where is the young man you were with?' the old man asked.

'We lost each other,' I said, as I crawled nearer the kitchen fire where there would be warmth. I couldn't feel the heat at first, but gradually, it rushed at me. Then I could feel the current of my blood, flowing through veins thinned by the cold, as it rushed all the way to the ends of my toes. Seeing my state, the old man understood there was nothing more to ask, and went into the kitchen. He returned with a bowl heaped with rice, a plate of picked cabbage and five boiled potatoes. As the old man turned round to fetch me a spoon, I said, 'Thank you, sir,' to his back, but perhaps there was nothing left in me, for no sound emerged.

He watched as I ate, shovelling spoonful after spoonful of rice into my mouth. He smoked one cigarette after another. As I ate, I could not say a word. It was not because I was rushing to sate my hunger after eating nothing for days, but because of my streaming tears. I was so grateful for the old man's kindness, but tears were my only expression.

'There are potatoes aplenty here,' he said. 'Tell me if you want some more. It would have been nice to see your friend again.'

At those words, I suddenly regained my senses. 'Sir, please may I use your phone to make a call? There's somebody whose number both my friend and I know. I want to ask him about my friend's whereabouts.'

He nodded and showed me his landline. It was an old-fashioned rotary phone, and the numbers were worn with use. Too hasty in dialling the numbers, I had to start again. I pressed the receiver tight against my ear, hoping and hoping I would hear Young-min's voice at the other end instead of Mr Shin's. But from the other end, all I could hear was Chinese. The old man listened for a moment and told me that the phone had been switched off. Over the next hour, I told the old man what had happened since we'd left his house. Then I tried to call again. There was only the same recorded message.

When the old man heard that the men at the church in Yanji had attempted to report us to the authorities, he became furious, as if it was he himself who had been insulted. He was extremely apologetic and said it had been his fault to make the recommendation. We sat in silence. He had lived on his own for some years now. He pointed to a picture of his wife on the wall, and the old photograph showed a smiling woman in her mid-fifties. Below that there was a small television set and the rotary telephone. In the small room beyond, through the open sliding door, I could see traditional wooden furniture and a sewing machine. Just as the old man had told me, his home hadn't changed since his wife died.

'Stay at my place until you can contact your friend,' he offered. 'In fact, just as you made your way here, he might find his way here too. Then you can be together again.'

'Thank you. I'm sure we will find each other in the next day or so. Until then, please let me help you around the house. Ask anything of me.'

The next day, I tried Mr Shin's number again as soon as I woke up. To my great relief, I could hear a ringing tone instead of the recorded message.

Mr Shin picked up the phone. 'Hello?'

'Hello, it's me. I'm calling you because I lost Young-min.'

'Make it quick,' he replied. 'Where are you now?'

I didn't understand why Mr Shin was speaking in such an urgent tone. 'I'm in Longjing. Do you know if—?'

He cut me short. 'Listen to me now. You have to leave there at once.'

'Why? Has something happened to Young-min?'

'Trust me, you have to get out of there. If you're at that house you went to with Young-min, hang up and call me from somewhere else.'

I said, 'I can't call you from anywhere else, and I don't have any coins. Please, tell me what happened. I need to know before I try to make my way alone.'

Mr Shin explained: 'Young-min came to me two mornings ago. It must have been several hours after you'd both parted. The authorities suddenly arrived and began to search the village, so he had to run. He came all the way here to Yanji, and do you know what he said to me? You won't believe it. He asked me to take him to his cousin's house!'

I replied, 'So, you said no, right? Where's that stupid boy now?'

He said, 'I had to take him back to my place, because he said you would call my number. At my flat, he kept demanding that I take him to his cousin's house. In the end, I was able to make contact with Young-min's uncle through my friend who works at the local broadcasting station.

'The uncle was much more sympathetic than the cousin, perhaps because he's a closer blood relative. He said his nephew would never murder anyone, and that he really wanted to see Young-min.

'When Young-min heard the news, he left the house and didn't come home even when it'd turned dark. Then yesterday, around four in the afternoon, I received a call from Uncle Chang-yong's wife. She said that the authorities had come and taken Chang-yong away, claiming that you two had just been arrested.

'That got me scared, so I turned my phone off and packed. We're ready to move. I switched the phone back on briefly this morning and that's when you called. You've got to get out of there. If Young-min really has been arrested, it's only a matter of time before they work out where you are.'

My hands were clammy with sweat when I put the receiver down. I was sure that the door would swing open at any moment, and that soldiers would come rushing in, just as I had feared when Young-min and I were hiding together.

The rays of morning sun that pierced the windows looked as sharp as silver blades. Where could I go from here? I had no money and the snow outside came up to my ankles. There was no way I could survive away from the village. For a fleeting moment, I was too frightened even to open my eyes, and I thought that surrender was the best option. I opened my eyes when a thought occurred to me – Chang-yong had received $700 from us. I had given that amount to him not merely to transport us a couple of miles, but because I had mistakenly believed that the road to South Korea would be easy after coming into town. Of course, it was embarrassing to ask for the return of money I had already given someone, but what did that matter in my current situation?

First, I called Mr Shin to find out Chang-yong's phone number. When his wife answered, I said, 'Hello. Is Chang-yong home yet?'

At first, Chang-yong's wife, in a terrified voice, asked who I was. When I explained that I was the one who had given him the $700, she began to complain, almost in tears. 'What's happening?' she asked. 'The officers said he'd be back home by morning, but he's still not home. If you're going to escape, you should have gone far away from here! Why on earth have you been sitting round in Yanji?'

I asked, 'Did the officers really say that my friend had been arrested too?'

'That's what they said yesterday. Why would they drag away my poor husband without any evidence? It's all right if they interrogate him, but if they fine him, we're ruined! They'll ask us to pay back twenty times the amount we received, and we'll be left out on the streets with nothing!'

I wanted to curse at her. So preoccupied was she with the fine she might have to pay that she'd volunteered not a single word of concern for my friend, whose life was in jeopardy. As I struggled to compose myself, I realised that I had an excuse to sink as low as I needed to resort to blackmail for survival. 'Hey, listen to me,' I told her. 'My friend doesn't know that I gave your husband any money, because I was the one who gave it to him. So you don't need to worry. But if I were to be caught, I can't guarantee that I'll keep my mouth shut. So that I can escape far away, promise Mr Shin that you will give him $100. Tell him you will transfer the money to him right away.'

She didn't hesitate for a second and promised to do as I'd asked there and then. When I checked three times that she would keep her word, she said she would swear by her entire family wealth, which consisted of two oxen. That was enough.

'Sir, I'll come back to repay you if I make it to South Korea,' I said to the old man as he walked me all the way to the road out of the village. Then I put my sunglasses back on.

A few hours later, I met Mr Shin at Yanji Station. He took out 800 yuan, the equivalent of about US$120, and handed it to me. I wasn't sure how much two oxen were worth, but Chang-yong's wife had kept her word. He looked at me awkwardly as he said, 'I know my uncle and his wife very well. She's not the kind of woman to just hand over a large sum of money like this. You know, I was born with a knack for getting hunches right. I'm sure you'll make it to South Korea.'

I put 400 yuan in my pocket and placed the rest of the money back in Mr Shin's hand. I said, 'If Young-min comes to find you, please deliver this money to him. And please, keep your phone switched on!'

I got on a bus to Shenyang and collapsed onto the furthest seat at the back. The bus was half-full, but most of the passengers were sitting near the front. So much had happened in such a short time. I wanted to close my eyes and rest my mind for just a few minutes, but everything I had seen and heard in the past few days rushed into my head. Young-min's face was the strongest image, and it took me completely by surprise. Why was I planning to run away when my friend had been captured? We had crossed the river together with a resolve to kill ourselves if we faced repatriation. What had gone wrong? Why was Young-min so set on going to his cousin's house, when he knew it was surrounded?

I went over everything Mr Shin had told me from the very beginning. Chang-yong had been taken by the authorities, who claimed that the pair of us had already been arrested. They'd said that he would be returned home after a night of questioning. But they had made no demands for the fine Chang-yong needed to pay, although there would have been no stronger grounds for his arrest than their knowledge about the money. In fact, Chang-yong's wife had returned $100 to me so as to send the secret of the other six hundred far away from her and her husband. And I was sure that Young-min would not have been so reckless as to go to his cousin's house. He would have first kept watch on the house from afar – he had that sort of introverted patience.

Out of the bus window, I could see enormous fields and large heaps of grain piled here and there. As we passed each one, I repeated to myself how everything would turn out well, and how we would be reunited. When the bus crossed a wide river, I stopped repeating my prayer and experienced a moment of relief. I looked up at the blue sky, where there was the silhouette of a bird. Seeing the speck, I dearly wished for a bird's eye view and a bird's heart too, so that I might look down on the earth and all its trivial suffering with indifferent contempt, and soar on through the air.

Only then did I become curious about the contents of the small bag that the old man at Longjing had given me when we said goodbye. Inside were six wheat rolls. Reasoning that an empty stomach would only exacerbate my anxiety, I put a piece of bread in my mouth, and decided not to use any of the money that remained after purchasing my bus ticket. How long could I survive on the remaining five wheat rolls? One week, perhaps. I would have to make it to South Korea in that time in order to stay alive. And, to do that, I needed to get some sleep.

When I opened my eyes at the sound of a loud Chinese voice ringing from the bus speakers, I was shocked to find myself on another planet altogether. Outside the window was a sea of city lights. This world, brightly lit up by electricity, made me reflect on the boldness of mankind in defying nature's darkness. In the blackness of North

Korea, the only places that had electricity twenty-four hours a day were the areas around statues of Kim Il-sung.

In North Korea, light was power, and this display of power was most evident at night. Changwang-dong of Joong-gu Area in Pyongyang, where I worked, along with the military buildings and residences at Seokchong-dong of Seoseong Area, were literally the beacons of the city: if they remained unlit for more than three hours, then the other areas of Pyongyang could not expect to have any electricity the following night. I could not comprehend how Chinese reforms could lead to a daily increase in the country's prosperity when they were even wasting electricity in such an obvious way. The overwhelming world of lights made me feel that I had the whole expanse of China's wealth before my eyes.

Speeding towards the centre of all this made me excited, as if I were entering into a bold new world. Yet I also wished I had waited a little longer for Young-min, so that he might see these lights with me. This regret pulsed through me.

When the bus stopped in the city, I became very aware of the police who would be on patrol. I dreaded the thought of getting out of the vehicle again, and peered through the dirty bus window to reassure myself that they weren't out there waiting for me.

The large clock in the bus terminal showed that it was just after midnight, so the journey had taken some six hours. I stretched my cramped arms as I climbed down from the bus. In the village I'd set out from, both sky and earth were pitch dark, but in this city where even night was like day, I felt I could seek shelter anywhere.

Yet the police were here too, a group of them, dressed in their military-green uniforms. I lowered my outstretched arms and walked quickly away. The first brightly lit shop I entered was a large room full of computers. To my relief, the people in this room were intent on their screens and didn't notice me at all. There were empty seats, and I sat down in one near the corner. Facing the computer's blank screen, I vacantly watched the others in the room and then fell asleep.

It didn't seem as if I'd been asleep long when someone shook me hard. I woke up in surprise to see a woman with shocking pink hair yelling as she stepped away from me. It was because she'd seen the five rolls fall from my lap when I'd stirred in my sleep. Those rolls were my lifeline, but she looked at them with disgust as if they were lumps of shit. As I bent down to pick them up, she cursed at my back in Chinese. I didn't dare respond, but snapped back at her under my breath in turn: 'In North Korea, girls like you would be dragged off to a prison camp just for the colour of your hair!'

I stumbled outside in a daze. It seemed as though I had only been in the shop for a brief moment, but it was already daylight outside. When I turned to look at the sign of that strange shop, it read in large English letters: 'PC'. If I needed to find another place to spend the night, I would find another 'PC' shop, I thought to myself – but one without the danger of pink-haired women.

As I walked the streets, my footsteps felt much lighter than when I was in Yanji. It was fairly crowded, and I felt I would not attract attention walking alone. Coming face to face with huge advertising hoardings that covered the whole sides of buildings, I could not but stop and stare. It was the most exotic scene I'd ever witnessed. In North Korea, it's inconceivable for there to exist a display more impressive than the iconography of the Kim cult. Every available space is taken by Kim murals or slogans of loyalty, and there is nowhere else for the eye to rest.

This was the first major city in China I had come to, and the scale and extravagance of it was breathtaking. One billboard depicted a couple kissing, each with a drink in their hands. In another, a woman was wearing nothing but her underwear. But as I wandered into a part of town where the billboards grew smaller, anxiety set in. Near the bus station, there had been Korean signs dotted here and there, but the further I walked, the less Korean there was. By the time that all the signs I saw were in Chinese, I came to a halt. I was astonished to learn from an ethnic Korean-Chinese passer-by that I had arrived not in Shenyang, but in Changchun. I had not realised that there was a stopover at Changchun, where I should have taken another bus on to Shenyang.

Thanking the man who had kindly given me instructions on how to make my way back to the bus terminal, I began to retrace my steps. I could now vaguely remember that Mr Shin had said something about changing buses in Changchun to get to Shenyang. But my head had been full of worry for Young-min, and nothing else had mattered.

I called Mr Shin again from a phone booth. 'Hello! I'm in Changchun. Is there any news about Young-min or Chang-yong?'

He replied, 'Well, congratulations on making it there on your own! Don't worry about Uncle Chang-yong. He's safely home. You know that Chinese woman you met right after you crossed the river? He was being investigated because of her report – nothing more. From what he says, it seems as if Young-min hasn't been caught yet. Anyway, Changchun is still quite close to here so it's better for you to go further, and Shenyang is safer. If your friend calls, I'll send him to Shenyang.'

I had thought of 400 yuan as a large sum, but after the bus fare from Yanji to Changchun, and then from there to Shenyang, I found I had only 3 yuan left. At least I had been able to afford the bus ticket to Shenyang, I thought, and tried to comfort myself with this. There was nothing I wanted more than for Young-min to make it to Shenyang. Perhaps he would appear at my side tomorrow.

I decided to test fate with a toss of a coin. If the face with the number showed, he would be here by tomorrow. After I'd tossed it up and before lifting my palm from it, the coin felt solid, containing our future. *Please let it show the number*, I prayed while holding the coin up to my forehead. But when I looked at the coin, it was the other side. I tried tossing it several more times, but the coin refused to comfort me.

I put the coin back into my pocket and thought of how a lot of things had not turned out as I'd thought they might, only for them to turn out better. Perhaps the flip side of this coin was plotting such a fate for me. I didn't toss the coin again, fearing that touching it might destroy that power.

As I got on a bus for Shenyang, I could not contain my excitement at the thought that Young-min might be safe. Even a man in beige clothes sitting in front of me on the bus seemed to look like Young-min from behind. In my optimism, I decided that I could afford to eat two more bread rolls. I looked at the remaining three and convinced myself that there were now fewer days to wait before I would see Young-min again.

As I idly played the piano on the back of the empty seat in front me, my fingers paused. In the netted pocket of the seat before me, there was a tourist leaflet printed in Korean. I flipped through it, and almost shouted out loud when I noticed the phone number of the South Korean consulate in Shenyang. I looked at it again, focusing carefully. Yes, it really was the number for the South Korean consulate. Had it been this easy to reach South Korea?

I had the sensation that my chest would explode with excitement, and squeezed my hands together as hard as I could to get rid of the excess energy. Why had Mr Shin not given us a phone number that was available so publicly? Granted, he was a country boy, but why had we sophisticated Pyongyang city boys not thought of this ourselves? I grew impatient to get off the bus. Unlike the trip to Changchun, this journey to Shenyang seemed excruciatingly slow.

Finding the consulate in Shenyang would not be difficult, and now there seemed no reason to leave the buns uneaten. I finished them off. As I crumpled the plastic bag in my hand, I was happy. All the suffering that I carried with me had become trivial. The bus's four wheels turned slowly on solid earth while my thoughts raced ahead.

Only after dark did the bus eventually crawl into the Shenyang bus terminal. Thankfully, the driver opened the door as soon as the bus came to a halt. I was the first to get off, having made my way to the front as we slowed to a stop. I ran about in search of a phone box. It seemed as if I had been rushing about like this ever since crossing the river, but only now did I feel that I was directing my own steps.

When I found a phone box and shut the door behind me, the sound of my breathing filled the booth. As I pressed a coin into the slot and dialled the number, my hands shook wildly. After I pressed the last number, it began to ring. I felt that someone would be waiting for my call on the end of this line.

'Hello.' A man answered in Korean. I held my breath.

'Hello. This is the South Korean consulate, is that right?'

'Yes it is, who's speaking?'

'Thank you, thank you.' I bowed my head towards the phone in a dream-like state, in amazement that the South Korean consulate had answered my call.

'Who's speaking?' the man asked again.

I took a deep breath and then spoke as courteously as if I had been stood in front of their national flag. 'I've come from North Korea. A friend has come with me. I wish to request asylum in South Korea.' There was no response, and I realised that the line had gone dead.

I banged the receiver several times. The stupid phone had decided to break at the most crucial moment, and I hurriedly went in search of another phone box. At the same time, tears streamed down my cheeks. South Korea had just heard my request for asylum. I had made it to the end of my journey. As I wiped my face with my fists, I could see three phone booths on a main road outside the station area. The first one looked beaten up, so I went into the newer-looking booth of the other two.

'Hello!' This time I spoke first.

'Yes, who am I speaking to?'

'I was the one who called earlier. I would like to request asylum in South Korea. I have my identification documents with me. The authorities have framed us for murder and are looking for us. But we are not murderers.'

'Hello, listen now. This phone is not very safe, do you understand?' I glanced all around me.

'It's difficult to get to South Korea from here,' the voice continued. 'At the South Korean consulate in Shenyang, China does not allow visas to be issued to North Korean refugees. If you would like to go to South Korea, you have to get to the South Korean Embassy in Beijing. We can't help you here.'

We can't help you here.

But we were both Koreans, he and I!

'How do I find the Embassy in Beijing? Please help me, I don't know where to go from here, and I have a friend in Yanji on the run with me too,' I pleaded.

'All the other refugees make it on their own. How can you expect us to help with such basic details? I can't stay on the phone for long, I'll have to hang up now.'

With those words, the line went dead. The flat dial tone felt like the whoosh of a bullet about to enter my skull. For a while, I stood there holding the receiver, unable to put it back in its cradle. Surely, the man I had just spoken to was a South Korean consulate employee, speaking in our language. Was there a chance that he had not understood my words? Perhaps I had rushed my explanation. Had I messed it all up after getting this far?

I fumbled in my pocket for another coin. I panicked that there might be nothing left, but I found a single yuan. It was not only my last coin, but also my last chance at life.

I dialled again. This time, I would explain my situation in detail. I would speak slowly, so the man at the other end would understand exactly what I was saying. The phone rang over ten times, but no one picked up. When the line went dead, I tried to get my coin back, but even the phone was indifferent and refused to return it.

I slid to the ground. I put my arms round my knees and leant forward, hiding my face in my hands. I could feel with my fingers the blood pumping hard through my temples. When I put my hands on the ground to lever myself up, my vision blurred. Although I strained my eyes and opened them as wide as I could, I saw nothing but darkness.

I knelt, breathing deeply in and out. As my sight gradually returned through thick fog, infinite spots of light swirled in front me. The painful and nauseating swirling gradually slowed and my sight began to clear. I stood up carefully.

Leaving the phone booth, I resigned myself to a miserable end, in anticipation of being pushed off the edge of the world. There were no more tears, and I realised that tears are only shed when we know there is another's hand to wipe them.

Dazed before the blackness of night, I was a mere speck of dust tumbling beneath foreign skies. Impoverished North Korea, surviving on Chinese aid, could afford to send its agents on the rampage with the cooperation of the Chinese authorities. But South Korea, an economic ally of China that invested in Chinese reform, seemed to have no will or authority to rescue one of its own. Did I have a homeland at all?

I looked back at the phone booth, because if I didn't at least fix my fruitless gaze on it, both my body and my hopes might collapse into nothing. I had said I was requesting asylum but the employee had told me the phone wasn't safe. Yes, he would have been cold to me on purpose, aware that we were being listened to.

He said that I had to go to the Embassy in Beijing. I had come all the way to Shenyang on my own, and of course I could make it to Beijing. When I was reunited with Young-min, we'd go straight to the Embassy in Beijing. I also told myself that although I might be penniless, I was in a city and not some remote village in the countryside. As for food, it would be more plentiful in the urban areas than in the countryside. Surely I could also manage to borrow a phone to check in with Mr Shin when I could. I looked for a 'PC' sign like the one I remembered from Changchun, and I spent my first night in Shenyang in an Internet café.

The next morning, armed with renewed determination, I went in search of somewhere where they might let me use their phone without paying. I needed to look polite, and I wasn't so near the border with North Korea any more, so I felt I could do without my sunglasses. Mr Shin was probably right, wearing them might make me look strange. But finding a phone I could use for free was not as easy as I thought. In the reformed economy of China, everything required money. I noticed several people who were charging people to use their landlines out on the street, and I had no courage to approach any of them. I decided that, as in Yanji and Longjing, the most helpful thing would be to find someone who spoke Korean. Where could I start looking? It was not as if I could easily tell apart ethnic Koreans from Chinese.

I walked to a street that was relatively busy. It was an entrance to a market alley. To my right there were clothes stalls, and to the left, there was a row of small restaurants. As it was too crowded, it was awkward to stand there, so I walked to a part of the street that seemed less congested.

I then called out in a low voice to each passer-by. When a man walked by, I called out, 'Sir!' in Korean; when a woman passed me, I called out 'Madam!' If they were Chinese, they would ignore me; but surely Korean speakers would turn their heads to see who had called out to them?

For the rest of the morning, I stood on that street calling out to each passer-by. I held my ground, calling out courteously, although my body wanted to collapse to the ground with hunger. By four in the afternoon, a sense of urgency came over me. If the sun were to set again with no result, I might become weaker in the dark.

2 | A FATEFUL MEETING WITH WANG CHO-RIN

I RAISED my eyes. About twenty metres away, a young woman was coming towards me. Her haircut was what we would call 'bucket-style' back home, because it looked as if the barber had put a bucket on a woman's head and cut around it. In North Korea, women were not permitted to grow their hair or let it down, as long hair symbolised the corruption of a Capitalist society. Only female dancers were allowed to have long hair, because it was part of the traditional look. But even they had to keep their hair tied back in their everyday lives. A lot of North Korean women permed their hair because it made short hair look better. Otherwise they just wore it plain.

The woman coming towards me with the bucket-style haircut was of medium height, and wearing leather boots. Her jacket was yellow with a black stripe across the shoulders. Her handbag was in brown chequered cloth. In terms of her clothing, even her handbag, she looked no different from the hundreds of other young Chinese women who had passed me by without so much as turning their heads.

As I had done with every previous greeting, I promised myself that this would be the last one. I waited for her. If I called out when a pedestrian was facing me, even if they didn't understand what I was saying, they would usually respond if only to check what they had just heard. So I spoke as soon as she was within distance.

'Madam!'

The young woman stopped and turned to look at me, blinking her large eyes, as if to ask whether I had spoken to her. 'Do you need help with something?' the young woman asked, in what was unmistakeably Korean. Although it was the language I had desperately longed to hear, I didn't at first know how to respond.

'Do you need help with something?' she asked again.

'Yes, yes!' I replied a little too earnestly.

'Well, how can I help you?' She even took a couple of steps towards me. As she drew nearer, gratitude filled me. The very fact that she was interested in helping me seemed to confirm that I was, after all, a human being.

'Do you need directions?' she asked.

As she stood facing me, I feared that she might be put off by my stench. I had not washed for days. 'Please promise me that you will hear my story to the end,' I said.

She hesitated and frowned. Was she regretting that she had approached me? She looked me up and down very quickly, as if she might move away.

'I'm not a weirdo. It's just that I don't speak Chinese, so I've been looking for someone like you, madam.' If I wasn't being careful, I might easily have called her 'comrade'. 'Please, would you spare five minutes to hear me out?'

She glanced at her watch, as if to say I had exactly five minutes. 'Go ahead,' she said. 'I'll listen.'

'Thank you,' I replied.

I explained that I had crossed from North Korea and that I'd been evading the authorities. I left out the bit about being wanted for murder. I described how Young-min and I had lost each other, and ended by asking her for directions to reach the South Korean Embassy in Beijing on foot.

'On foot? Why, you can catch a bus to Beijing!' She seemed surprised, but appraising my situation from my appearance, she went on, 'You can't possibly walk all the way to Beijing! It's too far.'

'Is there another way to get to South Korea?'

She took a step forward and began to explain, as if to reward me for having put faith in her charity. She said that most North Koreans went to the Embassy in Beijing rather than to the consulate in Shenyang. She said that if I went via the city of Dalian, the journey might be made easier by the fact that many there spoke Korean. If I made some money in Dalian, perhaps I might get hold of a forged Chinese passport, and enter South Korea with that.

'How do you know all this?' I asked in amazement.

'My father who lives in Helong, he's helped many like you.'

Hearing that, I found myself telling her about the people I had met between Yanji and Shenyang: Chang-yong, Mr Shin, and the old man in Longjing. The woman stepped even closer to me.

'Do you have family in Shenyang?' she asked.

I smiled awkwardly, and shook my head.

'Then where will you spend the night? Have you eaten?' I could not bring myself to say that I had already eaten, yet neither could I bring myself to tell a woman that I had not eaten for two days. I started gesturing with my hand, looking for an excuse, but she had already taken out her mobile phone. Was she about to report me to the authorities? I looked at her phone and listened anxiously as she spoke in rapid Chinese, which I could not understand.

When she folded the phone shut, her expression was brighter. 'I have two vouchers for a sauna-motel. I was going to go with my fiancé, but I've just called him, and he's happy for you to have them. Would you like to stay there tonight? It's not far from here.'

Lost in the thought that the girl before me appeared to be just as kind as the father she'd mentioned, I didn't answer.

She continued, 'You can wash and sleep there. As I said, it's not far.'

She turned towards the road as if to say, 'Let's go.' I felt awkward as she drew closer to my fugitive's stench. We walked slowly because I tried to keep one step behind her, while she slowed down to keep pace with me.

'Thanks for helping me like this,' I said. 'May I ask you something?'

'Yes,' she replied.

'You said you have two vouchers for the sauna. You said you were going to go with your "fiancé". Is that the name of your friend?'

'Oh, my fiancé!' She grinned. 'It means we're engaged. We're going to get married. Here in China, the one you are going to marry is your "fiancé". I guess it's like the North Korean equivalent of … hmm! I'm not sure.'

Although I was a writer who lived with words, I had never thought there could be such a special word in Korean to refer to the person you were going to marry.

She continued, 'Anyway, he says you can have both vouchers. Which means you can stay there for two nights. Isn't he sweet?'

I wanted to say that they were both sweet. 'He's a great man! Thank you! Please send him my best regards. May I ask your name? I want to be able to remember your help.'

'Me? Wang Cho-rin.'

'Wang Cho Ing?'

She laughed as I struggled to pronounce her name. She repeated each syllable slowly, and then laughed again. I had arrived at an oasis of intelligible language and was so grateful for it, but she did not notice my astonishment and spoke in Korean as if it were the most natural thing to do in China. I wanted to say something to please her.

'Let me guess your age. I'll get it right,' I said.

'You think so?' she replied. Pointing to a food stall by the side of the road, she said, 'If you get it right, I'll buy you a lamb kebab from that stall.'

I became very serious. It was the first and only time in my life that I wanted to guess a woman's age correctly in exchange for food. I must have really wanted it because while I meant to say 'twenty-six', I muttered 'lamb kebab' instead. I blushed. Although she wore only light make-up, her skin glowed radiantly, and I guessed that she would be in her mid-twenties.

'Twenty-five.'

'Hmm? You think so?'

'Well, how old are you?' I asked.

'Twenty-seven.'

I was devastated but Cho-rin had a good heart. In return for my guessing she was younger than she actually was, she rushed off and bought not just one, but four lamb kebabs. In fact, she kept one for herself, and offered me the three others. The smell of cooked meat overwhelmed me.

Her kindness awoke in me the notion that, however weak-willed we might grow, we are all still entitled to life. In such a world as this, no misfortune could be random. And because of the vouchers that Cho-rin gave me, I was able to wash with warm water that night.

As I was sat in a tub overflowing with hot water, I wondered where Young-min might be. I so wished he were with me. The baths here were much bigger and there were more people than there had been at the bathhouse Mr Shin had taken us to in Yanji. Some people were eating as they walked around, and the noise of chatter and water was so loud that nobody noticed I was there.

Scrubbing off my fugitive's dirt off with orange-scented soap, I mulled over what had been said between Cho-rin and me during our encounter. The most memorable thing was that she referred to the man she was going to marry as her fiancé. In the institutionalism of life in North Korea, anyone who was older than you or ranked higher at work was called *dongji* (comrade), and everyone else who was your equal was *dongmu* (comrade-friend). These were our comrades in loyal obedience. With the hierarchy of respect based on age and seniority so clear-cut in everyday life, it felt like a natural form of respect – and not a political or legal thing – to be loyal and obedient to the Leader.

Even among lovers it was the same. Women addressed all men as *dongji*, and men addressed all women as *dongmu*. It was considered subversive to refer to your lover by any other address or title, as they seemed to do here in China. Unconditional love was reserved exclusively for Kim Il-sung and Kim Jong-il, whose portraits were always displayed on the badge that everyone wore. If anyone were to place another human above them in any way, they would be reduced to second priority. Strange as it may seem to outsiders, it was unthinkable to us that we should love anyone more than Kim Il-sung and Kim Jong-il. I had lived my life according to the totalitarian lexicon of a self-serving despot, who encroached on our most intimate emotions in order to steal them away from the individual. So I could not stop marvelling at the beauty of the word 'fiancé' as taught to me by Cho-rin.

After my bath, I opened my locker to retrieve my clothes. As my eyes fell on my precious bundle of handwritten poems from Pyongyang, rescued for me by Young-min from the shed near Chang-yong's mother-in-law's house, I felt awful for having run off to Shenyang, thinking only of my own survival.

I wandered around the motel in search of a phone. Given that this was a day on which I had been offered two nights of shelter by a woman I had met by chance on the street, I wondered whether I might strike lucky twice. Perhaps if I called Mr Shin, he would have good news for me. There were two pay phones in a corner of the motel foyer. I sat below them, as if a one-yuan coin might drop on me from heaven, and eventually fell asleep with my head on my knees.

'Hello?'

When I woke, it was the next morning. Someone was prodding me gently and I closed my eyes tighter. I didn't have the courage to open them, because I was afraid to find myself in the grip of the authorities. But when I realised that the voice belonged to a woman, not a man, I was reassured by the thought that it might be one of the female employees at the motel, and sat up.

Still, I didn't dare turn my head towards the person who'd spoken. Ever since crossing the Tumen River, I had stopped being the first to look another in the eye.

'You're the man I met yesterday, aren't you?'

I looked up and could not trust my eyes when I saw her. It was Wang Cho-rin, whom I had believed I would never meet again. It looked like she had just bathed, as her hair was still wet.

'How did you find me?' I exclaimed. In my joy at this surprise meeting with a friend on Chinese soil, I didn't realise that I was shouting out in a loud Pyongyang accent.

'Ta-daa!' Cho-rin grinned as she opened a plastic container full of hot white buns, but at that moment I was truly more delighted to see her than the food.

'How did you find me?' I repeated. 'Did you come with your – fiancé?'

'No, he's got other things to do. I came to bring you something to eat. I was passing by this area anyway and I thought if I didn't bring you something, you might not eat at all today. I did well, right?'

I wanted to give her something in return as she handed me a bun. I dearly longed for the money in my rucksack, which the authorities had taken when we were hiding near the house of Chang-yong's mother-in-law.

'I told him everything,' she continued. 'I boasted about how I was able to help someone like you.'

As she said these words I worried over what she meant by 'everything'. I glanced up and caught sight of the veins on her pale neck. Her delicate skin looked translucent, a sheet of glass that seemed to reveal her kindness. Every time she smiled, her eyes closed in the shape of two small crescent moons like innocence itself. But, in her small soft face, her upturned nose hinted at an inner defiance that might sting like a bee if provoked.

'What did your fiancé say? Is he Chinese?' I asked.

She waved at the box of buns. 'I've already eaten, you have them all. Oh, what did you just ask me? Yes, he's Han Chinese. He said it was very good of me to help you, and so he's taking me shopping on Sunday! He really hates Kim Jong-il too. I bet most Chinese hate him, if only because of his pot belly.'

I laughed. I then wondered about their relationship. 'Do many Han Chinese marry ethnic Koreans?'

'Yes, why not? While they're the dominant ethnic group and we're only a minority among fifty-six others, we're known to be among the most hard-working. Plus, with increased ties to South Korea, more of us have become wealthy. I will admit, though, that it's not as common for Han Chinese women to marry an ethnic Korean man, as it's harder for a man like that to establish himself on a new social ladder. But it happens a lot the other way. You know what? We Korean women are good with housework, and the Han Chinese men know it!'

I was grateful for the food, but even more for her companionship. I wanted to do something for her and looked round to see if I could get her a cup of water. But she beat me to it. 'Oh, let me get you something to drink,' she said. As I watched her hurry off to get me water, I became convinced that an ordinary, domestic life would soon be granted to me. A moment later, Cho-rin returned, walking carefully with a paper cup in each hand. I leapt to my feet to greet her. We found a bench and I sat down, and Cho-rin wiped her wet hand on her shorts before sitting down next to me.

As she bent down, I glimpsed her pale cleavage and quickly looked away. I felt I had done something disrespectful to someone who had offered me help. I had been about to take a bite out of a bun, but I put it back down. I was reassured a little when I heard her press the keypad of her mobile phone, but I still could not face making eye contact with her.

'Eat your bun. It'll go cold,' she said, then added more playfully, 'Can I ask you something? I heard that there is cannibalism in North Korea because of hunger. Is that true?' 'There were rumours of that kind of thing from time to time, but neither I nor any of my friends actually saw it happen. But I did once witness a mother trying to sell her daughter in the marketplace.'

'Really? Her daughter? You saw that with your own eyes?'

It was 1999, on a day that had started out just like any other. I was walking past Dongdaewon Area on my way somewhere. Even though it was situated in Pyongyang, Dongdaewon was an impoverished district where the city's poorest people were concentrated. The market was shabbier than most, and vendors who couldn't afford the rent grasped in desperation at passers-by. One of them approached me and held out some bread.

'Please buy a packet of bread for 100 won. Please, help me!'

Her wrinkled hand was swollen and split in many places as she held out a packet containing five little buns each the size of a baby's fist. I just wanted to give her 100 won (worth around 10 US cents) and not take the packet, but I realised that I had left my wallet in my other coat at home.

'I'm sorry, I left my wallet at home. Really.'

She might have pleaded with me one more time, but instead she shook her head from side to side with disdain as she looked me up and down, taking in my well-dressed appearance. It didn't help that I was wearing a formal suit and tie.

I wanted to get away from the embarrassing situation as quickly as I could. But just then, several people ran past, one of them bumping into me. A throng of people was gathering up ahead, to my annoyance. I had wanted to pass through quickly, because the distinctive smell of the marketplace revolted me. Meat and fish that had gone off in the scorching heat were still on display, with vendors trying to keep the flies away with their fly swats. The ground was unpaved, and food waste and sewage pooled on the muddy earth. The stench of body odour and human excrement added to the other smells, and I had to try hard to keep myself from throwing up.

'Can I get through, please? I have to be on my way.'

I tried to make my way past but the crowd was becoming so tightly packed together that every step I took seemed to push the whole mob along. When I got to a spot where I could at least see the ground beneath my feet, my eyes settled on the sight in front of me before I could wipe the sweat off my forehead.

In the square where all the buyers and sellers usually gathered, there stood a woman and a young girl, like prisoners about to be shot at a public execution. I stiffened with disgust when I saw what was written on the piece of paper hanging from the girl's neck. She looked to be about seven years old. The note read: 'I sell my daughter for 100 won.'

The woman standing next to her, who seemed to be her mother, had her head hung low. I'd often heard of cases where a mother would abandon her child or give it away, but never had I come across someone who was selling her own child for as little as 100 won.

The other onlookers, thinking the same thought, were hurling curses at her.

'That bitch is out of her head!'

'You cunt! Even if you're starving, how can you sell your own daughter?'

'She looks as pretty as a whore, but her soul is rotten.'

'What scum you see nowadays.'

An old man asked the girl in a loud voice, 'Child, is that woman really your mother? You can tell the truth; we're here to help. Is she really your mother?'

I watched the girl's lips. As she hesitated, shouts rang out from here and there in the crowd. When someone shouted, 'Everyone, be quiet! Let's hear what the girl has to say!' even the middle-aged man standing next to me, who kept scratching at different parts of his body, stopped what he was doing. The girl mumbled an answer while clutching at the woman's clothes.

'She *is* my mother.'

Her mother? And that mother was selling her daughter for 100 won? The circle of onlookers grew more agitated.

'Tut-tut. Poor child!'

'Hey bitch, if you're going to sell your child, price her right!'

'Even a dog goes for 3000 won! Is your daughter worth less than that?'

'Who's going to buy a girl when no one can even feed themselves?'

'Absolutely, maybe if she begged someone to take her daughter away, she might get some sympathy.'

'Stupid woman! What are you going to do with 100 won?'

The woman, strangely, did not react. With her eyes cast to the ground, she didn't move an inch. This seemed to irk the crowd even more, until someone yelled, 'Say something, you stupid whore! Hey, are you deaf and dumb or something?'

The insults soon turned into gossiping murmurs.

'She's deaf?'

'Hey, she's deaf!'

It seemed to me as well that there was something wrong with the woman. Another voice rang out from the mob asking the girl whether she had a father, as if resigned to the fact that it was no use cursing at a deaf and dumb woman.

'No, I don't have a father anymore. He didn't have enough food …'

The girl mumbled her answer again, then suddenly looked up and screamed, 'Stop saying bad things about my mother! They say she's only got a few more days to live! She's going to die!'

The child's shriek pierced the air. Some began to tut, as if to acknowledge that waiting for a certain death was worse than death itself. Looking at the mother and daughter in that place, I felt sure that we were living in the end days of the world. An old woman near me began to cry. As she wiped her tears, she said that if the mother at least had a voice, she would be able to grieve and to share her pain with others.

The deaf woman had a waxy look about her, as if she had already become a corpse, and there seemed to be no blood in her skeletal hands. The sleeves of her shirt and her trouser bottoms were thickly padded, patched over many times. The immaculate stitching was pathetic evidence of one human being's defiant struggle against poverty.

I was reminded of a saying that handicapped people were skilled with their hands. The child, taking after the mother, was pretty. Although her cheekbones stuck out, you could see that with a bit of flesh, she would be attractive. On her chin just beneath her lips, she had a beauty spot. My elders used to say that that if a girl had a mole where it was visible, it was bad luck. That was certainly the case here.

By this time, no more curses were being cast at the woman, only sympathetic murmurs.

'So how will the girl carry on after the mother dies?'

'If only there was a way for both to stay alive.'

'Maybe there's a relative who could take the girl in?'

A female market vendor, who looked as if she could not stand it any longer, took out 200 won and offered it to the mother. 'Missus, we're all struggling to make ends meet here,' she said. 'No one will take your daughter in. Here, take this.'

Others spoke out in agreement.

'She's right, take her money.'

'Go on, if you stay on the streets, it will only quicken your death. You've got to stay alive for your daughter.'

Whether it was because she couldn't understand, or because she felt patronised by this offer of charity, the mother kept her hands clenched and refused to take the money. The vendor tried to demonstrate to her that 200 won was worth more than 100 won, but the mother didn't budge. When the vendor tried to put the money in the daughter's hand instead, the mother angrily took it and stuffed the money back in the trader's pocket.

She then took the paper sign from her daughter's neck and hung it around her own.

'Clear the way! Clear the way!' Stern shouting and the blowing of a whistle began to draw nearer. It was a security agent in military uniform. Perhaps someone had notified him. He went straight to the mother and hit her on the shoulders with the palm of his hand. 'Are you out of your fucking mind? Do you think this is one of those rotten Capitalist societies where you can buy and sell human beings like slaves? Get out of here! Take off your fucking sign!' He snatched at the piece of paper and ripped it up. As the torn paper fell to the ground, the crowd became agitated again.

'Hey you, she's got a terminal disease. You should at least find out what's going on!' somebody shouted.

Encouraged by this, the anger of the others was stirred, and mocking voices began to call out.

'You think you're in charge just because you're with fucking security? What's the point of tearing up her sign?'

'Look at that arsehole, he looks like a fucking rat.'

'That son of a bitch is the kind of man who will sell off his own wife.'

The agent, absolutely furious, turned to identify the source of the insults.

Another voice rang out: 'What? Can't you see us? Open your fucking eyes!'

Spontaneously, the whole square rang with laughter. His face now red with fury, the agent began to take his anger out on the deaf woman. 'You're coming with me, you cunt!' he bellowed. 'How dare you sell your daughter and defy Socialism? You love money? Are you promoting Capitalism? Try eating bean rice, cunt.'

The young girl had begun to cry, but the man dragged at the woman's arm as if to break it. She stumbled and strained to hold her ground. The anger of the onlookers was at a climax, yet no one dared to take a step towards a man in military uniform. Then someone approached him and seized his arm. It was an officer, with a first lieutenant's stripes.

'I'll take the girl. That will solve it, right?'

'What?' The security agent turned towards the voice, about to strike its owner, but stopped as soon as he registered the officer's rank.

The lieutenant pulled the security agent away from the woman. He looked very strong. 'I receive military rations from the state,' he explained. 'I'm confident I can take responsibility for the girl. So here, take 100 won for her.' The officer's words revealed that he was not buying the daughter for 100 won, but taking on the role of motherhood. In order to make his point clear to the woman, he picked the girl up in his arms.

The mother reacted in the most unexpected way. After she had accepted the 100-won note from the lieutenant, she hesitated for a moment. Then she broke through the crowd and disappeared. The officer, confused, stood there with the girl still in his arms. Had the mother run off for fear that he might change his mind? If so, that was certainly stupid. But perhaps she was mentally ill, which would explain why she had tried to sell her daughter.

The onlookers made wild guesses. Suddenly, someone from the back shouted out, 'She's back! Make way! The mother's here!' The crowd made a narrow corridor for the returning woman, who was stumbling and out of breath. She was carrying bread, of the very kind that I had been offered just outside the marketplace.

Had she resolved to commit such a wretched act for that miserable packet of bread? Had she not even 100 won to give her daughter for a last meal, as a last act of motherhood?

To my astonishment the mother opened her mouth and began to wail, 'Forgive me! Forgive your mother! What a wretched woman I am! This is all I can give you before I go.' She knelt in front of her daughter, sobbing violently and putting pieces of bread into her daughter's mouth.

'She's not deaf and dumb!'

'She could hear us all along!'

'How much pain she must feel inside.'

Several in the crowd began to sob. Standing among them, I could not but cry with them.

BECOMING A PIANO TEACHER 3

I HAD finished speaking but Cho-rin's shoulders were still shaking. She wiped her wet hands on her robe and raised them up to her eyes again, wiping away more tears.

'How can Kim Jong-il call himself a great leader? He's a bad man.' She sipped some water and blew her nose.

'You did well to leave that country,' Cho-rin said. 'Why would you stay there?' She turned round to face me, patting her cheeks in embarrassment. 'I never cry. Really, I never do.'

Composing herself, she continued, 'How will you get to South Korea? Even North Korean refugees who make it as far as the Embassy in Beijing get arrested at the gate. You hear it on the news quite often. You'll have to find a safer route.'

She flicked her hair behind her ears, determined that we should work on the problem together. She would take care of Young-min's whereabouts by contacting Mr Shin, she said, but the immediate problem was my safety. I couldn't stay in the sauna-motel for ever, and each meal presented a problem in itself. She was not a single woman; she was engaged, and she could not be with me all the time. Whether in finding shelter, or travelling to South Korea, the problem was money. She suddenly looked up and asked, 'Is there something you can do to earn money?'

I said wryly that since I'd crossed the Tumen River, the only thing I was practised in was looking out for police and keeping under the radar. I added that I could play the piano, not that it would be of any use. But Cho-rin clapped her hands in delight.

'Really? You can play? You know, like, with both hands?'

Watching Cho-rin flail her arms like a drowning woman, I broke into a grin.

'Well, yes. Not well enough to play professionally, but I've played for friends.'

Cho-rin clapped her hands again and then looked at me in surprise as an idea occurred to her. Her uncle lived in the nearby Xita District, she explained, where there were many Korean-Chinese. In fact, he had been looking for a piano tutor for his son. He was quite wealthy and if I taught his son piano, I would have a place to stay and be able to earn some money on the side. The suggestion made sense to me. As well as being able to earn some money, the time I spent in Xita, also known as the 'Korea Town' of Shenyang, would surely help me find a way to get to South Korea.

Cho-rin pulled her phone out of her pocket and dialled her uncle's number straight away. She talked to him for over half an hour, blurting out entire sentences in Chinese whenever the conversation seemed to become more tense. When she finally slipped her phone away, I waved my hands dismissively and said, 'If he says no, it's fine. I need to leave China as soon as I can anyway.'

'No, it's all right! He says I'm to take you to his house tonight.'

In the few hours we had before the meeting, I tried to call Mr Shin several times with the money Cho-rin had given me. I used a public phone because if the Chinese authorities were tapping Mr Shin's phone, I didn't want Cho-rin's mobile number to come up. At around seven in the evening, I finally got through to Mr Shin.

He said that there was still no news from Young-min. When he heard from him, I said, he should stress that Young-min must not return to his cousin's house, but should instead travel to Shenyang. Mr Shin gave me his wife's mobile number, in case I might not be able to get through on his. He said that when I had established a way to reach South Korea safely, I should inform them, so that his wife could join me. I asked Mr Shin to please leave his phone connected, because I knew Young-min would be calling back.

That night, Cho-rin and I took a cab to her uncle's house. Instead of taking the main roads, we seemed to be going through lots of alleyways. Cho-rin explained that the driver was taking a short cut because it was rush hour, but the journey still took over twenty minutes. She paid the fare at the end. It seemed like a fortune: over 25 yuan.

At the entrance to a luxurious apartment building, Cho-rin turned to me and said, very seriously, as though my life depended on it, 'When my uncle asks, just say you play piano really well. He's not musical at all, so you don't have to worry. If you feel uncomfortable about playing, just say your hands hurt. You know how musicians don't play when their hands are injured – that sort of thing.'

The apartment was on the eighth floor. As Cho-rin had said, her uncle was indeed a wealthy man. The fittings and furnishings were expensive. Unlike Mr Shin's flat, which had a heated floor covered in old-fashioned linoleum, this house had a marble floor covered with areas of plush carpet. This was only the second private home I had seen in my life with a marble floor.

In North Korea, the most luxurious private homes were in Eundok Village in East Pyongyang, where Kim Jong-il's closest associates lived. Its surroundings were beautifully landscaped, with many trees and the Daedong River flowing nearby. As the residential area was said to have been constructed as a special favour from Kim Jong-il, it was named 'Eundok' (Korean for 'favour').

Director Im lived there, and I was often invited into his home. Eundok Village was encircled with electric fencing and patrolled by armed guards. There were six buildings within the compound, and the village had its own diesel generator to provide an uninterrupted electricity supply for its residents. All six buildings had four storeys and were the same rectangular shape and size. The ground floor consisted of garages, and the family apartments were from the first floor upwards. Only one generation of a family lived on each floor. The lifts were made by Mitsubishi in Japan. Director Im lived on the second floor of his building.

The lift doors on the second floor opened directly into his home. The hallway was full of bicycles, tennis rackets and assorted boxes. When you took your shoes off to enter the main living area you put them in a shoe cabinet that reached from the floor to the high ceiling. There was a main corridor in the middle of the apartment, and the doors to the rooms on either side of the corridor faced each other. The first large space was the living room, and the kitchen was at the far end of the corridor. There were two bathrooms, and a total of ten rooms excluding the bathrooms.

The walls of the living room were covered in framed photographs showing Director Im with Kim Il-sung or Kim Jong-il. Three mahogany display cabinets stood against one wall. The cabinets displayed state medals, gold watches and other special gifts, and the wine glasses into which Kim Il-sung or Kim Jong-il had poured wine for him. One of the items I found most interesting in Director Im's private study was a telephone. It was a black rotary phone with the red Workers' Party emblem in the centre of the dial. Director Im explained to me that ordinary phones weren't as reliable; and besides, they might be bugged. His hotline to Kim Jong-il was an old-fashioned model specially built for this purpose, he explained. Behind the phone there was a small antenna and a red LED light, which came on when there was a call from Kim Jong-il.

The apartments indeed could only have been built as a 'favour' from Kim Jong-il. Even in the kitchen, incongruously, there was a large chandelier with countless glittering crystals. Director Im explained that this was a high-end design specially imported from Germany. Each crystal had three hundred and twenty sides, he said, and – just as with diamonds – the cutting of the crystals had a crucial effect on how the light was reflected.

For me, though, the marble floor was the most striking feature of his home. Most ordinary North Korean homes had flooring that was little more than a version of wallpaper. Those who were better off had decorated linoleum flooring or wooden floorboards imported from China or Japan. But that wasn't what surprised me about the marble floor: before stepping into Director Im's home, I had thought that marble floors were an exclusively First Class construction feature, which could only be used in sanctified buildings directly related to Kim Il-sung and Kim Jong-il, such as the Revolutionary Rooms attached to all schools and workplaces. In these Rooms, students received ideological indoctrination appropriate to their age group so that, as they moved up each year from nursery all the way to the end of university, the entire span of Kim Il-sung and Kim Jong-il's formative years would be covered by the sessions. For working adults, various kinds of political and self-criticism sessions took place in the Rooms, the workplace equivalents being covered with photographs of Kim Jong-il conducting relevant on-site guidance. Revolutionary Rooms nationwide had to have their displays updated at least once every three years, for which purpose funds for the maintenance of the cult of Kim were set aside. When I asked about Director Im's marble floor, he crouched down and rapped it with his knuckles, explaining that it was made from pink Italian marble. Although Cho-rin's uncle also had a marble floor in his apartment, it was yellowish and looked as if it had lost its original colour. And instead of photographs taken with Kim Il-sung and Kim Jong-il, there were just three paintings hanging on the living-room wall. Although I couldn't see a stove, the apartment was comfortably heated. In each of the four corners of the living room there stood a traditional Chinese vase glazed in red and as tall as a grown man. Dark brown curtains were draped from the huge windows.

When I sat on the black leather couch, I sank into its cushioned depths.

'Nice to meet you,' said the uncle. He was a man in his early fifties, wearing a brown cardigan. His gaze was gentle, and his lips were plump. His accent was not very different from Mr Shin's. As he had already heard my story from Cho-rin, he seemed uninterested in hearing further details. That was a relief.

He asked, 'So you used to be a pianist?'

'Yes.' I tried to stick to a short answer at Cho-rin's earlier insistence, but uneasy with this exaggeration of my piano-playing skills, I felt I needed to provide more of an explanation: 'My music teacher was a famous violinist. Before he moved to North Korea during the Chinese Cultural Revolution, he was a member of the Shanghai Symphony Orchestra. I never trained to be a professional pianist, but I learned to play a little from my teacher.'

The uncle looked over at Cho-rin.

She said, 'Yes, that's right, his teacher was a famous musician. That's wonderful, isn't it? Just like you, Uncle, you're a successful businessman, but, to be honest, you can't claim to be a world-class business expert, now can you?' She glanced at her hands as she spoke, and looked a bit uncomfortable.

The uncle said, 'Yes, yes, Cho-rin, you've already said that. Well, can you play something for us?'

As he rose from the sofa, Cho-rin rushed to my side. 'Do you think you can play? Are you sure your hands are not injured? Uncle, can't you just take my word for it?'

'No, I can't.'

Cho-rin assumed a mock-angry expression. It was clear that they were very close, as he laughed heartily at her pretend petulance.

Passing a corridor that led off to the right of the living room, we entered a room in which there stood a black upright Yamaha. It looked far more impressive than the Yamaha we had had at home in

North Korea. I tested the pedals. My foot was met not with a smooth resistance, but some kind of scraping sensation. The piano seemed never to have been played.

I proceeded to play a scale from the lower notes all the way to the top. Fortunately, the instrument was not too much out of tune, although I was sure it had not been touched since it was bought. I explained that a piano was a living, breathing thing. If it were not looked after regularly, the changes in weather would affect its tone. I saw Cho-rin smiling broadly, looking pleased with my demonstration of expertise.

'Play us a song!' she urged me.

What should I play? I decided to go for an easy piece, 'Autumn Whispers' by Richard Clayderman, which I could play from memory. Already, images from home filled my mind and one in particular made me smile. Once, on a state holiday, I had played 'Autumn Whispers' in a mini-concert I had put on for guests at our home. The security agent responsible for my residential area, who must have received a complaint from nearby, came to break up the party. In North Korea, you were not allowed to enjoy or share foreign culture unless the performance was authorised, as in the case of students studying Western music at university level for example. But even for them, this was supposed to remain a restricted privilege. Putting on a performance for laypeople, as I had been doing with my private concert, was strictly prohibited.

The security agent pleaded with me, saying that he would have let us continue on any other state holiday, but this was the occasion of the General's birthday. He really could not risk others finding out about our concert on such a day, he said. Someone in the audience offered the agent a glass of wine, and he finally relented, sitting down among the guests. After hearing one piece, he was the one who paid me the most enthusiastic compliments, saying that the sound of the piano was beautiful.

The faces I longed for among that audience came to me one by one. As I played each melodic phrase, I recalled their names in my mind. From the periphery of my vision, I could see that Cho-rin had clasped her hands.

This autumnal piece proceeded to pull me deeper into my memories, with images of the family I had left behind. The sofa where my mother sat to listen to my piano practice when I was still a child; the smoke drifting from the end of my father's cigarette as he sat next to her with his eyes closed. Then later, when my elder sisters came to visit with their husbands, the tiny hands of my infant nephew as he suckled at my sister's breast, and the sparkling eyes of my other nephews and nieces as they rushed into their uncle's arms.

In the interlude, the quickening pace of the melody evoked a story of broken calm, of unspoken goodbyes and of terror; my ears ringing with the pounding of my feet as I crossed the Tumen River, the stomp of military boots in pursuit. When I returned to the autumn fields of the coda, the sky was a stark blue. Wanting to allow the resonant last note to linger, I lifted my foot from the pedal slowly. I waited for the tips of my fingers to rise and leave the sensitive touch of the keyboard, before gently returning my hands to rest on my knees.

As the last notes faded, I could hear Cho-rin sniff. 'Someone with your musical talents, why have you had to suffer like this? You haven't been able to eat. You've even been sleeping rough. Oh, I don't know what else to say. I'm sorry I keep on crying.'

Cho-rin's uncle didn't say anything, but he came to stand next to me and rested his hand on my shoulder. After we had moved back into the living room, where he sat on the sofa, he took a cigarette from his pocket only to put it away again. He still said nothing and spun the lighter in his fingers. When he finally lit his cigarette and blew out the smoke, he spoke intensely and with sincerity.

'To be honest, I only let Cho-rin bring you here because she was so insistent about it. I asked around before you arrived. The crackdown on North Korean refugees here is pretty bad at the moment. They say it's become much worse in recent days.'

'Uncle, how can a man go back on his word?' Cho-rin interrupted.

'I've seen a lot in my lifetime. I don't think you're the sort who escaped out of hunger. Am I right?'

'There were certain circumstances that led me to flee,' I replied.

'Of course, but in that case, neither North Korea nor our own authorities here in China are going to give up on you easily.'

I lowered my head in silent agreement.

'Well, do you have contacts in South Korea? What brought you all the way to Shenyang?'

'Actually, I crossed the river with a friend. But we were separated in Yanji. It wasn't part of the plan.'

'Why was that? You left North Korea together?'

I sketched the trajectory of what had happened since we crossed the river.

Tapping the ash from his cigarette into the ashtray, Cho-rin's uncle made a proposal. 'This is what we'll do,' he said. 'I don't know when your friend will show up, but you can stay here until then. Promise me two things, though. First, you mustn't leave the house. Here in Xita there are more police officers than there are cockroaches. The other thing is that I can't have two of you in the house. You'll have to leave as soon as your friend arrives.'

Cho-rin tugged at her uncle's sleeve. 'Uncle, even if his friend arrives, can't they stay as long as they need to, if he teaches piano?' she asked.

'To tell you the truth, that son of mine has no musical aptitude whatsoever. In fact, he doesn't care for music. I only bought a piano to see if it might civilise him. Besides, you've got to earn your keep. Until you see your friend again, you can teach my boy some piano. It won't be easy, though. He's like an untamed horse.' He sighed and continued, 'You can stay in our spare room; I'll make sure you have enough bedding. I'll pay you separately for the piano tuition, so when you see your friend again, you'll have enough to make the journey to Beijing together. As for me, I'll ask around for South Korean contacts. How about that? Does that sound good?'

'Thank you, thank you!' I got out of my seat and bowed with gratitude. As he asked me to sit back down, he smiled brightly. Then his expression darkened as he asked me for my opinion on how music lessons might help improve his son's attitude.

'First, it will be good for him to acquaint himself with the sound of the piano,' I replied. 'By the time he can distinguish harmony from dissonance, I hope he'll have become more perceptive of the world around him.'

The man slapped his hand on the coffee table and spoke in Chinese to Cho-rin, who looked delighted. Suddenly, we were startled by a loud bang as a young boy burst into the room, practically hurling the door off its hinges. Although Cho-rin's uncle shouted at him in Chinese, the child ignored him and ran about in search of something, throwing everything out of place. Finally, he grabbed a toy sword from under the table. He then stormed out of the room, slamming the door as if to break its frame, just as he had when he came into the room. It all happened so quickly, as if a tornado had whirled through rather than a ten-year-old.

'What's his name?' I asked, still grinning with the shock and surprise of the boy's energy.

'Wang Hou.' The boy's father looked despairingly at me. 'You can only have one child in China, and my wife and I were well into our middle age by the time he was born. We named him "Hou", meaning tiger, so he'd grow to be strong and independent. Perhaps children are destined to resemble not their parents, but the name they're given ...'

Indeed, the boy seemed wilder than I could have imagined. None of the family knew where his energy came from, his father explained.

From the moment he woke to the moment he fell asleep, he was either running about or throwing a tantrum. He wasn't interested in things like junk food, but he had an obsession with historical dramas on television, and the only toys he would play with were plastic swords. Propped against one wall of his bedroom was a tightly packed row of toy swords, each one different from its neighbour. I could see that I would have a battle on my hands.

It was January, and the boy was on winter vacation. We blocked out ten to eleven for piano tuition each morning, and three to five in the afternoon. Cho-rin would act as an interpreter for us. She usually worked as an accountant at her uncle's company, but she would take some time off and stay in the house with us.

I had to admit defeat in our very first session. That morning, I called Mr Shin's wife and left her the number of the house I was staying in. The thought of being reunited with Young-min had given me a positive start to the day, but the boy did not listen to a word I said.

When Cho-rin relayed my instructions to him, Wang Hou ignored them. He continued with his strange jumping and odd movements, as if he were a martial arts character on television. He even insisted on climbing onto Cho-rin's back as if he were riding a horse. When I lost my temper and banged on the keys to get the boy's attention, he showed no fear. Instead, he sat on the stool and made even more noise by stomping on the keys with his heels. When I moved to close the cover of the keyboard, he screamed at the top of his voice.

His desperate mother, holding a stick in one hand and a kitchen knife in the other, tried to intimidate the boy into compliance. Seeing my surprised look, Cho-rin explained that if his mother held up only the stick, the boy would run into the kitchen and pick up a kitchen knife in response. Once, he had even cut her on the leg; and from then on, she kept the kitchen knife in her own hand. No one in the family knew what to do with him.

I realised that I had to find a way of my own to get through to him. Determined, I waited until three in the afternoon. When the clock struck three times, I collected the knife from the kitchen and knocked on the boy's bedroom door. There was no response, so I knocked again. I heard a thump on the other side of the door. I knocked with my knuckles, but he responded with his toy sword.

I said, 'Cho-rin, tell him that his piano tutor is looking for him.'

When Cho-rin translated for me, the boy shouted something in response. Judging from Cho-rin's sharp intake of breath, it was clear that the boy had used bad language. Holding the kitchen knife behind my back, I opened the door and walked into his room.

'Cho-rin, tell him that I am the most terrifying piano teacher in the world, and that I shall show him no mercy.'

As Cho-rin blustered, the boy put his hands on his hips and chuckled. I picked up a toy sword from his collection and went into the living room with a deliberate and slow stride. Making sure the boy was watching, I held up the kitchen knife above the plastic toy sword. I struck down hard and the toy sword broke into two pieces with a smack, and then fell silently onto the plush carpet. The boy screamed. As if witnessing his fear of a grown-up for the first time, his mother and cousin stood in silent astonishment.

I gestured towards the piano room with the kitchen knife. 'Go and sit in there.'

The boy clenched his fists in fury but he remained where he was, making it clear that he would not back down. I went into his bedroom again, and this time I returned with an armful of toy swords. I scattered them onto the carpet and pointed again towards the music room.

'Go sit in there.'

Before I could finish my short sentence, the boy spat on the carpet. I sliced a second toy sword into two pieces, and his lips began to tremble.

I told Cho-rin, 'Tell him that I wouldn't mind chopping up another toy sword. Ask him to sit at the piano. Tell him I'm not his mother or father. Cho-rin, are you listening?'

I felt like a strange caricature of a grown-up as I said those words, and remembered how much I had feared Choi Liang when he was my music teacher in Sariwon. Now I knew what it felt like to be a teacher disciplining a student, and I could see in my mind's eye the deep wrinkles on Choi Liang's forehead.

Cho-rin translated my message, but without much conviction. Then something miraculous happened. The boy shuffled reluctantly into the piano room. He looked anxiously at me and at the kitchen knife I was holding, as if to entreat me to save the rest of his toy swords from harm. As I returned the knife to his mother, I gave her a wink. She looked into my eyes in wonder. Until now, I had felt like an unwelcome guest in her house, and she had made an effort to avoid making eye contact with me.

When I returned to the room, the boy was standing quietly next to the piano. I pointed to the stool.

'Come, Wang Hou. Sit here.'

Although I spoke in Korean, he understood and complied without hesitation. I could hear the mother speaking excitedly on the phone to her husband from the kitchen. Cho-rin took the phone from her and laughed as she spoke. While the grown-ups were now in good spirits, the boy looked utterly defeated and I felt sorry for him. That evening, perhaps exhausted by the first surrender of his life, he went to sleep well before his bedtime. When his astonished father returned home, he sat beside his sleeping son for a long time.

4 | THE KIM JONG-IL STRATEGY

'L ET's have a drink.'

After dinner, Cho-rin's uncle placed a bottle of Shaoxing wine on the table. I had thought all Chinese wines were white, but this one was a pale red. It was one of the top ten best-known wines of China, he explained, and was considered to have been a favourite of Chiang Kai-shek, the leader of the Chinese Nationalists who retreated to Taiwan after losing to the Communists. The northerners living in a colder climate preferred white wine, whereas the southerners were said to prefer red; he declared that one of the best of these was Shaoxing wine. I confessed that I didn't hold my drink very well. He replied that this was a wine enjoyed by women for its lightness, and went on to pour me a very large glass of it.

I had believed that Chinese wines were all as strong as liquor, but the Shaoxing wine defied my expectations. Wang Hou's mother retired to bed after dinner, but Cho-rin and her uncle stayed at the table to drink with me. While she and I drank the Shaoxing, her uncle chose Kaoliang wine. As we started getting tipsy, he lit another cigarette and asked me a question.

'You know, seeing you here, it strikes me that there must be a certain spirit of defiance in you North Koreans. Look, even a powerful country such as the US remains at the mercy of Kim Jong-il. Even though the country is dirt poor! I've always wanted to know, what's the secret behind it all? How do you North Koreans get away with it?'

'It's simple,' I replied. 'The US negotiates as a matter of diplomacy, to seek common ground on an issue; but when North Korea comes to the table, it's a counter-intelligence operation. In other words, North Korea uses dialogue as a tool of deception rather than of negotiation, with the objective being the maintenance of misplaced trust in the other party. And why not? North Korea's opacity is its greatest strength. It allows things to be done on its own terms while other countries continue to take what North Korea says at face value. In fact, Kim Jong-il formally set these three principles as a basis for diplomatic engagement: "The US will buy any lie, as long as it is logically presented"; "Japan is susceptible to emotional manipulation"; and "South Korea can be ignored or blackmailed".'

Cho-rin's uncle laughed. 'So South Korea is the most pitiful one, eh! But how does the North go about ignoring South Korea's demands? Doesn't North Korea need their cooperation?'

'Yes, but we know how to make it happen on our own terms.'

At the time of my escape, North Korea's secret diplomatic weapon against the South was the Northern Limit Line (NLL) Strategy. This issue remains extremely sensitive to this day.

The NLL is a demarcation of territorial waters established in the Yellow Sea by the UN, and contested by North Korea, after the armistice signed on 27 July 1953 by the UN Command, North Korea and China at the end of the Korean War. It became the focal point of North Korea's military provocations against the South during the era of the Sunshine Policy.

In February 1998, when the left-wing administration of then president Kim Dae-joong came into power, South Korea embarked on a foreign policy focused on warming relations with the North and softening North Korea's perception of the South as adversarial. This was the Sunshine Policy, whose name was inspired by an Aesop fable in which a strong wind (a hard-line policy) was unable to force the coat off a man, but the sunshine (a conciliatory policy) managed to do so with its embracing warmth. Ironically, the policy only served to entrench Kim Jong-il's slipping control, and enabled the Party to consolidate and adapt its political and economic powers for a new era.

By 1999, there was a dire need to secure the North Korean system domestically, as it was the fifth consecutive year that state rations had not been distributed. With mass starvation and resulting economic hardship, loyalty to the Party among the populace was waning at an alarming rate. Leaving aside the core central institutions in Pyongyang, many organisations had become paralysed in terms of their departmental or regional functions, and there were increasing incidents of their putting their own and their staff's needs for survival before their duty to the Party. This was a dangerous situation: Kim Jong-il had painted himself into a corner he could not get out of, and was slowly losing his iron grip over the people. It was then – to the Party's profound relief – that South Korea's Sunshine Policy came unwittingly to the rescue.

At first, North Korea criticised the policy, saying its real purpose was to collapse the system through soft-power tactics. But by mid-1998, Kim Jong-il had ordered the United Front Department to formulate a Sunshine Exploitation strategy that would allow the Party to extract much-needed economic benefits from South Korea while making as few concessions as possible.

All available UFD resources were deployed on this mission. In order to lure South Korean companies into investing by means of collaborative ventures, the UFD prepared strategies for reconciliation and negotiation. The visit in June and October of Jung Joo-young, CEO of South Korea's Hyundai conglomerate, was a great coup that helped to legitimise the new status quo of 'cooperation' between the two Koreas. As international and South Korean food aid entered the system, the Party was able to resume to a certain extent its provision of rations, allowing it to return to the use of stronger levels of enforcement to secure the obedience it needed from the people.

At the time, the highest priority for the Party was to acquire the minimum resources it needed to reverse its diminishing control over the nation. But just as its priority today remains the satisfaction of the nation's economic demands at the lowest possible level required for stability of power, and to ensure that access to all opportunities remain routed through Party-vetted channels, Kim Jong-il had then to focus on the next most pressing priority after a degree of control had been regained: unconditional aid and joint economic ventures were to be managed so as to prevent the North from having to reciprocate or accept demands made by the outside world.

In the first move of the Sunshine Policy, South Korea's Kim Dae-joong administration suggested that inter-Korean family reunions be allowed to take place, in exchange for fertiliser aid from the South. South Korea's opposition party at the time, the conservatives, criticised the Sunshine Policy as pouring resources into a bottomless pit. They argued that there should instead be a principle whereby the North would have to make tangible compromises in return, such as a reduction in military spending or the implementation of reforms.

'Perhaps they had a point?' asked Cho-rin's uncle.

'Maybe,' I said wryly. In order to stem the erosion of the Party's control that had begun during the years of famine, Kim Jong-il urgently needed to accept South Korean aid and investment. But if the Kim Dae-joong administration bowed to pressure from the opposition party and decided to apply the principle of reciprocity, Kim Jong-il might be forced to refuse the aid and risk even more decentralisation of power.

Acts of military provocation could prevent such a scenario from being realised, because North Korea could use the bargaining chip of offering to cease provocations, as a contingency to be held in reserve. Moreover, not only would our position be strengthened if it did come to give-and-take, but once the Sunshine Policy's unconditional aid began to flow in, a lurking threat of military confrontation might even ensure the policy's longevity. While South Korea had money to offer on its side, which the North really wanted, North Korea would have peace to offer, which the South would need as much, or even more. The underlying logic was simple: South Korea must continue to provide unconditional aid and keep its engagement with the North separate from political issues, or give up its peace again.

'Wait a moment,' interrupted Cho-rin. 'At the very same time North Korea was planning to benefit from the Sunshine Policy, it was prepared to take military action against South Korea? That's crazy, isn't it?'

I shrugged. This sort of thinking wasn't new to me. In early February 1999, Kim Jong-il ordered the UFD to plan our first military provocation against South Korea. At the time, I was staying at the Ui-Am Guesthouse at Director Im's invitation, completing Kim Jong-il's poem 'Spring Rests on the Gun Barrel of the Lord'. The guesthouse was not far from Director Im's home in Eundok Village, and it served as his control hub for coordinating the Sunshine Exploitation strategy and the strategy of military provocations. With staff from various sections all summoned to the UFD guesthouse to make their contributions, I witnessed its progress at close quarters and over a prolonged period. I can still recall many of the conversations that took place in my presence, such as the following exchange between Policy Director Chae Chang-guk and Director Im:

'When Hyundai CEO Jung Joo-young met with us last year, we had already made agreements on investment plans. We're struggling as it is to proceed with reconciliation and negotiations designed to bring South Korean companies on board. How on earth are we supposed to accommodate military provocations with the Sunshine Exploitation strategy?' Policy Director Chae Chang-guk had asked Director Im, his exasperation clearly visible.

Director Im pursed his thick lips but didn't respond immediately.

His silence on this occasion was a mark of the sworn obedience of North Korea's most powerful men, who might command the highest authority, but who for that very reason could not engage in the questioning of an order sanctioned by Kim Jong-il. His gaze rested on Chae Chang-guk, perhaps envious of his subordinate's freedom to voice a complaint, however trivial.

After a pause, he said, 'Come now, Chae Chang-guk. Figure it out. You choose the people you need for the job. Give it your best.'

A week after that conversation, the UFD began to crystallise the strategy whereby, on land, North Korea would remain focused on receiving aid and pursuing economic cooperation with the South; but at sea – and only at sea – it would carry out military provocations. This arrangement, which allowed room for both the Sunshine Exploitation strategy and military provocations, was North Korea's carefully prepared response to South Korea's Sunshine Policy. To the outside world, we referred to our stance as the *Uriminzokkiri* policy, meaning 'just between us Koreans', in order to highlight that we had entered into a new era of 'goodwill' with South Korea. Internally, we christened it the Northern Limit Line – NLL – Strategy.

When the UFD presented the strategy to Kim Jong-il, he was extremely pleased.

To support the strategy, the Party newspaper *Rodong Sinmun* published an increasing number of articles suggesting that North Korea's naval power could be strengthened by means of using the distinctive coastal shape of the Korean peninsula to our advantage. More overt declarations were also made in these pieces, stating how the military border between the Koreas was not restricted to the DMZ, but stretched to the Northern Limit Line at sea.

The First Battle of Yeonpyeong on 15 June 1999 marked the initial main clash in the NLL region. Presented by the North as an act of provocation by the South, it was actually ordered by Kim Jong-il himself, planned by the UFD and executed by the naval command.

The confrontation began with the North's vessels ramming South Korean ships, and ended with a clear naval defeat for North Korea.

Although South Korea had been unambiguously provoked by the North, the Kim Dae-joong administration played this down and did not escalate the conflict. The UFD had been holding its breath and celebrated this outcome with considerable relief, because we could now proceed further with the NLL Strategy. In fact, encouraged by the patient peace-making efforts of South Korea, the North decided to focus on military provocation as the long-term basis of its foreign policy strategy, which was to be guided by the three-stage framework of Provocation, Marking Position and Maintenance. This would be carried out through the development of nuclear weapons at an international level, and through naval provocations at the inter-Korean level.

There was a specific reason behind the UFD's decision to choose June 2002, the time of the Seoul World Cup, as the date for the second naval confrontation in the NLL region. Their goal was to move the territorial dispute from the initial stage of Provocation to the second stage of Marking Position by publicising the issue on the international stage. Following the instructions of the UFD, Naval Commander Kim Yoon-sim coordinated the Second Battle of Yeonpyeong, in which gunfire was exchanged and both sides suffered casualties and fatalities. Kim Yoon-sim had been a commander in the West Sea Force before his promotion to Navy Commander in April 2002, succeeding Armed Forces Director Kim Il-chul to the post.

On 1 May 2002, Kim Jong-il broke with his International Labour Day tradition of making on-site inspections of factories. Instead, he went to inspect the naval command post and facilities relating to the Yellow Sea engagement. Photographs published in the 2 May 2002 edition of the *Rodong Sinmun* show military figures standing next to Kim Jong-il. Most of these had taken part in the naval engagement. On

29 June 2002, the day of the World Cup third place play-off between South Korea and Turkey, North Korea began provocations that led to the second major confrontation in the NLL region. The UFD took special precautions to keep the details of the plan hidden, in order to make the clash look like an accidental escalation. The captain of the mission was given his assignment only after being summoned to Kim Yoon-sim's private office, so as to avoid wiretapping by joint US–South Korean forces.

In December 2003, during the UFD end-of-year meeting in which we explored our agenda for the year ahead, Director Im announced the following in his speech:

'Our objectives remain clear. The Kaesong Industrial Complex is an important source of foreign-currency earnings. Such developments must be continued, but restricted to the South–North Korean collaboration zones on land. At the same time, we must continue with systematic provocations against South Korea at sea.'

I explained this much to my drinking companions. After completing my escape to the outside world, I would later come to appreciate – from the state of inter-Korean affairs and the South's perceptions of it – that the UFD's coordinated response to the Sunshine Policy could not have been a more phenomenal success.

After I had concluded my long response, neither Cho-rin's uncle nor Cho-rin said anything. I had thought Cho-rin might be uninterested in such details of policy, but she too looked stunned. Her uncle had finished his glass of wine and held it out so that Cho-rin could pour him another, but she was too preoccupied to notice.

'I thought Kim Jong-il was just a stupid man who didn't know how to feed his own people,' she said. 'I had no idea that North Korea put this much thought into policy-making.'

Cho-rin's uncle looked up as if she had just intruded into his silent thoughts, then reached for the wine bottle. He poured himself a glass and lit another cigarette. 'I don't suppose I will get to meet someone like you ever again. North Korea is a very interesting place. What does it think of China? Surely North Korea doesn't have anyone else to lean on?'

It was now past midnight, but I was burning to tell them what relations between North Korea and China were really like.

'The country Kim Jong-il hates the most is China,' I said.

Both Cho-rin and her uncle seemed suddenly to sober up.

'What do you mean? Isn't North Korea grateful for China's support? How could Kim Jong-il hate China?' Cho-rin's uncle asked.

His surprise, like many other things outsiders find incomprehensible about North Korea, has its roots in the cult of Kim, which goes beyond mere ideology or politics. There is a Korean saying that if you tell a lie one hundred times, even the person who made up the lie will eventually come to believe it. Having consolidated a cult for the North Korean people in which the Leader was omnipotent, Kim Jong-il came to believe himself in his entitlement to absolute authority. But China, more than anyone else, proved to be the thorn in his side.

The US could easily be cast as the embodiment of imperialism and corrupt Capitalism, which allowed North Korea to portray itself as the plucky underdog that dared to remain defiant against a superpower. China, however, which was supposed to be a fellow Socialist nation and on the same side as North Korea, posed endless challenges that undermined Kim Jong-il's authority. Even in terms of ideology, China was considered a dangerous enemy to the *Juche* ideology of self-reliance, forever tempting the isolated North Korean people with the fruits of reform and openness from over the border.

Above all, the Chinese Communist Party's pursuit of economic relations with South Korea aroused in Kim Jong-il an acute sense of betrayal. As South Korean corporations entered the market in the three north-eastern provinces of China, the Chinese public began to warm towards South Korea, but their regard for North Korea did not improve correspondingly. The increasing flow of North Korean refugees into China only made matters worse, and Kim Jong-il issued an internal Party declaration in 1997 stating: 'The Sino-DPRK border is an ideological border, just like the 38th parallel.'

The 38th parallel is the line on the Korean peninsula which the USSR and US agreed would mark the zones of control between North and South Korea after the end of the Second World War. Through his 1997 statement, Kim Jong-il decreed that the Sino-DPRK border, which separated North Korea's isolation from China's openness, was a border of ideological demarcation just as the 38th parallel represented the divide between Communism and Capitalism.

It was at this time that border patrol units along the Sino-DPRK border were promoted from rear guard and given military corps status, to reflect the importance of their work. Operatives whose work had previously focused on the US, South Korea and Japan increasingly transferred their attention to China. Several UFD colleagues who worked through the Jochongryon (Association of Chosun People in Japan) were asked to establish equivalent operations in China. As these cadres had the most extensive experience of collaborating with overseas Koreans, they were to apply their knowledge in a new context. I recalled a conversation with one of them, a former classmate from Kim Il-sung University, who aired his frustrations with me one drunken night at his home.

'Koreans in Japan are sympathetic and have money to spare, but ethnic Koreans in China are poor scum. All they think about is how to make money through South Koreans, so why would they have anything to do with us? Even if they had information to offer in lieu of money, what would we pay them with? I don't know if I can keep my earnings up any more.'

As with the UFD, Office 35, which was responsible for overseas intelligence operations, was also asked to turn its focus towards China in earnest. Kim Jong-il feared the intentions of his ally much more than those of his sworn enemies. While the policy leanings of the US and other Western nations were relatively openly exposed to scrutiny by their press, the extent of China's knowledge about North Korea was harder to establish. As China's economy boomed, loyal cadres set up numerous companies as fronts to establish their presence in the three north-eastern provinces.

I knew this background well from my work in the UFD, but the reason behind Kim Jong-il's visits to China in May 2000 and then again in January 2001 remained a mystery to me. I asked my Kim Il-sung University classmate, who by then was running well-established operations in China, to explain.

'Birds listen in to private conversations in the daytime, and mice do the same at night.' He muttered the old saying as he checked that the windows in the room were shut.

Once he was sure we could not be overheard, he began, 'You remember when our General visited the Chinese Embassy here in Pyongyang, right? On 5 March 2000? He went with the Director of the General Political Bureau Cho Myong-rok, the Military Chief of Staff Kim Young-chun and the PAF Director Kim Il-chul.

'You know the reason he went to their Embassy? He went to boast to China about a document we'd obtained, regarding China's current stance on the anti-US/pro-DPRK pact made between China and North Korea in the 1950s. The document includes statements made by some of China's top cadres, saying that China should delete the clause in the pact that automatically involved its military if war were to break out on the Korean peninsula. There are even statements in there proposing that China should request reparations from Pyongyang for its support during the Korean War. No one in China was notified before our General went to their Embassy in Pyongyang, and our state news agency announced it publicly without telling China first. It was nothing short of a diplomatic insult to China.

'When our General met Chinese ambassador Wan Yongxiang in

Pyongyang, he said he knew about China's proposed amendments to the pact and its intention to demand reparations for the Korean War. Our General threatened that if China did proceed in such a direction, North Korea would sell weapons to Taiwan. The Chinese ambassador tried to explain that the views in the document did not reflect the official stance of the Chinese leadership, but rather views held by certain individuals.

'You won't believe how it all backfired. The Chinese leadership dismissed ambassador Wan immediately afterwards, to show their displeasure at his weak retort to Kim Jong-il. At the time, China's appointment of a new ambassador to Pyongyang had been postponed and was four months past its due date, because Wan Yongxiang had a good relationship with Kim Jong-il. But now they decided to replace Wan with hard-liner Wang Guozhang.

'China's swift decision was reported to our General on the day it happened. The following day, as you know, Central Party cadres were notified. In response, our General issued an internal order for the staff at our Embassy in Beijing to prepare for withdrawal. Everyone packed their bags. But I bet that's the first and last time our General tries to play with China the kind of games he plays with the US. We all know that if they squeeze us, we're dead.

'Two months later, between May 29 and 31, Beijing invited our General to make an informal visit. He probably had to sit through lectures about economic reform or something. Whatever it was, it would have been really bad, because we had to deal with the damned Shenyang Incident after that.'

The Shenyang Incident was the crisis that occurred when cadres of North Korea's Office 35 were caught grooming Chinese Communist Party cadres in local government, police and border units. The number of people arrested by China's Ministry of State Security in relation to the Shenyang Incident numbered over sixty. Ultimately, while an owner could get away with kicking his dog, the dog – in this case, North Korea – would not so easily be forgiven for biting its owner.

My former classmate continued, 'China's Ministry of State Security had been keeping an eye on us anyway, to show South Korea it was committed to protecting their investments in the north-eastern regions. They hadn't really laid a finger on us before, but they were really determined to send us a message this time round. In addition to the arrests, they even put a stop to material aid to North Korea. All our General could do in retaliation was to execute a few Party cadres who had studied in China, and purge so-called supporters of Chinese-style reform.

'What more could he possibly do in the face of China's wrath? If they decide that our regime must go, it will go. When our General was summoned to Beijing in January 2001, he had no choice but to make the trip again. They made him and the rest of the delegation wait outside the city for days even though they'd sent the invitation in the first place. Eventually, our General had no choice but to grovel and go on a tour of Shanghai's Pudong special economic zone, declaring his "admiration" for China's economic reform. Then the media all reported the trip as a demonstration of our General's interest in Chinese-style reforms. They really know how to twist the blade! You know what those of us working for him in China say? Our Great General went once to the Chinese Embassy full of bluster, but was dragged off to China twice as a punishment.'

Friends like us could share this sort of dangerous information because a conversation between two cadres in North Korea, no matter how treacherous, cannot be used as the basis for prosecution unless there is independent evidence of its having taken place. The Party had established this as an internal regulation within the Ministry of State Security in an attempt to prevent personal vendettas among powerful cadres from spiralling out of control, as they often did. This regulation is also the very loophole that the North Korean elite employ to establish mutual trust and forge alliances. In fact, there is no more valuable currency of trust than sharing the truths behind the official narrative: in a system where we loyally upheld the fabricated cult of Kim to avoid the penalty of treason, we acknowledged no greater token of faith in another.

In 2002, so as to reduce his people's dependence on China, Kim Jong-il issued an order for North Korean companies trading under Party auspices to cease business activities with China. But, among other factors, the North Korean economy was already much too reliant on cheap imports from China. Cracking down on the sale of Chinese goods in the markets could only lead to rising prices and a strengthening of the black market economy. As economic decentralisation would result in the loss of societal and political control, Kim Jong-il rescinded his order after just three months.

When I wound up my explanation, Cho-rin's uncle shook his head slowly as if in disbelief. 'Is this really true, what you're saying?' he asked. Muttering that only someone from the heart of such a corrupt regime could know these things, he took a final large gulp from his glass and repeated the number 'three' several times, as if it were his prophecy that the current North Korean regime would not last beyond three generations. 'Tell you something,' he said, 'I might be in an ethnic minority, but all the same I'm glad – no, grateful – to have been born a citizen of China, not North Korea.'

5 | MEETING CHO-RIN'S 'INTENDED'

AFTER these conversations, Cho-rin's uncle treated me with great respect. When he left for work in the morning he made sure to knock on my door and say goodbye. He phoned the house at least twice a day to ask if there was any snack or small treat I wanted him to bring home. Each time, Cho-rin would take advantage of the opportunity to ask for various delicacies that she wanted too.

I enjoyed an extravagant three days in this manner. Nevertheless, every morning, I made it my first task to phone Mr Shin. He kept reassuring me that I had luck on my side, but the more I heard this, the greater I feared for Young-min. What if he had forgotten Mr Shin's phone number through some trauma he'd suffered? I mentioned this to Mr Shin in a roundabout way. Mr Shin said that the graver danger was that Young-min might give away his phone number under interrogation, as the authorities would then track us both down.

I understood his concern. His wife was a North Korean refugee too. When I asked about sending someone to check Young-min's relative's home again, Mr Shin made the excuse that he was very busy. Cho-rin, who was standing next to me, asked me to pass the phone to her. I wondered if she'd had an excellent idea that a man wouldn't have thought of.

'Hello!' Cho-rin's voice was cheery as always. She continued, 'Please help find his friend. After all, it's only locals like us who can help, as we speak the language and know the area. And please come with him to Shenyang! I'll take you all out for a delicious meal.' She was about to return the receiver to me when she paused for a moment, took it back and added, 'Well, goodbye for now!'

Mr Shin was very curious. Was she my girlfriend? How was it that we were staying in the same house? He remarked that she had a distinctive way of speaking, full of affection, and, without giving me a chance to explain, added, 'Congratulations!' Then he assured me, promising several times, that he would send someone to Young-min's relative's house that very day.

In terms of her cousin's piano tuition, Cho-rin was also one step ahead of me. If I played the tyrant, wielding a kitchen knife in front of the child, Cho-rin led the way with empathy. When the boy was about to lose his temper because he was unable to get the notes right, she got the answers right on his behalf, so that his pride wouldn't be injured. To deal with his whingeing, Cho-rin appealed to the family ties between them. Now and then, she would pretend to get very upset and tearful, saying that she would get in trouble with the scary piano teacher if he continued to misbehave – although of course I had no such thing in mind. Nevertheless, it worked, and the fierce tiger would return to being a ten-year-old boy.

Once, saying he was tired, the boy bolted from the room. When words couldn't coax him back, Cho-rin tried a new tactic. In order to pique his jealousy, she sat next to me on the piano stool. It must have irked him, to see us ignoring him like that, because he screamed from the other room that if she didn't get off the stool at once, he would hurl it out of the window. As she translated those words for me, she rested her head on my shoulder.

The lemon scent of her hair infused my body. All at once, I forgot about the boy. When the boy screamed again, Cho-rin took her act to another level, putting her hand on mine as it rested on the keyboard, then lifting it to put my arm around her shoulders. I was overcome by the sense of intimacy. In North Korea, no man would dare make bodily contact with someone else's betrothed, and a woman would never take the lead in such a way. Moreover, from Pyongyang to Shenyang, all I had had to touch were rough things. Even when I'd grasped Young-min's hand, my hand had been met by trembling and the sense of a life that was barely holding on. The warmth of Cho-rin's hand on mine awoke in me the touch of life. I became focused on my breathing and worried that my slightest movement might shatter the stillness of the moment. When Cho-rin lifted her head again, I wondered if she too felt that time had stopped for us alone.

As Cho-rin tried to allay her cousin's tantrum, I went into the bathroom and splashed my face with cold water. I wanted to wash off my shamelessness. Yet, even after I'd wiped my face with the towel, I felt the same. When I looked at myself in the mirror, I saw too many layers hiding my real self from the world.

I told myself that there would have been no double meaning behind Cho-rin's actions. She genuinely wanted to help me, and she was satisfied with that. If that weren't the case, she wouldn't still enjoy laughing with me in the same way as when we'd first met. Neither would she put her head on my shoulder and take my hand as a mischievous ploy to annoy the boy. I had no right at all to expect Cho-rin to have for me any of the feelings that she had towards her fiancé. In fact, I was indebted to her for her many kindnesses and felt obliged to repay them in such a way that I would never regret it.

Suddenly, I heard Cho-rin scream from the other room. The sound was all the more shocking because the scream came when I had been re-examining my emotions for her and feeling repentant. As I ran out of the bathroom, I saw that the boy had embarked on another outrage while I was out of sight. With Cho-rin resisting, he was attempting to put his hands under her shirt.

Cho-rin struggled to push him away, but the boy did not budge. She was not strong enough to stop him grabbing at her breasts. I rushed to pull him off her from behind, and he yelled so loudly that his body trembled in my arms. Seeing that Cho-rin was on the verge of tears, I gave the boy a hard smack on his backside, then pulled him off her with all my strength. Just as I was about to start shouting at him, I realised that clenched in the boy's hands were Cho-rin's bra and a piece of cloth torn from her shirt. At the same time, Cho-rin gave a cry. I quickly shut my eyes as Cho-rin stood there almost naked, covering her breasts.

I swung the boy round to face me and block her from my view. As I turned, I heard Cho-rin run out of the room. The boy flailed in my arms, and at that moment I was full of hatred for him. I held him tightly by the wrist and dragged him to his room. I wanted to confine his energy in there until he offered an apology.

Although I spoke no Chinese, the boy must have understood my resolve. 'Sit there!' I commanded. The boy complied with my Korean and put his arms around his knees. Once, when I'd thrown a tantrum as a young boy, my father had confined me to my room. When I heard my mother argue with him, saying I should be allowed out to join the family for dinner, hers had been the most welcome voice in the world. But my father insisted that discipline was more important than dinner, and I was not allowed out until after the meal. That was perhaps the first time in my life that I thought of one's right to eat as something important.

I leaned over the boy and pointed my finger at him. 'Don't you dare leave this room.'

With those words, I left him in his bedroom. But in the living room, the awkwardness remained in the air. It was so quiet that, when I sat on the couch, I flinched at the sound of the leather underneath me. At first, I worried about how upset the boy must be. But as the minutes went by, I became more concerned about Cho-rin. Would she be sitting down in the other room, or would she be standing? I didn't know what to do with myself. Perhaps twenty minutes later, I heard the boy's bedroom door swinging open.

Although I had left him to calm down, he had spent the time stoking his rage. I had no strength left to deal with him when the boy ran to the front door. Holding up his shoes to put them on, he turned to me and shouted, '*Shabi zai zi!*' As he opened the front door to leave, he shouted, '*Shabi, wo da si ni!*'

He slammed the front door behind him and the words continued to ring in my ears. With the boy gone, it was even more awkward. Without knowing what the words meant, I muttered to myself, '*Shabi zai zi, shabi, wo da si ni.*' Looking up absently, I started at the sight of Cho-rin.

She was standing at the other end of the living room, seemingly unable to come near or to look at me. Even her hand, which touched her eyebrow and then her lips, moved unnaturally. As if her change of clothes did not fit her well, she pulled distractedly at the hem of her shirt. When I caught myself standing there in a daze, I too felt awkward. Then our gazes met and we both blushed. She was the girl whose modesty had been compromised, and I was the boy embarrassed by it.

I escaped into the piano room. This part of the house comforted me more than anywhere else. I sat on the stool and opened the lid of the piano. The black and white keys were like black pupils set against the white of an eye, all of them looking into my heart.

'Play me something, please.'

From behind me, Cho-rin's voice sounded very close, as if confirming that we two were the only ones in this part of the house. It seemed that no music could transcend the sound of her voice, but what should I play?

I wanted to play a short and simple piece that would linger. I remembered teacher Choi Liang's words, which he often repeated in our music history lessons: 'All his life, Beethoven composed dark music. There was one bright song among them that he wrote for a lover: "For Elise".' I began to play this piece for Cho-rin. She seemed to enjoy the all too familiar tune, but for me, this time it was different. With every phrase, I felt the plight of Beethoven, who had lost his love in life but left his music behind him for eternity.

About half an hour later, Cho-rin's uncle and aunt came through the door together. Before he had finished taking off his shoes, the father called for his son. At the noise, Cho-rin frowned and went to greet her uncle. It sounded as though she were making a long complaint. The mother said she would go look for the boy, who was probably playing video games in the nearby arcade. But the father replied in an irritated voice that she should not bother. When she brought out the tea, her husband called me into the living room. I took my seat and he asked me to repeat exactly what his son had said to me. Not knowing the context, I did as I was told.

'*Shabi, wo da si ni! Shabi zai zi!*'

The wife tutted and Cho-rin said agitatedly, 'See, there's nothing he won't say!'

I was curious to know what the words meant, but kept quiet on seeing the seriousness of the father's reaction. 'Anyway, that's that,' he said eventually, massaging his temples. 'Is there any news about your friend?' He spoke kindly, perhaps to change the subject.

'No, not yet. I called my contact in Yanji this morning and he said he was sending someone to the relative's house.'

'Good. I've been using my connections too, to find a way through South Korean businesses, so we may have some good news soon. You've had a long day. Let me treat you tonight.' He took 350 yuan from his wallet, and continued, 'You haven't been out since coming to stay here. Tonight, why don't you go out on the town? I'll allow it just for this evening. Cho-rin, show him the sights of the city!'

'Good thinking, uncle. Great minds think alike! My fiancé returned today from his business trip to Shanghai, so we'd planned to go out anyway.' Turning swiftly towards me, Cho-rin said, 'Let's all go out together. My fiancé wants to meet you. He's richer than me, so he can buy dinner. How does that sound?'

I felt a little embarrassed. In fact, I felt very uncomfortable at Cho-rin's excitement at the prospect of our night out together, my emotions in turmoil at the thought of spending an evening with both her and her fiancé. I made the excuse that I wasn't feeling well, so that the two of them could spend some time without me. Cho-rin didn't reply, but lingered as she did up the buttons of her coat. Her uncle and aunt both urged me to go out with Cho-rin and her fiancé. As I slipped the money into my pocket, I resolved to go, because I could now repay Cho-rin's kindness one way or another. She had taken the time and trouble to help me, although I'd had nothing to offer her in return. But now, I did have something. It wasn't so much the money as that, with it, I had regained a dignity that I had lost while on the run with no possessions other than my tattered bundle of poems.

'Yes, Cho-rin, I'll join you for dinner.'

Cho-rin was excited to be seeing her fiancé and, now that I'd made up my mind to go with them, I was excited at the prospect of leaving the house for the first time. We were both impatient to leave. When her aunt told her to be careful and avoid attracting the attention of the authorities, Cho-rin waved away her warnings and left the flat first. Five minutes later, she called the house phone and I went down to find a taxi waiting for me outside the building. Cho-rin waved at me through the taxi window, telling me to hurry up. She was wearing mittens. It occurred to me that I might buy her a pair of leather gloves.

As I looked out of the taxi window, I was amazed more by the number of people on the streets than by the brightly lit streetlamps and dazzling neon lights. I asked, 'Is it a national holiday in China today?'

'No, why do you ask?' she replied.

'Then where are they all headed to? Is there a mass-mobilisation event happening?'

'We don't have stupid things like that in China! It's like this every day. Actually, the crowds are smaller than usual today because of the cold.'

It still didn't make sense to me. In Pyongyang, the busiest time of the day was the evening rush hour, between 7 and 8 p.m. Within one or two hours at most, the streets cleared like a tide gone out. And because everything in North Korea ran according to a centralised system, you couldn't go out for a meal just because you wanted to. Even Pyongyang's famous Okryugwan cold-noodle restaurant shut at 8 p.m., and you couldn't just pay with cash. To enter the restaurant you needed a special coupon issued as a privilege by the Light Industry Section of the Workers' Party. This coupon system first appeared around 1992, when food rations began to shrink. The system was introduced in an attempt to uphold the integrity of state-determined prices, which were the pride of North Korea's Socialism. But from 1994 onwards, by which point the ration distribution system had completely collapsed, many of the state-run shops and restaurants that accepted special coupons and state prices began to close down.

As prices determined by market forces took hold in the economy and overrode the prices set by the state, the notion that a state salary could support one's livelihood was undermined. The average monthly salary of around 150 North Korean won became so worthless that it could not feed one person for even a day, let alone for a whole month. Unable to provide for its people, the Party had no choice but to turn a blind eye to illegal trade and the markets that popped up all over the country. But as this 'grey' economy quickly mushroomed and ordinary North Koreans stopped turning up for their state jobs in order to fend for themselves, the situation became a black hole that sucked in the Party's ability to retain control over its people.

On 1 July 2000, North Korea announced the 7.1 Measures in a

desperate attempt to claw back its monopoly of control, as channels of livelihood spiralled beyond its reach. Ironically, the international community welcomed the measures, referring to them as evidence of North Korea's willingness to consider reform. In reality, the non-state-controlled economy had had a declaration of war made against it by the Party, which had become drawn into a battle that continues today, as it struggles to retain its monopoly of control in the face of unplanned market forces.

The 7.1 Measures implicitly acknowledged that there was a discrepancy between state prices and market prices, by increasing the average state salary from 150 won to 2000 won. The Party urged the people to return to their state jobs, saying that it would actively oversee the regulation of market prices. But the toxic combination of sudden salary rises and severe crackdowns on market prices resulted in soaring inflation. As prices spiked along with the rise in salary, an average monthly income from the state could buy just five eggs. Finally the Party could impose some form of control over the markets only by legalising some of them, charging rent and restricting opening times.

In Pyongyang, the Party's powerbase, none of the pedestrians out on a dark night could have been mistaken for individuals out to enjoy the evening. Instead, all of them – including children, university students and soldiers – would be citizens mobilised for political events or training exercises such as Pyongyang's Gathering of One Million, Arirang Mass Games or a Troop Review. Seeing the busy streets of Shenyang and marvelling at the combination of lights and people, I wondered how this could possibly be a regular occurrence and not a festive exception. How did all these people earn enough to live like this? How did the Chinese Communist Party come to tolerate it? It was astonishing to me.

Lost in these thoughts, I realised too late that we had arrived at our destination and that Cho-rin had handed over the cab fare. If

Cho-rin insisted on paying for the small things today, I told myself, I would pay for the large things.

'Cho-rin, when are we meeting your fiancé?' I asked.

'Seven-thirty. We still have some time.'

'Is there a department store nearby?'

'Why? Would you like to have a look round inside?'

'Yes. You did say we had time.'

The department store was close by, not more than fifty metres away. On the side of the building, a large Coca-Cola advertisement lit up the surrounding area. The entrance was a set of revolving doors. Full of excitement, I led the way, then panicked and turned back, coming out as I had entered. I had almost fallen into the arms of a police officer with a pistol guarding the entrance. Cho-rin looked puzzled, then playfully nudged my arm and giggled.

'He isn't a real officer, dummy! He's just a security guard! The pistol's probably a dummy too, just for show.' I felt mortified, thinking that Cho-rin might now take me for a coward. I took the lead again. In Pyongyang too there were department stores selling imported goods, but they only accepted foreign currency and most ordinary people could not shop there. The first department store I saw in Shenyang had more goods on sale than the ones in Pyongyang, but I was disappointed to see that these were not foreign imports, but products made in China. I noticed a stall displaying leather gloves, and walked quickly towards it. To redeem myself for having fallen for a fake, I picked out a pair of genuine leather gloves.

I showed them to Cho-rin, 'Here, try these.'

'Why?' she asked.

When I replied that I wanted to buy her a pair, she shook her head and told me not to be so silly. She said she had several pairs at home; and, anyway, I mustn't waste my money on useless things. When I looked at the price tag, I was deflated. Four hundred yuan for a pair of gloves? Feeling mortified yet again, I could only follow Cho-rin meekly out of the store as she urged me on, saying that now we would be late.

Just inside the main entrance I noticed a toy stall. I picked out two toy swords from the display. They were modern ones with batteries in the handles and, when you pressed the button, lights flashed in different colours. I imagined that when Cho-rin's cousin saw the swords, he would be delighted and we would make up our differences. A moment later, Cho-rin appeared by my side and pinched my arm, saying that she had gone outside and, thinking she'd lost me, panicked and rushed back to look for me. Then, when she saw what I'd bought, she told me off and asked me to get a refund. I struggled to convince her, insisting that it was part of my teaching method.

Outside, Cho-rin became even more excited than I was, grinning and slicing a toy sword in arabesques through the air. Every time the sword flashed, Cho-rin looked more beautiful.

Cho-rin had arranged to meet her fiancé at an expensive restaurant where waiters greeted us in a long entranceway. I was startled to see them bowing, as it seemed as if they were grovelling. When we followed two waitresses to our table, we found that Cho-rin's fiancé was waiting for us in a private room. Even from first impressions, he seemed to be a good man. His name in Korean pronunciation was Ju Yun-bal. Cho-rin introduced us, adding that he had the same name as a famous Chinese actor. I liked his smile very much, and his youthful good looks seemed to confirm that couples are often similar-looking people. Although the only Chinese I'd picked up was the greeting Ni hao! he seemed very pleased with that one phrase of mine. He was well mannered, helping Cho-rin take off her coat and smoothing its shoulders before hanging it up. He would clearly make her a wonderful husband.

When the waiter brought us the menu, Cho-rin glanced at it and then handed it to me. I was intending to pay for dinner, and began to flick through the pages with pleasure. Although I couldn't read the Chinese characters, I despaired at the numbers next to each item – a starter was priced at 50 yuan upwards. I had 340 yuan left after buying the toy swords.

I passed the menu to Cho-rin's fiancé who called the waiter and ordered dish after dish. I asked Cho-rin in Korean, 'I wanted to buy dinner, but this is all I have. What can we order?'

'Forget it,' she replied. 'I didn't bring you out for that reason.'

She then changed the subject, as if warning me not to mention payment again. Cho-rin explained that in China, ordering food was for show in many ways. For example, if you asked for beer, they would understand it not as one bottle but as a box of ten. I wondered whether this was related to China's size, or a result of economic reforms leading to a show of purchasing power serving as the marker of status.

Soon the large round table was filled with all kinds of dishes. There was far too much for the three of us, and probably more than enough for nine. I guessed that the bill would be over 1500 yuan. And sure enough, they did us a box of ten bottles of beer, just as Cho-rin had said.

I excused myself to use the bathroom and rose from the table. I remembered that when we entered the restaurant, we had walked past a glass cabinet displaying wines. Although I couldn't afford the food, I wanted at least to buy them a nice bottle of wine, especially after Ju Yun-bal's generous orders, even if it was really just for show. Fortunately, there was a reasonably good-looking bottle of wine for 350 yuan. I showed the waiter my money and, although he saw that it amounted to 10 yuan less than the asking price, I was relieved that he accepted the notes and handed me the bottle with a smile.

I suddenly recalled the argument I had had with Young-min in an alleyway in Yanji over a paltry 10 yuan, and felt guilty that I was spending this money on wine when he might be hungrily wandering the streets. When we met again and he discovered how I had been getting on without him, he would surely feel let down by his friend. I quickly prayed that the 400 yuan I had left with Mr Shin in Yanji would be delivered to Young-min, and that he would arrive safely in Shenyang with the money. As I compared that sum with what I was paying for the wine, the bottle felt even more precious. Still, thinking how I had nothing to my name when I met Cho-rin, I felt proud that I could at least afford to buy her this bottle of wine by way of thanks.

As I walked back to our table with the wine, Cho-rin, who was taking a sip of water, slammed down her glass hard enough to make a noise. I said that I had known she would react like this, and that it was too late – the bottle had already been opened. Unexpectedly though, when she looked at the label, she relented, saying it was a very nice wine. After handing the bottle to her fiancé, she shot me a look, and said in a threatening tone that she would ask for the money back from her uncle, as I had wastefully spent my money on them.

From then on, we put the beer mugs to one side and made our toasts with wine glasses. I was astonished to find that in Chinese too, you said *Gunbae!* when you made a toast, just as we do in North Korea. We were discussing where the word had originated from when Cho-rin's fiancé received a phone call.

I filled Cho-rin's glass and my own. 'Cho-rin, can I ask you something?'

'Ask me anything you want.'

'You know what your cousin shouted earlier today, what does that mean? You know, *shabi zai zi*.'

'Shh!' she said, nodding at her fiancé. 'He might hear.'

'What does it mean?'

'You know they say that you won't live long if you know all the answers to life!'

'I'll ask Ju Yun-bal then.'

'No, don't do that! I'll tell you. Quietly.'

'So, *shabi*?'

'Mother … fucker.'

'The brat! What's *wo da si ni*?'

'I'm going to beat you to death.'

'Wow. What's *zai zi* then?'

'You don't need to know.'

'I'll ask your fiancé then.'

'No, I'll tell you.' She hesitated and then said, 'It means "prick".'

I didn't understand. 'What does that mean?'

'You know, like the male organ.'

Maybe because she was tipsy, Cho-rin blushed to the tips of her ears. When I said that I would demand that her cousin apologise for the insult as well as for his assault on her before I presented him with his toys, Cho-rin clapped her hands and smiled. As her fiancé finished his call, he asked what we had been talking about.

Cho-rin asked me, 'What should I tell him?' Her face was full of mischief.

'Tell him that if he ever makes you cry, you'll talk to him in the way that your cousin does.'

She threw her head back and laughed. Her fiancé seemed even more curious now and I worried that she might translate exactly what I'd said. When he put his thumbs up, I was relieved but confused. Cho-rin explained that she had told him it was his turn to buy wine now. I learned anew that human relations are built on careful words.

After dinner, we went for a walk. It wasn't snowing, and that made it a magnificent winter's night. Cho-rin walked between us with a man on each arm. I wanted to walk all the way back to Xita just like this, but a taxi slowed as it passed, although we had not flagged it down. We decided to get in. When we arrived in Xita, Cho-rin was the last to get out of the cab. Her fiancé scolded her for not leaving the change with the driver. Cho-rin replied indignantly as he walked on ahead, and slipped her hand into the pocket of my coat. She undid my clenched fist and pressed the change into my hand. As I tried to take the money out of my pocket, Cho-rin held my hand down. When I tried again, she pinched the back of my hand. When my hand surrendered, she patted it with her fingers, as if to reward it for its good behaviour.

At the entrance to the building, Cho-rin's fiancé almost tumbled on the ice. As Cho-rin and I rushed to support him, we all lost our balance and laughed. Cho-rin, giddy with wine and insistent on walking up the stairs, made us climb eight flights with her instead of taking the lift. That suited me fine, but by the time we reached the apartment, our evening together seemed to be over far too soon.

Cho-rin rang the doorbell and then knocked impatiently, emboldened by the two men at her side. We were all in good spirits, but staggered back when the door opened to reveal a grim-faced police officer. And there, just behind him, stood another.

THE officer who had opened the door came and stood behind the three of us. My heart was beating fast, but I was surprised to find that it wasn't as bad as it had been at other times of crisis. As we walked into the living room, Cho-rin's uncle explained in rapid Korean, 'I had spoken to my wife briefly about you, but the boy must have overheard. He asked questions, and my wife made him promise several times that he mustn't tell anyone there's a North Korean staying with us. But he's not the kind to do as he's told, is he? So he came back with these men, having told them we had a North Korean hiding in the house.' Through clenched teeth he added, 'I'm going to break his legs tonight. But stay calm, I've told them that you're South Korean.'

One of the men motioned to the uncle to stop him from talking, and then gestured towards the sofa, where the boy was sitting. When he called for him, the boy bounced up eagerly, and that made me uneasy. The way that Cho-rin said something to him gave me the premonition that things weren't going to go well, and this was confirmed when he walked towards me with a big boy's swagger. He pointed his finger at me, then poked my stomach with it several times.

My hands, which had been clenched in anxiety, lost their grip, and the bag containing his two toy swords fell to the floor. When the boy saw them, his eyes glittered with joy. Looking at me to check that I wouldn't stop him, he seized them and rushed back to the sofa. The two officers moved confidently towards me.

'They're saying you must show them your passport. Say something in Korean, I'll tell them in Chinese that you lost your bag,' Cho-rin instructed rapidly, taking my arm as though we were lovers.

As we went back and forth in translation with the men, the boy interrupted several times with stubborn insistence, perhaps to point out how we were lying. The father eventually smacked him on the back of the head to shut him up and the boy screamed, ran into his bedroom and slammed the door very loudly.

Cho-rin's fiancé, who had remained silent until then, yelled something at the officers. One of them shoved him in the chest to intimidate him. Ju Yun-bal shouted again at the officer in defiance, stepping forward threateningly. As Cho-rin came between them, the other man made a call on his phone. Everyone was quiet for a second, and Cho-rin turned deathly pale.

'You've got to run. They've just called for reinforcements.'

The officer put his phone back in his pocket and unclipped a pair of handcuffs from his belt. These Chinese handcuffs were shiny and new, just as one of the girls at Mr Shin's house had described them. Trying hard to speak in a calm voice, I told Cho-rin, 'Buy me a little time.'

I strode across the living room, doing my best to appear unconcerned, and to my surprise no one tried to stop me. I walked into the piano room and collected my manuscript of poems, my identification documents bearing my true identity, and my sunglasses.

I turned and walked towards the front door, but the two men moved to block my path. Cho-rin screeched and at the same time her fiancé lunged at one of the officers, grabbing him at the waist. Cho-rin rushed towards the other officer, shouting, 'Run! Quickly!'

Without pausing to look round, I ran down the stairs, leaping several steps at a time. As I hurtled from landing to landing, I could hear shouting behind me, then Cho-rin's scream, and then a loud thud as the building absorbed the shock of a body hitting the floor. I could hear the sounds of more struggle, and a door crashing against the wall. Suddenly the sound of heavy boots filled the stairwell.

Running out of the building, I tripped on the step, almost fell, then doubled back down the alley next to the apartment block, where I hid myself among the rubbish bins. The officers would leave sooner or later, and then I could say a final goodbye to Cho-rin and Ju Yun-bal, and to her uncle's family. I hoped that Cho-rin would find a way to slip out and say goodbye.

But the situation was only getting worse. Boots stomped down into the lobby of the building, and an officer dashed outside. His cap was gone and his shirt buttons were undone; it must have been a violent struggle upstairs. Sirens sounded and a police vehicle appeared. Two more vans followed, and eight officers rushed out of the vehicles. They rallied near the cap-less officer, listened to his instructions, and then proceeded to carry out his orders. Four of them went back into the apartment, and the rest went off in different directions.

Two of them began to come my way. They were only ten metres from me. If I stayed there any longer, I would be caught. I lowered my head and began to run.

'Zhan zhu! Zhan zhu!'

One of them spotted me and starting yelling. I broke into a sprint. Terrifying shouts came from all sides, and I imagined a rough hand seizing my collar at any moment. Just as when I'd crossed the Tumen River, my legs trembled beneath me. I was panting and my chest felt tight. I had turned into an alley with high walls on either side, and the sound of the officers' boots echoed all around me.

I feared I'd run into a dead-end and panicked, realising that the streets here were different from those in Yanji, where the roads had been open. I was out of breath and could not sprint for much longer. My legs were so heavy that it felt like I was dragging them with each step. I considered giving up.

Seeing a steel drum in front of me, I hurled it behind me with all my might, and heard the officers' shouts as the drum crashed into their path – sweet harmony for my pitch-perfect ears. The sound of the pursuing boots seemed to stop. But no, there were the boots again. This man was stronger than the one who'd fallen, and gaining ground. Twenty metres, fifteen metres, ten metres … I had to make a decision. I picked up a piece of metal piping. Screaming at the top of my voice, I turned to face the oncoming officer.

He stiffened and almost fell forward as he stopped in his tracks. Although it was dark, he was standing so close that I could make out his eyelashes. I lifted the pipe high above my head, and as the pole scraped on one of the cement walls that rose on either side, it screeched loudly. Gaining confidence, I swung the pole and scraped again, as hard as I could. Sparks flew from the end of the pipe. I yelled, like a dragon breathing flames, '*Shabi, wo da si ni! Shabi zai zi!*'

Lifting the pipe high over my head again, I ran at the officer. He stepped back a few paces, then turned and ran. Chasing him a few metres, I saw an alley leading off to the right. I scraped the pipe again on the cement wall to let him know I was intent on following him. In case he changed his mind and decided to pursue me again, I shouted again for good measure, '*Shabi, wo da si ni! Shabi zai zi!*' Then I darted into the alley.

Perhaps I ran for about ten minutes through the alleyways. I slowed to a walk when I came to a deserted area, but I kept moving. I had dropped the pipe by then, and there was no feeling from my hand to my shoulder. When I felt the limb with my other hand, there was no sensation at all – it was like touching an alien object. The ends of my fingers trembled and twitched.

I checked my pockets, and my poems were still safe. Or rather, the poems, my lucky charm, were keeping me safe. In fact, every time I had been separated from my poems, something bad had happened. In Yanji, Young-min had returned them to me, and in Shenyang,

Cho-rin had bought me time to retrieve them. I folded my arms across my chest, resolving never to take my manuscript out of my jacket pocket again.

What had happened to Cho-rin? She and her fiancé, her uncle and aunt – how shocked they must have been! I feared that the authorities would impose harsh penalties on them. I had run so far into the outskirts that I was now surrounded by darkness. I could see an area in the distance where the bright city lights were concentrated. Perhaps it was the glow of the police lights surrounding Cho-rin's uncle's house.

Her cousin would be in serious trouble with his father. Cho-rin would not just let the matter drop, either. And then I remembered the toy swords. Where had I left them? Had I taken them into the apartment? Yes, I remembered the boy picking them up. I had intended to make a present of them, but it ended up as his reward for reporting me to the authorities. What a fool I'd made of myself! I laughed out loud like a madman, until I realised that the boy had helped me in some respects. I'd been able to summon up the courage to wield steel piping in front of an officer's face because I'd been imitating the boy. And the lesson in Chinese I had received from him couldn't have been more useful: *Shabi, wo da si ni! Shabi zai zi!*

I repeated the words to myself and reached an area lit with streetlamps. Cho-rin would be overjoyed to know I was alive and well. If I saw her again, I would describe to her my feat of martial arts, fending off an armed officer with metal piping. She would pat me on the head as a mother would a boy. And seeing me safe, Wang Hou's parents would forgive him.

I began to walk more quickly. If I did see Cho-rin again, we would have to say goodbye, and I would have to leave for Beijing. If I saw her again, I wasn't sure if I could hold back a flood of tears.

As I continued to walk my body began to shiver involuntarily, and I realised I was drenched with sweat. I found it hard to believe that I had been able to spend two nights out in the mountains near Yanji, and that we had not frozen to death.

When I began to see signs in Korean here and there, I realised I must be back in the Xita District. If I walked a little further, I might reach that familiar apartment building, and perhaps Cho-rin would be waiting there. Perhaps the police would have moved on and I could steal back into the flat? My hopes were rising wildly and, as if that thought was becoming manifest, I saw a familiar Coca-Cola advert up ahead. It was the same advert as the one on the wall of the department store I had entered with Cho-rin. But why had the advert moved to a wall of a different building? When I came closer, I realised that the building housed a restaurant, not a department store.

I walked further and saw another advert, exactly the same, dancing in the neon lights. I was in a street I did not recognise at all. People were walking everywhere, not caring whether they were stepping on the pavement or road. The overwhelming chaos of pedestrians, combined with the traffic noise coming from all directions, made it even more difficult for me to regain my sense of direction.

Panic overtook me. Today was the first time I had left the house. When we'd arrived at Cho-rin's uncle's house, and when we went to the restaurant with her fiançe, we had used cabs. I realised I had no way of knowing which way was which.

The rumble of a train in the distance reminded me that over the rooftops of low-rise buildings, I had been able to see many intersecting rail tracks when I'd looked out from Cho-rin's uncle's apartment. If I reached the railway intersection, I thought I might be able to gain my bearings.

I walked for more than half an hour, but realised I was utterly lost. My surroundings turned shabby. Beyond the flyovers tangled like snakes overhead, all the apartment buildings looked the same. I tried to remember where I'd ended up after evading the officers, but it was no good. By the time I returned to what looked like the centre of

Xita, the streets were emptier and there were fewer cars and people. A police vehicle shot past me with its sirens silent and lights flashing.

I was furious with myself. I had let my guard down while staying with Cho-rin's uncle. How careless I had been, not bothering to prepare for a possible confrontation. How could I hope to make the long and dangerous journey to South Korea? *How could I? How could I? How could I?*

That night, I slept in the stairwell of an apartment building somewhere, huddled against the cold, drawing up my knees and pressing my face against them. The position must have been bad for my circulation, because when I opened my eyes, it felt as though ice had started to form inside my body. My teeth clattered uncontrollably. When I tried to stretch my limbs, I thought I could hear the cracks of breaking ice. There was nowhere that did not ache – my arms, legs and back all throbbed with pain. I feared that I might have broken a bone – it was difficult enough to be on the run without a plan, but an injury would be the end of me. When I saw the bruises on my body after last night's headlong flight, I was relieved to discover the source of my aches and pains.

Watching the sky unfurl into colour with the coming of the dawn, it seemed for a moment that I might find my way back in no time at all. But the city turned out to be much more complex than I had appreciated in the dark. I despaired as the map of familiar places that I had carefully pieced together in my head scattered and was replaced by the chaos of this inscrutable city.

As midday passed into afternoon, my stomach started to grumble. Only when I thought of food did I realise that I was penniless once more. For a panicked few seconds I rushed to retrace my steps, thinking that I had dropped 350 yuan on the ground. I grinned ruefully when I remembered that, of course, I had spent it on a bottle of wine over dinner, and that Cho-rin had appreciated my choice as she read the label. Building on this positive memory, an idea came to me. I could call Mr Shin: his wife would have the landline of Cho-rin's uncle registered on her mobile phone. All I needed to do was to retrieve that number, and I would be able to see Cho-rin one last time.

Walking quickly at first in my excitement, I slowed down as I figured out how to find the coins to make a call. One yuan was all I needed. Then I recalled that Cho-rin had mentioned something about Xita Church. A lot of North Korean refugees went there looking for help, she'd said, and South Koreans provided money to help them. One refugee had even received enough to purchase a false passport, and had been able to fly to South Korea. I decided I would make my way to this Xita Church. I wouldn't be begging for assistance with my entire escape, merely asking for one yuan on compassionate grounds. Anyone could find themselves in that situation, and one yuan wouldn't be too much to give away. I put on my sunglasses and stood at a crossroads.

I noticed a Korean sign that read 'Kyonghoeru'. It was a familiar name, which I had come across at the UFD as I studied Seoul. 'Kyonghoe' referred to a virtuous meeting between a master and servant, and was the name of a tower built near Kyongbok Palace in Seoul by a Chosun king in the fourteenth century. Just as the history behind the name was grand, the restaurant was large. When I entered, there was only one woman cleaning up, as they had finished serving lunch. Fortunately, she spoke Korean. She kindly gave me directions to Xita Church, and even drew me a map.

I managed to find the church without difficulty after about fifteen minutes' walk. There were several groups of people gathered in conversation outside the church. As I neared them, I could hear fragments of Korean. Recognising my own language, I desperately wanted to join in and become one of them. This group of Koreans seemed to stand out from the Chinese even in the way they dressed, with a distinctive fashion sense of their own. One young man was wearing a bright jacket and trousers, with a smart white shirt. Nearby, a tall couple engaged in conversation, both wearing smart long black coats. I felt proud that my fellow Koreans looked so good, and felt as if I were already one of them, standing equal among them. Perhaps it was for this reason that I couldn't countenance the thought of begging from them. Even though I only wanted one yuan, I couldn't bring myself to ask for money. I remembered what my parents used to say when I was younger, that one must never scrounge from others. It was almost more acceptable simply to ask for safe passage to South Korea.

As I approached the front door of the building with this thought, two men prevented me from entering.

'Who are you looking for?'

'I have some business inside.'

'You don't look like a member of our congregation.'

'No, I've come from North Korea. I've something important to talk about. It's dangerous out here, I really must go—'

Before I could finish, one of the men seized my arm to stop it reaching the handle and the other shoved me back.

'Come back on Sunday. We might give you money then. Not today.'

Immediately, I retorted, 'I'm not here to beg for money. Believe me. I didn't come to ask for money. I'm not that kind of person.'

'This isn't a place for North Korean refugees! And what's with your sunglasses? Get out of here. Go find a consulate or embassy, you piece of shit. It's because filth like you keep coming here that the authorities won't leave us alone. Can't you hear me? Get out of here, out!'

I fell back. As I moved quickly away, I thought I could hear the tread of military boots behind me. My face was hot with humiliation, and I grew angry as I imagined the crowd outside the building mocking me behind my back. I slowed to a defiantly upbeat pace to preserve my dignity, but inside I was screaming: *Am I not making a plea for help in a common language? Are we not fellow human beings, speaking the same tongue?*

I sat down on a bench in a park not too far from the church. Even when I looked up at the sky's expanse, there was not a piece of it I could claim as my own. I had imagined that freedom as wide as the universe under these skies would allow me to choose my own life. But freedom turned out to be no more than a shrinking cold hole. Were there certain people that had been set apart as free? Was freedom a predetermined fate that I had no right to enjoy?

I remembered how Young-min said we would never make it to South Korea after we were thrown out of the church in Yanji. Perhaps his purchase of a blade with our last 10 yuan had been the right decision. I fidgeted in desperation, opening and closing my hands inside my pockets, where my fingers found a small crumpled ball of paper. I took it out and threw it to the ground. My gaze rested upon it blankly until I realised it wasn't just a piece of trash but some precious yuan. I reached to pick it up and found two one-yuan notes. A gift from heaven?

Where had it come from? In my befuddlement, it took a while before my mind came to rest on an image of Cho-rin's face. It was the change from our cab ride together.

I called out her name: 'Cho-rin!'

I leapt out of my seat and actually began to run, looking for a phone booth, but instead found an old woman who was on the street selling phone calls from her landline. I handed her my money and took the receiver with my other hand. The number I dialled began to ring, and in the short moment before Mr Shin answered, Cho-rin's face flashed in my mind.

'Hello?' Mr Shin answered.

'Hi, it's me. You know that number on your wife's phone?' I said quickly, trying to make the message as brief as possible so I could call Cho-rin. 'I don't have any more money, so before I run out of minutes on this phone, you know that number I called from, can you read it out to me? I'll call you back soon!'

'What on earth are you talking about?' Mr Shin asked. Annoyed, I began to repeat my sentences, but Mr Shin interrupted. 'Your friend has died. What are you going on about?'

I didn't respond.

Mr Shin continued, 'Are you listening? Your friend Young-min – he's dead.'

I doubted that what I had just heard had been a real voice, and checked that I was still holding the phone.

'What? What did you just say?' I managed to say. The receiver was shaking in my hand.

'Stay calm. Just listen to what I'm saying. Yesterday, I got a call from Young-min's uncle, asking to meet me urgently. He wouldn't say why. When we met, the man was too distressed to speak. Then he broke down in tears, telling me that his nephew had died, and that it had been a terrible end. He said that Young-min was taken away in a car by the Chinese authorities, and they were driving over a mountain pass when he apparently asked to relieve himself by the side of the road. He used the opportunity to kill himself by jumping off the rock face. Young-min had been on the streets for a week before he was caught near the house. The uncle was asked to identify his body, which he did.'

I couldn't hear what Mr Shin said after that. I lowered the receiver. Even when the old woman took the phone away from me, complaining that I had gone beyond my allotted time, I felt nothing.

The evening sun was reflected on the glass buildings all around us. As the world drowned in a tide of red, I felt certain I had seen this sky before. It was the same sunset that Young-min and I had seen on that first night, on the way to stay with Chang-yong's mother-in-law. It had been a beautiful sunset, full of hope. From that distant place, I felt the presence of Young-min drawing nearer. As he became clearer in my eyes, my vision clouded. Young-min could not have died. It could not be true, even if his own father had been the one to identify his body. How could he be no longer here in this world with me? I bit my lip to stop myself from crying. If I cried, it would seal the truth of his death. But if I held back my tears, I knew he would come back to me.

I walked a few steps and then collapsed to my knees when I remembered how Young-min had desperately wanted to buy a drink in Yanji market. All he had wanted was to lose himself for a moment as we fled from our pursuers. But I had denied him even that small final comfort. Even if it meant abandoning our hopes of freedom, even if it meant surrendering, I wished, in vain, that we had shared that one last night of drunkenness.

Filled with bitter regret, I knelt down on the pavement and wept. I was not there with him to the end. He had thrown himself off that rock face because I was not there to take his hand. What pain did he feel as he knew he was going to fall? What did my kind friend pray for in those last few moments? I groaned, and the tears would not stop. What had I been doing as Young-min killed himself? I was playing the piano, making music, though that music truly belonged to him.

I wept in an agony made all the more bitter by not having anything left for Young-min, not even a drink with which to toast his memory. I had nothing left to my name. All I had as an offering for Young-min's ghost were my own wretched tears.

Dawn came. The new day offered me a challenge, and I snapped the bridge of my sunglasses, tossing the broken halves on the ground and crushing them underfoot. After Young-min had confronted death itself, I couldn't justify my timidity, my remaining hidden behind dark glass to conceal myself from the world. If I remained hidden, Young-min would mock me from above. I was ashamed of being alive without him, and it was a worse betrayal to continue in cowardice.

From that moment on, I was no longer a fugitive. I was no longer fleeing out of terror, but fighting for my freedom, so that I could expose the lies of Kim Jong-il. I wasn't afraid to die if I died a free man, and this released me from fear. I did not even flinch when I passed a police officer. If I must follow the path Young-min had taken, so be it. Silently, I swore at each passing officer: *Shabi, wo da si ni! Shabi zai zi!*

I had two paths to choose between. Not the way I had come and the way I would go, but a path I knew and a path that was unknown. I wanted to confront the latter, and I would find a way to Beijing. When I came across the Korean restaurant sign 'Kyonghoeru' again, I felt I would try whatever had been put in my way.

When I opened the door, I spotted the woman who had given me directions to Xita Church the day before.

'Come on in,' she said. She recognised me, and even asked whether I had managed to find the church all right.

'Yes, I did. You were so kind to me. Thank you.'

The woman smiled shyly at my compliment. 'What would you like to order?' she asked.

'I'm not eating, thanks. Would you please call the owner of the restaurant?'

'Do you know him?'

'Please tell him someone would like to meet him, thanks!'

'Sir! Sir!' The woman's voice became distant as she ran off to fetch the owner. It was too early for lunch, so there were no other customers. I looked at my reflection in the window and patted my hair down. I brushed the dust and grime off my shoulders as best I could, rubbing spit into the cloth of my jacket to darken the marks.

'He'll be down in five minutes. He's just cleaning his teeth. Please wait here – take a seat.' The woman gestured to a chair and went into the kitchen. Perhaps she was going to have her own meal before customers began to arrive.

I prepared myself to make a good first impression on the owner of the restaurant. Though I might be shabby in appearance, I wanted to convey courtesy and gravitas, so that the man would see me as a fellow human being. Should I sit with a straight back in a display of confidence? Or should I sit more modestly, but hold my head up? As I tried out different positions, I noticed a newspaper on another table. I decided that there would be no more natural pose than to wait with an open newspaper in my hands. I sat back, crossed my legs and opened the paper, but immediately sat up straight when I saw what it was. The newspaper was a South Korean broadsheet that I used to enjoy reading with my UFD clearance back home.

The UFD acquired South Korean newspapers through China so they were always out of date by the time they reached us, three days old at best. But now here I was, reading today's paper! I felt as if I had already settled into a world of freedom. As this was a paper that had arrived from my final destination, I couldn't just flip through the pages. I didn't want to miss a single story.

I saw a phone number that readers could call to provide leads for stories. Before I turned the page, I looked again at the number. How could I make use of it? The contact was there to solicit scoops; it was not a helpline for asylum-seekers. If even the South Korean consulate in Shenyang didn't give a damn about my situation, why should a journalist? Besides, if I did provide them with information, I would only put myself in more danger.

Reporters had nothing to do with spies. Yet those who worked for a free press might be willing to risk their safety to uncover a lie. If I could meet one of them in person, they might listen to me. Right now, though, the most important thing was to get enough money for my fare to Beijing.

'Are you looking for me?' A man in his mid-forties stood opposite me. When I noticed his pursed lips, I knew that if this did not work, it would be the end.

'Yes, I came to tell you something. It'll only take five minutes.'

'Bring two cups of tea here!' the man shouted, turning towards the kitchen. He picked up the newspaper I had been reading, rolled it up, and swatted a fly on the table's edge. Then he threw the paper into the bin and turned to me again. His manner made me think that he wouldn't care what I said. Feeling guilty, I decided I would have to spin a story.

'I've come from North Korea,' I began.

The owner, who had been sitting back comfortably, turned to shout at the kitchen again. 'Breakfast for this gentleman!'

My stomach had been groaning and moaning since I first stepped into the restaurant, but I pretended to be taken aback by the suggestion of breakfast. 'I didn't come here for a free meal!' I exclaimed. 'I came to talk to you about something.'

The man looked quizzically at me and shouted again to the kitchen, 'Cancel that breakfast!'

My heart sank, but I tried not to show my disappointment. I

asked, 'Do you know about the Ace Bed Company, the South Korean furniture giant?'

He replied, 'I don't have any links to corporations like that, and I'm not interested either. What's your point?'

'The Chairman of Ace Bed, Ahn Yoo-su, is originally from North Korea.' I knew about Chairman Ahn's background from my work at the UFD. We had compiled extensive profiles of South Korean CEOs in order to manipulate South Korean conglomerates into providing us with aid. Ahn Yoo-su was the first one to come to mind because, like me, he had been born in Sariwon, my hometown in North Hwanghae Province. He had fled south in the course of the Korean War and, starting from scratch, had created the largest furniture company in South Korea. The main roads in Sariwon had been paved with asphalt through funds donated by Ahn.

I rattled off many personal details, so that the restaurateur wouldn't just dismiss me as a desperate refugee winging it. I paused for a moment, and uttered my next sentence with special emphasis: 'I'm Chairman Ahn's nephew.'

The man glanced up at me. He had been concentrating on the design painted on his teacup.

'My uncle has a subsidiary in Beijing,' I continued. 'As soon as I crossed the river from North Korea and reached Yanji, I called the managing director of the Beijing subsidiary. He said he'd deliver my message to the chairman, and that he'd be waiting for me at the office. All I ask of you is a bus fare to Beijing. I promise I will repay you. My uncle too will be forever grateful.'

None of this made any sense. Why would the nephew of a tycoon be short of a bus fare? And even if he was, why would the managing director in Beijing be waiting for me at the office instead of sending me a car? I was an idiot. Sweat ran cold down my back.

'I'm not the only Korean in this part of town. Why did you choose me to ask for your bus fare?'

I couldn't think of an answer to that question. I was sure he wanted me to leave. He wouldn't care even if I really was the penniless nephew of the rich uncle. A moment of silence passed between us. I opened my mouth to speak in the desperate hope that my heart would guide my words.

'Because you're the owner of Kyonghoeru, because you run the biggest Korean restaurant here in Shenyang, and because I knew I could trust you,' I said.

These words, at least, were sincere.

After I'd made myself vulnerable like this, there was nothing else I could think of doing but to leave the restaurant and wait outside the entrance for his verdict. He didn't say anything, but sat stroking his cheek with his huge hand, staring at me. Then he leaned to one side as if to rise from his chair. But before I could shut my eyes in terror, he pulled a wallet from his back pocket.

'The fare to Beijing is 250 yuan. As you said, I'm the owner of Kyonghoeru, so here's an extra hundred. Eat something on the way. Your lips are all cracked.'

The tears of despair that had been welling up inside me were transformed into tears of gratitude. Drops rolled down my cheeks and onto the backs of my hands. The owner of Kyonghoeru pretended not to have seen, and stood up. 'You don't need to pay me back,' he said, kindly. 'You have your fare now. Get some breakfast before you go.' His manner became brusquely managerial again when he called out to the kitchen, 'Breakfast for this gentleman!'

To hide my tears, I bowed my head as I stood up. Unable to look him in the eye, I bent my waist in a deeper bow. 'Thank you. I will repay your gratitude. Please remember me – my face and my voice. I will repay you.' I bowed again, then turned and left.

'Hey!' the man shouted. 'Have some breakfast!'

I ran outside, but didn't go far before I turned to look back at the sign: 'Kyong-hoe-ru'. I would cherish those three syllables for the rest of my life. And now, I would be able to make my way to Beijing, to the South Korean Embassy.

I headed straight to the Shenyang bus terminal. On the way, I stopped to make a call to Mr Shin. I wanted to give him my word, and Cho-rin too, that if I managed to be given asylum in South Korea, I would return to see them. But Mr Shin's phone was switched off, and his wife's phone was not connected either.

I called several times from the terminal, but I couldn't get through. I worried that the authorities, having successfully captured Young-min, might have seized Mr Shin. I told myself I would try again when I arrived in Beijing.

While waiting for the bus I remembered the telephone number for the Korean broadsheet that I had seen at the restaurant. My bad experience of talking to the South Korean consulate in Shenyang prepared me to try a different approach with the woman who answered the phone.

'Hello, how can I help you?' she said breezily.

'Hello! This is the number for tip-offs, isn't it?' I spoke as calmly as I could.

'Yes, it is. May I please have your name and address?'

'I've come over from North Korea.'

'Excuse me?'

'I'm not calling to seek asylum or anything like that. I work on inter-Korean affairs, at the United Front Department. I've come to China on business. I'm calling to provide your newspaper with an exclusive.'

'United Front Department, did you say? Inter-Korean affairs? Yes, please wait a moment.' She called out to someone else in the office. 'Sir, sir! Do you have a moment?'

I could picture the woman putting the phone down and running off to fetch the editor. A few seconds later, I heard the urgent voice of a man.

'Hello? Hello! Thank you so much for getting in touch, it can't have been easy. Where exactly are you at the moment? United Front Department, you said? Is that the section that deals with South Korea?'

'Yes,' I replied.

'I see! What an honour to speak to you. Could you please explain your position in the Department?'

'I can't stay on the line for long. You must understand.'

'Of course, I understand absolutely. Would you please tell me a little about the information you wish to provide us with? As for the rest of it, there's no hurry.'

'I've got my North Korean identification documents with me. But how can you trust that I'm genuine just by talking to me on the phone?'

'No, I trust you. When I heard your voice I could—'

'Sorry, I need to say this quickly: please give me the number of your Beijing correspondent. Not his office number, but his mobile number. It's got to be a private one too, so it won't be bugged.'

'Yes, please hold for a moment. I'm really sorry, it'll really only be a moment.'

South Korean journalists were quick off the mark. The editor was soon back on the line and gave me a private number for his Beijing correspondent. He said I should wait ten minutes before calling, and that he would call the correspondent right after we hung up to tell him to expect my call.

In those ten minutes of waiting, I considered, with the sort of intense concentration that I might apply to a poem, what I would say when I got through to the correspondent. I had just one phone call to get him on my side.

When I called, he answered the phone immediately.

'Hello,' I began, 'I used to work in the United Front Department of the Workers' Party.' Calling a private number like this, I felt more able to speak openly. To establish the legitimacy of my identity, I told him why I'd left North Korea, what information I could provide, and the fact that I had been framed for murder. I focused on the main points and kept it as concise as I could. I then said in a frank tone, 'If you decide to meet me, you must realise the risks. I am happy to tell you what I know, but I cannot guarantee your safety, let alone my own. If I make it to South Korea, I promise to repay you with many exclusives. Please help me.'

'What kind of help do you need?' he asked.

'Please connect me with a South Korean spy in Beijing.'

'I'm afraid I can't help you with that. I don't know any spies.'

'I'm not stupid. You're a journalist in a country like China, where North Korean agents operate freely, and if you don't know, you must be only one phone call away from someone who does. Please put yourself in my position. When you hang up, you can go back to your normal life, but the only thing left for me is suicide.'

For a moment there was only static on the line. I expected him to hang up, as the employee at the South Korean consulate had done.

'You said you're in Shenyang right now?'

I was elated by the mere fact of hearing his voice again. 'Yes, I'm at the bus terminal in Shenyang,' I said urgently. 'I've already bought a ticket for the noon bus to Beijing.'

He asked me to call him back as soon as I was in Beijing. He said that he would do his best to find help for me before my arrival.

The journey to Beijing took eight hours. During every moment of those eight long hours, I replayed in my mind the details of the conversation I'd had with the Beijing correspondent. Every word, the emphasis on each word, how his breath punctuated each sentence – I left nothing unexamined. Eventually, I was able to relax a little at the thought that I had spoken not to an ordinary local but to the correspondent of a major South Korean newspaper, and that he had promised to do his best. All I could do for now was to trust his word.

As soon as I got off the bus in Beijing, I looked around for a phone booth. The bus terminal was incomparably larger than the one in Shenyang. An enormous clock showed that it was ten minutes past nine, and off to the right I found a phone box. Dialling the number, I prayed that the correspondent would answer. I didn't care if he gave me a cold refusal at this point – I just wanted him to answer the phone.

'Hello?' he answered.

I exhaled in relief. 'I've just arrived in Beijing.'

'I'm going to read you a phone number,' he said. 'Please don't write it down, just memorise it. You should call it as soon as we hang up. Someone will be waiting on the other end. Just so you know, he's not with South Korean intelligence, but he can help you reach the South Korean Embassy.' The man made me repeat the number and then hung up.

My fingers shook as I dialled. The phone rang just once before someone answered.

'Hello, how are you?' he said.

'Yes! Hello! I am—'

He interrupted me. 'Don't say anything for now, sir, please just listen carefully. From where you're standing, there's a tree at ten o'clock. Do you see the rubbish bin next to it?'

There was indeed a tree at ten o'clock, and a rubbish bin beside it. Somebody must be watching me! As soon as I became conscious of this fact, the thought of North Korean agents filled my head, and I looked round in panic. To calm myself, I reasoned that North Korean agents would have jumped me by now, and I fixed my eyes on the tree and the rubbish bin.

'Yes, I can see those things,' I replied.

'If you look inside the rubbish bin, you'll find a black plastic bag. There's a mobile phone inside the plastic bag. Let's continue our conversation on that.'

Before I could ask any questions, the line went dead. I crossed to the rubbish bin and looked inside. It was too dark to make out what was inside, so I reached down into it and started to feel for the plastic bag. The first thing I pulled out was a torn sneaker. I tried again, and then I felt something like plastic. I pulled it out, opened the bag, and found a mobile phone and another object, thick and tightly wrapped in paper.

Taking out the phone, I flipped it open and turned it on. My hands were shaking wildly, and I could feel my pulse thumping in my neck.

The phone rang immediately. I answered, 'I found it!'

'Yes. It's great to meet you, sir. We already know who you are.'

We? As in South Korean spies? Or journalists?

'We've been trying to reach you, and it's wonderful to meet you at last. Please listen carefully now. You are in great danger. The Chinese authorities have not only sent out their border guards and police, but have also mobilised agents of the Ministry of State Security. And North Korean agents arrived at their Embassy here in Beijing a couple of days ago.'

The Chinese Ministry of State Security? That was their secret police. What crime had I committed against the Chinese Communist Party?

'So for the safety of us all, you must do exactly as I ask you to.'

'Yes, I understand.'

'First, I'd like to ask you something. When you were in Shenyang, did you provide the South Korean journalist with any information in the form of documents?'

'No, we only spoke on the phone.'

'I see. Good. Please make your way quickly towards the main road and flag a cab down. Call me back when you're in the cab and I'll tell the driver where to go.'

I did as I was told. I went out to the main road and I waved down a cab coming towards me with its light on. For a moment I thought the driver had not seen me. But then he stopped maybe ten metres ahead of where I was standing and reversed the vehicle until the car was right in front of me. When I got in he said something to me in Chinese, but I signalled for him to wait and called the South Korean man again.

'Hello? I'm in the cab,' I said.

'Good. Now pass the phone to the driver.'

Maybe the driver was annoyed by the soft foreign voice on the phone, because he responded roughly. He didn't even look back as he passed me the phone, and took off in a hurry.

As the taxi made its way to our unknown destination, I kept looking behind us. I was not so much concerned that hidden eyes were watching me but, rather, I was afraid that at this breakneck speed we might get too far ahead of my minder. I sat in anxiety and even gestured at the driver to slow down when he accelerated too hard for my liking.

The phone rang again. 'There's 2000 yuan in the plastic bag,' the voice said.

'Where?' Only then did I realise that the other object in the plastic bag was a bundle of cash.

'Give the driver 100 yuan when you get out. He can keep the change. After turning into the next street, the taxi will stop.'

When the taxi pulled up I found that we had come to a hotel, but I didn't have time to register its name. The voice on the phone guided me straight to the café in the hotel lobby. It instructed me to order a coffee and even told me how I should sit.

'Well, that's it from our end,' the voice concluded. 'In five minutes, a man will come to sit at your table. All you have to do from now on is whatever he says. Goodbye.'

When the call ended, my lifeline was gone too, and the mobile phone became an ordinary object again. I felt a rush of impending disaster. I feared that the man's words, 'from now on,' were an instruction to forge a new life as a fugitive with the 1850 yuan that remained after the cab fare and cup of coffee. Why else would they have given me so much cash?

As each minute passed on the mobile phone's tiny screen, my breathing grew louder. I had experienced more despair than I could ever have imagined when I lacked one yuan with which to make a phone call, or ten more yuan with which I could have shared a drink with Young-min. Yet the possession of 1850 yuan gave me no consolation. It lay heavy in my hands, and I clutched it because there was nothing else to hold on to.

'Mr Jang?' I started at the sound of a man's voice behind me. I made a move to stand but felt his hand on my shoulder. His arrival after exactly five minutes seemed to confirm his trustworthiness, and when he finally stood before me, his physical presence was as solid as a mountain. He was a smartly dressed man in his early fifties, dapper in his freshly pressed suit and gleaming glasses.

'Thank you! Thank you so much for coming here,' I said.

'Please stop looking round. Look only at me,' he muttered quietly as he took a cigarette from a red pack. 'I wanted to meet you, Mr Jang, in person,' he continued, 'so I asked a friend to guide you here. It's a relief that you two were able to connect at the station.'

'Thank you for organising that. I had no trouble getting here.'

He nodded. 'I have a contact in the Chinese authorities. About two weeks ago, he mentioned you. You crossed the river with a friend, is that right?'

'Yes, that's right.'

'Why did you separate?'

'We were looking for a place to stay the night, and we thought there was nowhere that would let two men into their house.'

'I understand. Just for routine verification, do you have your identification documents with you?'

'Yes, I do.'

I reached into my inside pocket but hesitated before taking them out, and put my empty hand slowly back on the table. My other hand, with which I had been rubbing my knee, I also placed on the table.

'And what if I don't have my papers?' I found myself saying. The man flinched, almost imperceptibly, and I saw something in his eyes that clashed with his suave façade. I looked into them as I spoke my next words: 'If I don't have my identification documents, will I be denied asylum? I'm speaking Korean right now. Is that not proof enough that I'm one of you? You said you learned of my situation from your contact in the Chinese authorities. Since then – as a matter of fact, only a couple of days ago – my friend committed suicide. He and I, we're not the only North Koreans being pursued on Chinese soil. There are thousands of us who are fleeing from North Korea. If we don't have our papers, do we all have to die like him?'

My voice had risen. The man looked quickly round the café and said quietly, 'If your friend hadn't made that decision, we would have rescued him by some means or other. To be honest, my colleagues and I, we're very sorry for your friend's death. Mr Jang, I understand what you've been through, and I won't ask you for your identification documents again. It's time. Let's go.'

I was surprised by the man's gentle response to my outburst. He even took the trouble to remind me not to forget the bundle of money, which had indeed completely slipped my mind.

We walked out of the hotel through the main entrance. A black sedan immediately pulled up in front of us. It must have been waiting. The man opened the back door for me and then sat in front with the driver. We had only been moving for about two minutes when the car pulled into an alley. Before I could register what was going on, both back doors opened and two other men slid in on either side of me, trapping me into the middle of the seat.

Their brute strength was in line with the viciousness of agents from North Korea's Ministry of State Security, whom I had constantly feared coming up against since crossing the Tumen River. I suddenly remembered the warning that Mr Shin had repeated several times as we left Yanji. He had explained that in a large Chinese city, it was not uncommon to meet a broker with connections to North Korea who might decide to betray a refugee in his care.

A faint whimper escaped my mouth and I coughed to hide it. Had South Korean spies really known all along about the details of my escape with Young-min, and even about his suicide? Why had I trusted so easily? My chest tightened with painful regret.

The two big men sitting on either side of me were probably carrying out the standard procedure used by North Korean agents to escort a criminal. I leaned slightly towards the man on my left, wondering if I might smell something distinctively North Korean about him, such as North Korean cigarettes or aftershave. If I did, I would put up a struggle. But neither he nor the man on my right smelled of anything. I noticed a scuffed patch on the knee of the man to my right. A man from a developed country such as South Korea wouldn't wear such scruffy trousers, I thought, and I shut my eyes in despair.

I remembered something I'd been told by a friend whose father worked in North Korea's Ministry of State Security. When their overseas agents brought home a criminal considered a flight risk, they would first break his limbs and then put him in a coffin for transport over the border. I started to believe that this car was headed not for the South Korean Embassy but for the North Korean one. There, these two men would break my limbs and my helpless body would be shipped back to North Korea in a coffin. I began to ache at the joints. I even envied Young-min, who had been able to kill himself quickly. As our vehicle hurtled towards what I was sure was hell, I considered whether I might now kill myself by biting my tongue and bleeding to death.

Perhaps fifteen minutes later, one of the men spoke to me. 'Mr

Jang, you are safe now. You can smile. Look over there – at that flag. It's the South Korean flag.'

I looked blankly towards the voice and then ducked my head to see where he was pointing. It was the national flag of South Korea. I could really see the flag with the white background against a sky turning blue, flying from the roof of the South Korean Embassy.

I looked in disbelief at the men in the car. They were all grinning.

I cannot describe in these pages how I was able to enter the Embassy compound safely. Neither can I say how I passed through the front gate without a passport, while Chinese officers stood guard. In fact, there are many things I cannot yet explain in this book, for the sake of all North Koreans seeking freedom after me.

But what I felt when I set foot in the Embassy compound, that experience is not mine alone to savour. It belongs to freedom, and I must share it for freedom's sake.

'Mr Jang, you're on South Korean soil. You're a free man now.'

As the embassy official embraced me with those words, I asked him to please repeat them again. Even after hearing him speak the words twice, I asked again. My desperation was never so intense as at that moment, before I was really sure that I had made it through.

As I stood there nervously, glancing at the backs of the Chinese officers at their posts just outside the gates, the embassy official hugged me tight and told me again, 'You have set foot on South Korean soil. Mr Jang, you are standing on South Korean soil.'

Only then, knowing that where I stood marked the end of my escape and the beginning of my life as a free man, I burst into tears. I had no words, only endless tears, both for myself and for Young-min.

The embassy official tried to calm me down and patted my back. But these were not my tears alone, and not for me to hold back. I cried from my heart in silence: *Long live freedom. Long live freedom. Long live freedom!*

EPILOGUE

TODAY, I live as a South Korean citizen. It wasn't easy to move into this world from a life that was dictated from above, and institutional in every detail.

When I was formally told that I was now a citizen of South Korea, my heart felt like bursting because I had been recognised as one among a nation of equals, rather than a subject who served one man alone. In North Korea, loyalty was the point of life; disobedience led to death. That was all.

My first day of freedom is fresh in my memory. I had spent eight months being debriefed in a safe house in Seoul, and set out on my own as a South Korean citizen on 17 December 2004. That night, I wandered the streets of Seoul into the early hours, taking in my newfound freedom.

Then, suddenly, a car screeched to a halt and a man cursed at me out of the window: 'Fucking son of a bitch! Watch where you're going!' It was a taxi driver who had had to brake hard for me as I crossed on a red light. The glow of freedom I'd been basking in was dispelled in an instant. The taxi driver gestured at me and cursed some more before driving on. As the shock subsided, I could only grin as I realised that I was now truly confirmed as a free man, no more or less entitled than anyone else. On that first night out on my own I tried to call Mr Shin, but his number was no longer listed. I hadn't been able to contact him immediately following my arrival in South Korea because I was in the safe house. Although I had no means of contacting him other than that number, we must have been destined to meet again, because three years later I ran into him unexpectedly in a public sauna in a northern Seoul district. When his North Korean refugee wife was granted asylum in South Korea, he too had been allowed to settle here. He was living in a government-sponsored flat for refugees in Seoul with his wife and two sons. He, a Korean-Chinese, and I, a North Korean, became very close: our friendship remains deep for we both live without an extended family in a foreign land.

Mr Shin didn't have Cho-rin's number any more. Although he couldn't help with that, he had good news to share about his uncle, Chang-yong. With the $700 we had given him (less the $100 I had taken back from his wife), he had eventually bought not the cultivator he'd talked so excitedly about, but two fine cows.

When I got a passport the following year, I made a trip back to Shenyang, where everything had become unrecognisable. I couldn't find Cho-rin, her uncle or her fiancé to thank them for their help. But I did meet the owner of Kyonghoeru, and was able not only to pay back my fare but to repay his kindness properly. I returned to the house of the old man in Longjing, but the building had been replaced by a modern construction and a new family had moved in. I was also able to enjoy a warm reunion with the Beijing correspondent of the South Korean newspaper. Recounting the experience, he said that he would never have dreamed of a North Korean defector reaching out to him like that, and I joked that the newspaper was very naïve.

In January 2005, I became a senior analyst at the National Security Research Institute in Seoul, which falls under the auspices of the National Intelligence Service. A former specialist on South Korea for the North, I was now in the opposite role.

While intelligence was my profession, in 2008 I decided to renew my career as a poet. This time, though, I was a free man and a poet in exile, no longer a poet of the state. My first publication was a book of poetry titled *I Sell my Daughter for 100 Won*, published under my pen-name, Jang Jin-sung, and based on the manuscript I had brought with me from Pyongyang. Perhaps through the grace of its having been rescued and protected by Young-min during our escape from North Korea, the book immediately became a bestseller, taking the number one position on the lists of major bookstores. The title poem of the book has been adapted for television, as a song, and as a play that was performed in South Korea's largest theatre at Seoul Arts Center.

More recently, I received an invitation to take part in Poetry Parnassus, hosted by the Southbank Centre as part of the London Olympic Games in the summer of 2012. One poet from each participating Olympic country was invited, and I had been chosen to represent North Korea in my exile among several other poets-in-exile. Such encounters with writers affirmed for me that a country could not truly be advanced in its human rights without also being advanced in its freedom of speech, and this strengthened my resolve to declare the truth about North Korea through the written word.

In 2010, I finally left my post and with it the world of institutions for good. I was able to spend more time writing and, with the entirety of my severance allowance, in 2011 I set up *New Focus*, the first news organisation run by North Korean exiles. I named it thus for two main reasons: in the hope that North Korea could pursue a new vision; and to show the outside world that there was a way of understanding North Korea beyond the way that existing frameworks of interpretation or government agendas allowed it. I wanted the knowledge and experience of North Koreans to be taken seriously into account. In April 2013, I wrote for a *New York Times* op-ed:

> [Back home] there are two North Koreas: one real and the other a fiction created by the regime. It was after my defection ... that I recognised the existence of a third North Korea: a theoretical one. This is the North Korea constructed by the outside world ...

After crossing the Tumen River, I had fled from the Chinese and North Korean authorities for thirty-five days. It was little more than a month of my life, yet the pain of that experience was akin to giving birth. And why wouldn't it be painful? Freedom is freely given to anyone born in a free land, but others have to risk their lives for it. In a free nation, freedom is a word that may be all too common and hollow in meaning; but my friend Young-min jumped from a rock face dreaming of it.

Even today, the Party brainwashes its subjects, telling them that the essence of their identity is based on their living in 'Kim Il-sung's homeland' and being 'Kim Jong-il's people'. My mentor Kim Sang-o replaced a country with a person by praising Kim Il-sung as 'My Homeland', but I, his student, could not follow in his footsteps. For me, my homeland was not the country I was born into, or the man I obeyed, but the world in which I wanted to be buried; so I escaped from a system where literature was permitted to serve only one man's legacy.

Writing the account of my escape required me to cry from the heart, *Freedom is my homeland*. And I was not its only author, because it was with Young-min that I made the journey. Nor am I the sole protagonist of this book. This story is also about my friend who testified to the desperation that drives millions of North Koreans who have stood, and still stand, before a cliff edge with nowhere else to go but over the precipice. It is also a tribute to those who helped me on my journey, those who helped me pull through because their loyalty was not to those in power, but to our shared humanity.

Today, there are over 25,000 North Koreans who have made it to South Korea. Some of them have had to hide out in caves for years; others have been captured and sent back to North Korea, only to make another miraculous escape. If all their stories could be put into words, my life would barely fill one page of that book.

One North Korean diplomat, captured by North Korean agents abroad and in the process of being returned to North Korea, had the good misfortune of a car accident – and was thus able to escape from the wreckage and seek asylum from the local authorities. Another, in shackles, leapt from the train taking him back to Pyongyang, and crawled back over the frozen Tumen River to reclaim his life. Risking his life once was not enough to buy his freedom, and neither was it for many others, who have been 'repatriated' three times and escaped three times. There are those who, innocent of any crime other than being the child of their parents, were sent to a prison camp, never given a name, yet managed to escape.

How many more North Koreans wandered through foreign lands and died namelessly? There is the tragedy of a couple who made it to South-East Asia after crossing China on foot; but in crossing the Mekong River, they entrusted the family's fate to a floating tyre inner-tube, and only their child survived. On another occasion, a mother and daughter were separated on the threshold of a South Korean consulate as Chinese authorities seized one while the other managed to dash to a terrible freedom.

In this way, all of us exiles not only had to escape from the system, but also, by risking death, to let go of our sense of entitlement to life. This is why, like many others, I had years of nightmares after settling in South Korea. At night, our fears take hold of us, as we are returned to the oppressive surveillance, or find ourselves arrested by secret police and hauled away to a prison camp. We say among ourselves that only when our nightly dreams are set in the safety of our new country, have we truly made it out of North Korea. Even in our waking hours, especially on any occasion marking the passage of time such as New Year or an anniversary, we are seized by overwhelming emotions that paralyse us and that we cannot begin to untangle.

North Korean exiles are a living testament that there does exist a difference between freedom and tyranny. Their stories are not merely a vehicle to evoke pity. They cry for justice on behalf of all those who have died without a voice and who have been buried with the world as their dumb witness. Their insistent voices are the triumph of humanity having survived a brutal struggle with a despot.

Kim Jong-il said that the word 'impossible' did not exist in his dictionary. This is the dictator's corruption of power, for whom a declaration that he wields a gun is as effective as his actually wielding it. For me, too, there is no 'impossible', but this is for me as an individual. The price of my survival was being lost to loved ones, and their being lost to me; and I can feel no greater pain or desolation, whatever hardships may lie ahead of me. Above all, I now know and fiercely possess my right to freedom, and that gives me the strength to rise a thousand times for every hundred times that I fall.

The North Korean regime has not finished with its persecution of me. It not only makes secret attempts to find and harm me physically, but it also threatens me openly through its media. In June 2013, for example, the Ministry of People's Security published an official statement through the North Korean state news organ, KCNA, saying it would 'remove my existence from this universe'. The tyranny of Kim has now been inherited by a third generation.

This is why my peace lies in waging war against despotism, until our people are freed. Without that, my privilege of freedom would be no more than selfishness. But if the regime has murder, deception and nuclear bombs in its arsenal, the weapon I wield is truth.

In freedom I have also found personal happiness. I am always accompanied by police escorts because of the North's continuing threats of assassination, but the woman who is now my wife did not begrudge the bulky chaperones who accompanied us on our dates for the three years of our courtship. When I said we should stop dating and, instead, offered her an engagement ring, I was grateful that she accepted it without hesitation. Last year, we had a healthy and handsome baby boy. The marriage of a man from Pyongyang with a woman from Seoul has given birth to a unified Korean child. Although Korea may be divided into North and South, our child was born into a union.

Whenever I do the dishes, my wife pats me on the back and says, 'Honey, you're settling nicely into a free and democratic world. If you continue like this, I know you'll succeed.' And I raise my hands in the air and confess, 'This must be my servile fate. I was ruled over by a dictator in North Korea and now, in the South, I'm ruled over by my wife!'

AFTERWORD
The Future of North Korea

THE outside world views North Korea through an outsider's lens. When Kim Jong-un began his rule following the death of his father, many interpreted the power hierarchy of the new regime according to the seven pall-bearers who were most visible at Kim Jong-il's funeral. But, in reality, not a single one of those seven figures held any real power as sanctioned by the Party's OGD.

Among the North Korean elite, real honour and power are conferred only through loyal obedience to the guidance of the Supreme Leader – with the OGD as its enforcer – and are not manifested through a formal post, but acquired through humility in the face of such guidance. As if in ironic confirmation, five of the seven pall-bearers whom the outside world saw as being North Korea's power brokers, among them Jang Song-thaek, have since been dispensed with by the OGD. The two who remain, Chairman of the Supreme People's Assembly Choe Tae-bok and Party Secretary for the Propaganda and Agitation Department Kim Ki-nam, are figureheads whose lives or deaths don't matter as far as the Party is concerned.

In order to understand how the country works, the outside world must look beneath North Korea's surface. Despite its civilian and diplomatic façades, the UFD is a highly focused operational entity specialising in counter-intelligence and psychological warfare; and the distorting influence of the OGD underpins many fundamental discrepancies between the apparent manifestations of power and its actual workings. Just as Jang Song-thaek's bloody history caught up with him with a vengeance in 2013, so Kim Jong-un has found himself slotted into a structure controlled by his father's men in the OGD. Even the North Korean military is an arm of the Party, and has no powers whatsoever to appoint its own staff or issue orders.

Jang Song-thaek's execution was the occasion through which the organisation that I founded, *New Focus International*, first revealed the reality and reach of the OGD to the world. Although there is still much more work to be done, our guiding principle from the start has been: Don't worry about going faster than those who have had a head start; worry only about being more honest. It may take a long time for the truth to come to light, but it will remain long after the lies have faded.

The single most powerful entity in North Korea has not been recognised as such by the outside world, nor by ordinary North Koreans, because the reality of the OGD is intertwined with the secret history of Kim Jong-il's rise to power. Kim Jong-il built up an entity whereby the OGD Party Secretary – himself – became more powerful than the Supreme Leader, leaving Kim Il-sung with only symbolic authority. The OGD must remain hidden because it is the entity that destroyed Kim Il-sung even as it upheld, on the surface, the most sacred legitimacy of the Supreme Leader.

The OGD is North Korea's engine of power. That engine might be concealed, but it nevertheless moves the vehicle. Just as the OGD's connection with Kim Jong-il's secret rise to power remains obscured, so its absolute authority is veiled by its operational secrecy. The world believes Kim Jong-il's succession was enabled by Kim Il-sung; but Kim Jong-il could not have obtained power without the OGD, and neither could Kim Jong-un remain in power without it. Through its meticulous and absolute control over personnel vetting and surveillance, not even the military – let alone any individual within the armed forces – can hold power away from the OGD. The situation is no different in the fields of authorised commerce or diplomacy. Moreover, the OGD not only runs North Korea's secret police and prison camps through the Ministry of State Security, it commands the ruling Kim's bodyguards and, as discussed elsewhere in this book, all policy proposals are routed through it.

Many approaches to the regime focus on its being the agent of possible reform. They therefore pursue sanctions towards it on the one hand, or use diplomacy, official exchanges and investment on the other. Yet the unleashing of unregulated market forces from below, which have amplified the flow of unofficial exchanges, has weakened the OGD's totalitarian grip more than anything else in history has done. North Korea might be ruled by a threatening regime as far as the outside world is concerned, but within the country itself, the regime no longer determines the price of a single egg. We must keep this reality in mind – along with the reality of power in North Korea – as we look to its future: while the OGD will not compromise on control of its own accord, its authority will diminish as long as livelihoods and opportunities lie in areas beyond its grasp. We must place our faith in the people of North Korea, not in the system that imprisons them.

GLOSSARY

Admitted, the – the tiny circle of elite whose presence Kim Jong-il has personally requested and who have spent more than twenty minutes with him behind closed doors.

Arduous March, the – the official North Korean term for the state of food emergency from 1995 to 1998.

Chosun – North Korea's name for itself.

Dear Leader – Kim Jong-il.

DMZ – Korean Demilitarised Zone: armistice line since 1953 that divides the Korean peninsula.

DPRK – Democratic People's Republic of Korea (North Korea).

General, the – Kim Jong-il.

Great Leader – Kim Il-sung or Kim Jong-il.

Gukgun – South Korea's National Army.

Jochongryon – Association of Chosun People in Japan: organisation run by the UFD that represents people of Korean origin in Japan.

Juche – state-ratified policy of North Korea based on the principle of self-reliance.

KPA – Korean People's Army (North Korean).

'Localisation' – UFD's policy of adopting South Korean ways of thought in order to influence South Korea.

NLL – Northern Limit Line: demarcation of territorial waters between North and South Korea in the Yellow Sea.

Office 101 – the policy-making section of the UFD.

OGD – Organisation and Guidance Department: the executive chain of command of the Workers' Party.

PAD – Propaganda and Agitation Department.

PAF – People's Armed Forces (North Korean).

PDS – Public Distribution System, which determines allocation of all necessities in North Korea.

Rodong Sinmun – the official newspaper of the Workers' Party.

Scrutiny, the – the North Korean term is *shimhwajo*, which can be translated literally as 'intensifying the scrutiny (of identification documents)'.

Section 5 – the section of the OGD responsible for the personal needs of Kim Jong-il.

Seed-bearing Strategy – the North Korean strategy of kidnapping foreign, especially Japanese citizens.

side-branch – a member of the Kim family to be 'pruned' for the tree to grow tall and strong.

Songun – the Military-First policy of North Korea.

southern Chosun – North Korean name for South Korea.

Sunshine Policy – South Korea's foreign policy towards North Korea, declared a failure by South Korea in 2010.

Supreme Leader – Kim Il-sung.

Suryong – Supreme Leader.

UFD – United Front Department: key section in the Workers' Party, which oversees inter-Korean espionage, policy-making and diplomacy.

Workers' Party – the official, ruling political party of North Korea.

INDEX